Study Guide

for

Rathus, Nevid, and Fitchner-Rathus

Human Sexuality in a World of Diversity
Fourth Edition

Lisa B. Fiore
Boston College

Allyn and Bacon
Boston   London   Toronto   Sydney   Tokyo   Singapore

Copyright © 2000 by Allyn & Bacon
A Pearson Education Company
160 Gould Street
Needham Heights, Massachusetts 02494-2130

Internet: www.abacon.com

All rights reserved. No part of the material protected by this copyright notice
may be reproduced or utilized in any form or by any means, electronic or
mechanical, including photocopying, recording, or by any information
storage and retrieval system, without the written permission of the copyright owner.

ISBN 0-205-30553-9

Printed in the United States of America

10 9 8 7 6 5 4 3 2 1   03 02 01 00

TABLE OF CONTENTS

Introduction v

Chapter 1: *What is Human Sexuality?* 1

Chapter 2: *Research Methods* 13

Chapter 3: *Female Sexual Anatomy and Physiology* 25

Chapter 4: *Male Sexual Anatomy and Physiology* 39

Chapter 5: *Sexual Arousal and Response* 51

Chapter 6: *Gender Identity and Gender Roles* 63

Chapter 7: *Attraction and Love* 75

Chapter 8: *Relationships, Intimacy, and Communication* 85

Chapter 9: *Sexual Techniques and Behavior Patterns* 97

Chapter 10: *Sexual Orientation* 107

Chapter 11: *Conception, Pregnancy, and Childbirth* 121

Chapter 12: *Contraception and Abortion* 139

Chapter 13: *Sexuality in Childhood and Adolescence* 153

Chapter 14: *Sexuality in Adulthood* 165

Chapter 15: *Sexual Dysfunctions* 177

Chapter 16: *Sexually Transmitted Infections* 189

Chapter 17: *Atypical Sexual Variations* 207

Chapter 18: *Sexual Coercion* 221

Chapter 19: *Commercial Sex* 231

Chapter 20: *Making Responsible Sexual Decisions—An Epilogue* 241

Appendix: *Answers to Chapter Exercises* 247

INTRODUCTION

Welcome to the fascinating study of human sexuality! The text chosen by your professor is highly interesting and well-organized. The components of each text chapter lend themselves well to effective, efficient study habits. Although you may have already developed your own methods of studying, read the following study tips and use them to evaluate the effectiveness of your methods.

Study Tips:

1. *Schedule your study time. Study regularly.* Make studying a priority and keep up with your reading assignments. Schedule times and places when you will have few distractions and interruptions. Study in small blocks of time — one half hour to one hour. Take breaks to ensure your full concentration during these blocks of time.

2. *Preview the material you plan to read.* Read the Chapter Outline and the Truth or Fiction questions which can be found at the beginning of each chapter. Page through the chapter, reading the large topic headings. Get a clear idea of what it is you will be reading.

3. *Read the text material.* Reading actively will increase your studying efficiency. As you read, stop periodically to summarize in your own words the content you have just read. Jot down notes about the major ideas. Try to relate the material you are reading to other knowledge you possess. These techniques will help you remember what you are reading.

4. *Review the text material.* Read the outline, glance at the large topic headings, and read the summary at the end of the chapter.

Now you're ready for the Study Guide! Each Study Guide chapter includes six components: **Chapter Summary, Learning Objectives, Fill-in-the-Blanks, Short Answer Questions, Matching Exercises, and Multiple-Choice Questions.** The following tips will help you make the best possible use of these components.

Tips for Using the Study Guide:

1. **Chapter Summary** Read the Chapter Summary. If any of the information sounds unfamiliar to you or raises questions in your mind, reread the relevant text section.

2. **Learning Objectives** Recite or write an answer to each of the Learning Objectives. Reread the relevant text section if you cannot address each objective.

3. **Fill-in-the-Blanks** This section provides a summary of the chapter; important facts and key terms are left blank. Complete this section with your text book closed. If you are unable to fill in all the blanks, search your text for the correct answers. Then, check your answers with those in the Appendix.

4. **Short Answer Questions** Write the answers to these questions with your text book closed. If necessary, search your text for the answers you do not know. Check your answers with those listed in the Appendix.

5. **Matching Exercises** Match the terms in the left-hand columns with the definitions in the right-hand columns. If you are unable to match all the terms, you can find the terms and definitions in the margin glossary of your text chapter. Check your answers with those listed in the Appendix.

6. **Multiple-Choice Questions** Choose the correct answer for each item. The Learning Objective (LO) on which the question is based and the text page on which the answer can be found are listed under each question. Check your answers with those listed in the Appendix.

All of the chapters in the Study Guide include the six components described above. Some chapters also include a section labeled **Other Activities**. Some of these activities are charts that require you to complete the information that is missing.

Why should you use these tips for studying and for using the Study Guide? So that *you* can take charge of your learning. *You* can choose the times and places you study. *You* can learn to study in the most efficient way and get the most out of each hour you study.

The topic of human sexuality and sexual behavior is one of the most interesting and most important topics you'll ever study. Knowledge in this field is critical to understanding many current controversial topics. And, knowledge about sexuality in conjunction with your value system will enable you to make the difficult sexual decisions we all must make. I hope this Study Guide will assist you in making this course one of the most beneficial courses you've ever taken.

Chapter 1

What is Human Sexuality?

Chapter Summary

This chapter begins with an exploration of the definition and the scope of the field of human sexuality. Anthropologists, biologists, medical researchers, sociologists and psychologists all contribute to the research in this field. The authors recognize the great diversity within and across cultures, subcultures, races, social classes and value systems and include such information throughout the text. Knowledge about human sexuality, the development of critical thinking skills, and values clarification skills help students make informed sexual decisions and take an active role in enhancing their sexual health.

Six perspectives on human sexuality are presented: the historical, biological, cross-species, cross-cultural, psychological and sociocultural perspectives. The history of sexuality is described beginning with the human groups who lived approximately 20,000 years ago and continuing through the ancient Hebrews, Greeks, Romans and early Christians. Sexuality in eastern religions is compared and contrasted with sexuality within western traditions. This section also includes European sexual history from the Middle Ages to the present and U.S. sexual history from colonial times to the present. Within each time period, topics such as the roles of men and women, attitudes toward sex, marriage customs, and sexual prohibitions are examined.

The biological perspective focuses on the genetic, hormonal, vascular and neural influences on human sexual behavior. The cross-species perspective searches within animal behavior for analogs of human sexual behavior. Anthropologists provide information for the cross-cultural perspective, which confirms that societies differ widely in their social attitudes, customs and practices.

Within the psychological perspective the authors examine the psychoanalytic and behavioral theories. The sociocultural perspective focuses on the behavioral and attitudinal differences in sexuality among subgroups within societies. Research from the six perspectives offers a vast amount of information that can help explain the complexity of human sexual behavior. As we approach the next millennium, human sexuality is sure to reflect changes in lifestyles and technology.

Learning Objectives

1. State the authors' definition of human sexuality.
2. Describe the contributions made by the many disciplines involved in the study of human sexuality.

3. Describe some of the cross-cultural variations in sexual behaviors and attitudes.
4. List the characteristics of critical thinking and discuss how critical thinking skills can be applied to the study of human sexuality.
5. Identify the sexual attitudes and practices characteristic of the historical eras described in this chapter.
6. Recognize that the origins of sexual attitudes and behaviors can often be traced to earlier eras.
7. Identify the major focuses of biological sexual research and its contributions to the field.
8. Explain what we can and cannot learn from cross-species comparisons of sexual behavior.
9. Discuss possible conclusions about the universality of human sexual behavior given the cross-cultural material presented.
10. Explain the psychoanalytic theory and several learning theories of human sexual behavior.
11. Describe the contributions that the sociocultural perspectives make to the study of human sexual behavior.

Fill-in-the-Blanks

_____ _____ is best defined as the way in which we experience and express ourselves as sexual beings. Science provides us with information we can use in making sexual decisions, but these decisions are also based on our _____.

Knowledge of paternity probably developed during the _____ era, around _____ BC. The _____ taboo may have been the first human taboo. During the Golden Age of Ancient Greece, Greek men in their thirties might take adolescent males as lovers and pupils. _____ means the sexual love of boys. Several of our modern sexual terms have roots that can be traced to Roman culture: _____, a sexual activity involving oral contact with the penis; _____, a sexual activity involving oral contact with the female genitals; and _____, sexual intercourse between people who are not married to one another. The _____ _____ is a sex manual that codified the sexual practices of the ancient Hindus of India. The two conflicting concepts of women, woman as Eve and woman as the Virgin Mary, originated during the _____ _____. During the Protestant Reformation, _____ and _____ were two of the Christian reformers who split off from the Roman Catholic church and formed their own sects. Although the Victorian Era became known for its repression of sexual pleasures, _____ flourished during this time. During the last 1800s and early 1900s, _____ _____ published a series of volumes on sexuality in which he argued against many of the prevailing Victorian ideas about sexuality.

The first large-scale studies of sexual behavior in the U.S. were completed during the 19___s and 19___s by a research group from Indiana University. The period from the _____ to the _____ is often referred to as the *sexual revolution*.

The biological perspective focuses on the roles of _____, _____, and _____ factors in explaining human sexual behavior. The study of the behaviors of other animal species defines the _____ perspective. _____ argue that there is a genetic basis to social behavior, including sexual behavior, among humans and other animals. Early in the twentieth century, research by anthropologists Mead and Malinowski spurred interest in the _____-_____ perspective on human sexuality. _____ (having more than one spouse) was practiced in a majority of the preliterate cultures studied by Ford and Beach, even though _____ (having one spouse) is more prevalent worldwide.

_____, a Viennese physician, formulated the theory of personality called _____. According to his theory of _____ _____, children undergo five stages of development: _____, _____, _____, _____, and _____.

_____ emphasize the importance of rewards and punishments in the learning process. _____-_____ theorists use these concepts but they emphasize the importance of cognitive activity and learning by observation. _____ _____ view sexual behavior as a form of social behavior occurring within a particular social system. One major focus is the examination of the influence of _____ _____ on sexual behavior.

Short Answer Questions

(LO = Learning Objective)

1. Name several areas of research that provide information to help individuals and society deal with sexual decisions and problems. (LO 2 – p. 5)

2. List the eight features of critical thinking described by the authors of the textbook. (LO 4 - pp. 9-10)

3. Describe the types of artifacts historians and anthropologists use to make conclusions about the role of sexuality in prehistory. (LO 5 – pp. 11-12)

4. Summarize the view of sexuality espoused by early Christians. (LO 5 - p. 14)

5. What general conclusions can be drawn from the historical information on sexuality? (LO 5 - pp. 20-21)

6. Cite areas of research within the study of the biology of sex? (LO 7 - p. 21)

7. Summarize the evolutionary process proposed by Darwin. (LO 8 - p. 22)

8. What general conclusions can be drawn from the cross-species research on sexual behaviors? (LO 8 – pp. 22-23)

9. How do sociobiologists explain why men are more promiscuous than women? (LO 8 - p. 23)

10. What general conclusions can be drawn from cross-cultural information on sexual practices? (LO 9 - p. 25)

11. How would behaviorists explain differences in sexual behaviors? (LO 10 – p. 27)

12. What are some of the important innovations and changes in lifestyles that the authors discuss as trends in human sexuality in the new millennium? (LO 1 – p. 31)

Matching Exercises

I. Individuals and Their Contributions

Directions: Match the individuals listed in the left-hand column with their contributions from the right-hand column.

a. Reverend Sylvester Graham (p. 18) ____ Compiled case histories of sexual deviation; viewed sexual deviations as mental diseases.

b. Havelock Ellis (p. 19) ____ Found great variety in sexual customs and beliefs among the almost 200 preliterate societies studied.

c. Richard von Krafft-Ebing (p. 19) ____ Led the research team that completed the first large-scale surveys of sexual behaviors in the United States.

d. Sigmund Freud (p. 26) ____ Ruled England from 1837 to 1901; her name has become virtually synonymous with sexual repression.

e. Charles Darwin (p. 22) ____ Concluded that gender roles are not inherent in our genetic heritage but are culturally acquired (an anthropologist).

f. Alfred Kinsey (p. 19) ____ Promoted in a series of books the views that women had natural sexual desires and that homosexuality should be viewed as a natural variation and tolerated.

g. Margaret Mead (p. 24) ____ Recommended that young men control their sexual appetites by eating simple foods, many based on whole grain flours.

h. Clellan Ford & Frank Beach (p. 24) ____ Early behaviorists who emphasized rewards and punishments in the learning process.

i. John B. Watson & B.F. Skinner (p. 27) ____ Founded the theory that animal and plant species evolved over time and through the process of natural selection.

j. Queen Victoria (p. 18) ____ Developed a theory of personality that emphasized sexual drives and the unconscious mind.

II. Vocabulary Exercise 1

Directions: Match each vocabulary term listed in the left-hand column with the correct definition in the right-hand column.

a. gender (p. 5) ____ Something that is similar or comparable to something else.

b. coitus (p. 5) ____ The prohibition against intercourse and reproduction among close blood relatives.

c. erotic (p. 5) ____ The practice of having one spouse.

d. gender identity (p. 5) ____ Sexually responsive to either gender.

e. gender roles (p. 5) ____ Images of the penis.

f. foreplay (p. 5) ____ A person who engages in the scientific study of sexual behavior.

g. phallic symbol (p. 12) ____ Complex clusters of ways in which males and females are expected to behave within a given culture.

h. incest taboo (p. 12) ____ The qualities in life that are deemed important or unimportant, right or wrong, desirable or undesirable.

i. polygamy (p. 12) ____ The state of being male or female.

j. monogamy (p. 12) ____ Mutual sexual stimulation that precedes sexual intercourse.

k. analogue (p. 21) ____ Sexual intercourse.

l. bisexual (p. 13) ____ The ways in which we experience and express ourselves as sexual beings.

m. values (p. 5) ____ Arousing sexual feelings or desires.

n. sexologist (p. 19) ____ The practice of having two or more spouses at the same time.

o. human sexuality (p. 5) ____ One's private experience of being male or Female.

III. Vocabulary Exercise 2

Directions: Match each vocabulary term listed in the left-hand column with the correct definition in the right-hand column.

a. evolution (p. 22) ____ A cognitively oriented learning theory in which observational learning, values and expectations play key roles in determining behavior.

b. natural selection (p. 22) ____ The tendency to treat standards of one's own culture as the norm by which to judge other cultures.

c. sociobiology (p. 22) ____ The theory of personality, originated by Sigmund Freud, that proposes that human behavior represents the outcome of clashing inner forces.

d. polygyny (p. 25) ____ A form of marriage in which a man has two or more wives.

e. polyandry (p. 25) ____ Acquiring knowledge and skills by observing others.

f. ethnocentric (p. 25) ____ Parts of the body, including but not limited to the sex organs, that are responsive to sexual stimulation.

g. psychoanalysis (p. 26) ____ Learning theorists who argue that a scientific approach to understanding behavior must refer only to observable and measurable behaviors.

h. erogenous zones (p. 26) ____ The theory that dispositions toward behavior patterns that enhance reproductive success may be genetically transmitted.

i. behaviorists (p. 27) ____ The development of a species to its present state, which is believed to involve adaptations to its environment.

j. social-learning theory (p. 28) ____ The evolutionary process by which adaptive traits enable members of a species to survive to reproductive age and transmit these traits to future generations.

k. modeling (p. 28) ____ A form of marriage in which a woman has two or more husbands.

Multiple-Choice Questions

(LO = Learning Objective)

1. Sociocultural theorists contribute to the interdisciplinary nature of the study of human sexuality by providing information relating to
    a. the relationship between the learning processes and sexual behavior.
    b. our physiological responses during arousal.
    c. the relationship between sexual behavior and religion, race, or social class.
    d. the cross-cultural similarities and differences in sexual behavior.
            p. 5   LO 2

2. Studying human sexuality can offer us all of the following benefits, *except*
    a. a better understanding of how sexuality is influenced by family, culture, and societal traditions and beliefs.
    b. assistance in recognizing and choosing appropriate intervention for sexually related problems.
    c. an increase in ability to communicate effectively with sexual partners.
    d. specifying which sexual behaviors are moral and which are not.
            pp. 5-7   LO 2

3. Critical thinking requires
    a. rejection of any claims and arguments of others.
    b. reliance upon our intuitive "gut impressions."
    c. examination of the logic of arguments.
    d. acceptance of conventional wisdom.
            pp. 9-10   LO 4

4. The Ancient Greeks viewed women and men as
    a. heterosexual.
    b. homosexual.
    c. bisexual.
    d. asexual.
            p. 13   LO 5

5. Alfred Kinsey's major goal was to
    a. study the physiology of sexual functioning.
    b. offer psychological advice about healthy types of sexual expression.
    c. describe patterns of sexual behavior in the united States.
    d. provide a guide book for improving one's sexual relationships.
            p. 19   LO 6

6. All of the following seemed to contribute to the sexual revolution of the 1960s and 1970s *except*
   a. the return to traditional values of family following the Vietnam War.
   b. the invention of oral contraceptives.
   c. increased sexual permissiveness and political liberalism.
   d. the widespread questioning of conventional social values of our country.
        p. 20   LO 6

7. Darwin proposed that members of a species who were better adapted to their environment would survive to ensure reproductive success. This mechanism is called
   a. Darwinistic adaptation.
   b. natural selection.
   c. cross-species comparison.
   d. sociobiology.
        p. 22   LO 8

8. _____ believe that sexual reproductive strategies, such as seeking many partners or limiting one's number of sexual partners, are genetically transmitted.
   a. Sociobiologists
   b. Behaviorists
   c. Psychoanalysts
   d. Social-Learning theorists
        p. 23   LO 8

9. Polygyny and polyandry are both
   a. forms of genetic transmission.
   b. forms of monogamy.
   c. forms of polygamy.
   d. chromosomal abnormalities.
        p. 25   LO 9

10. According to Freud, the three structures of the personality are the
    a. ego, unconscious, and id.
    b. superego, id, and ego.
    c. id, unconscious, and subconscious.
    d. id, ego, and superego.
        p. 26   LO 10

11. Watson is to Freud as
    a. behaviorism is to social-learning theory.
    b. sociobiology is to psychoanalysis.
    c. behaviorism is to psychoanalysis.
    d. social learning is to the cross-cultural perspective.
            p. 26-27   LO 10

12. According to social-learning theorists, your sexual preferences, values, and patterns of behaving are developed through
    a. the stages of psychosexual development.
    b. receiving direct rewards and punishments.
    c. observation and imitation of significant models.
    d. the unfolding of your genetic program.
            p. 28   LO 10

Chapter 2

Research Methods

Chapter Summary

This chapter begins by describing the scientific method: research question formulation, hypothesis formation, hypothesis testing, and drawing conclusions. The goals of the science of human sexuality are to describe, explain, predict and control behavior. To achieve these goals, researchers must always operationally define their terms.

Various sampling methods for choosing subjects within a population are discussed. The problem of volunteer bias is explained.

Five research methods (case-study, survey, observational, correlational, and experimental) are examined. For each method, the related terminology, the variations, the problems with generalizability, the advantages and disadvantages, and the limitations of its use are examined. Examples of studies using each method are described, and, where space permits, results are presented.

The case study method with its emphasis on an individual or a small group is presented, and the problems with generalizability are emphasized. The presentation of the survey method includes descriptions of classic and new surveys, magazine surveys, and several surveys of diverse populations. The sampling techniques of each are analyzed. The observational methods described include naturalistic observation of humans and animals, ethnographic observation, participant observation, and laboratory observation. The significance of statistical correlations between variables is explained, and the lack of cause-and-effect conclusions is emphasized. The terminology of the experimental method is explained and research examples are presented.

The chapter concludes with an examination of the ethical obligations sex researchers have to their subjects. The authors describe the role of institutional ethics review committees in protecting subjects from harm.

Learning Objectives

1. Explain the four essential elements of the research method.
2. List the four broad goals of the science of human sexuality.
3. Explain what operational definitions are and why they are necessary to the research process.
4. Describe the sampling methods used to choose research subjects and identify the problems associated with these methods.
5. Describe the case study method and its limitations.
6. Describe and analyze the sampling techniques used in several large-scale surveys discussed in this chapter.

7. Identify problems associated with using the survey method and give examples of each.
8. Describe the four observational methods and suggest situations in which each might be used.
9. Discuss several weaknesses of the various observational methods.
10. List the terms associated with the correlational method and explain why correlations do not indicate a cause-and-effect relationship.
11. Discuss the experimental method in terms of the variables involved and the assignment of subjects to groups.
12. Cite the limitations of the experimental method and give examples of situations in which it could not be used.
13. Discuss the major ethical issues researchers encounter when conducting sex research.

Fill-in-the-Blanks

The _____ _____ is a systematic way of gathering scientific evidence and testing assumptions through empirical research. Scientists use various research methods to study human sexuality, including the _____-_____, _____, _____ _____, and _____ _____ methods.

Scientists cannot study all members of a population, so they select a _____. If individuals selected for a study do not represent the target population, we cannot _____ the results to the population. A _____ sample is one in which every member of the target population has an equal chance of participating. The term _____ _____ is used to describe samples in which we know the probability of any member's being included in the sample.

A _____ _____ is an in-depth study of an individual or a small group of individuals. In the _____ method, interviews or questionnaires are used to gather information about behavior. A major advantage of using questionnaires instead of interviews is that questionnaires are _____. One problem in sex research is _____ _____, because the differences between those who volunteer to participate and those who refuse to participate can ruin the generalizability of the study.

There are several other limitations of the survey method. In _____ _____, respondents may recall their behavior inaccurately or purposefully misrepresent it. In _____-_____ _____

_____, respondents may be influenced by a fear of the disapproval of the interviewer or others, if their identify became known. In _____, they may report higher or lower numbers for their behaviors than they know are true, and in _____, participants may not acknowledge feelings or behaviors that elicit anxiety,.

In _____ methods of research scientists observe the behavior of animals and humans where it happens. In ethnographic observation, _____ observe the social and sexual customs of people in various cultures. In _____ _____ investigators learn about people's behavior by interacting directly with their subjects. One of the basic problems with observational research is the _____ _____, the possibility that the behavior under study may be altered by being observed.

_____ research describes the statistical relationship between two or more variables. Although correlations do not show _____ _____ _____, they can be used to make _____.

The best research method for studying cause-and-effect relationships is the _____ method. In this research method the _____ variable is manipulated or controlled by the researcher. The _____ variable is the outcome or the measured results. Subjects in the _____ group receive the independent variable, but the subjects in the _____ group do not.

_____ _____ _____ pass judgment on the acceptability of proposed studies before they may begin. Ethically, subjects cannot be exposed to unnecessary _____ and _____. Sex researchers must also guarantee _____ ; that is, they must protect subjects from the harm or embarrassment that might result if their responses were divulged. The principle of _____ _____ requires that subjects freely agree to participate after being given information about the research. In studies that involve _____, researchers must demonstrate that the effects of the treatment are not seriously harmful and that _____ of the information obtained outweigh the risks.

Short Answer Questions

(LO = Learning Objective)

1. List the four elements of the scientific method cited by the text authors. (LO 1 - pp. 36-37)

2. List the four goals of the science of human sexuality. (LO 2 - p. 37)

3. Why must sex researchers operationally define their terms? Give an example. (LO 3 - pp. 38-39)

4. Describe the difference between random samples and stratified random samples. (LO 4 - p. 41)

5. Why are the results of magazine surveys not generalizable? (LO 6 - p. 46)

6. What research method did the Kinsey team use? What research question did they attempt to answer? (LO 6 - pp. 44-45)

7. In what way might the choice of terms used in a survey influence the outcome? (LO 7 - p. 50)

8. A researcher wishes to study foreplay behaviors in couples in a laboratory setting. What limitations of laboratory observation does he/she need to consider? (LO 9 - pp. 52-53)

9. Explain why a control group (and not just an experimental group) is necessary in experimental research. (LO 11 - p. 55)

10. Why must researchers use other animals instead of humans in some studies? (LO 12 - pp. 55-56)

11. What is the most common mistake people make when interpreting correlations? (LO 10 - p. 54)

Matching Exercises

I. Research Reports and Their Descriptions

Directions: Match the research reports listed in the left-hand column with their descriptions from the right-hand column.

a. The Kinsey Reports (p. 44)   ____ Interviews were used to examine the sexual behavior of White and African American women in Los Angeles County.

b. The Playboy Foundation Survey (p. 45)   ____ These reports were based on a sample of 979 homosexuals and 477 heterosexuals, matched for various factors.

c. The Janus Report (p. 46)   ____ This first nationwide sex survey was based on interviews of 23,000 Chinese over a period of eighteen months.

d. The Hite Reports (p. 46)   ____ Also called the Hunt survey, this 1974 sex survey had participants from only 24 urban centers and no rural areas.

e. The Billings Indian Health Service Survey (p. 48)   ____ This research was among the first to report direct laboratory observations of individuals and couples engaged in sexual acts.

f. The Wyatt Survey (p. 49)   ____ Although two books were published from the data, these reports cannot be considered scientific studies because of low return rates and unrepresentative samples.

g. The Liu Report (p. 49)   ____ This research consisted of the data obtained from interviews of 5,300 males and 5,940 females between 1938 and 1949 on various types of sexual experiences.

h. The Masters and Johnson Research (p. 51)   ____ This recent nationwide study of sexual behavior in the United States surveyed 2,765 people.

i. The Kinsey Institute Reports on Gay People: 1978 and 1981 (p. 47)   ____ Published in 1994, this survey consisted of interviews of 3,432 people representative of the overall population in the United States.

j. The NHSLS Study (p. 45)   ____ This survey was one of the first surveys of the reproductive and health behavior of Native American women.

II. Vocabulary Exercise 1

Directions: Match each vocabulary term listed in the left-hand column with the correct definition in the right-hand column.

a. empirical (p. 36)   ____ The attributing of human characteristics to an animal.

b. hypothesis (p. 36)   ____ A detailed study of a sample obtained by means such as interviews and questionnaires.

c. anthropomorphism (p. 37)   ____ Part of a population.

d. variables (p. 38)   ____ Concerning the vital statistics (density, race, age, etc.) of human populations.

e. operational definition (p. 38-39)   ____ A slanting of research data that is caused by the characteristics of individuals who volunteer to participate, such as willingness to discuss intimate behavior.

f. survey (p. 43)   ____ A response bias to a questionnaire or interview in which the person provides a socially acceptable response.

g. sample (p. 40)   ____ A random sample in which known subgroups in a population are represented in proportion to their numbers in the population.

h. population (p. 40)   ____ With respect to tests, the degree to which a particular test measures the constructs or traits it purports to measure.

i. volunteer bias (p. 41)   ____ A precise prediction about behavior that is tested through research.

j. reliability (p. 44)   ____ A definition of a construct or variable in terms of the methods used to measure it.

k. validity (p. 45)   ____ Quantities or qualities that vary or may vary.

l. demographic (p. 38)   ____ The consistency or accuracy of a measure.

m. stratified random sample (p. 41)   ____ Derived from or based on observation and experimentation.

n. social desirability (p. 50)   ____ A complete group of organisms or events.

III. Vocabulary Exercise 2

Directions: Match each vocabulary term listed in the left-hand column with the correct definition in the right-hand column.

a. ethnography (p. 51) _____ A method in which observers interact with the people they study as they collect data.

b. naturalistic observation (p. 50) _____ A condition in a scientific study that is manipulated so that its effects may be observed.

c. participant observation (p. 51) _____ The measured results of an experiment, which are believed to be a function of the independent variables.

d. experiment (p. 54) _____ A group of study participants who do not receive the experimental treatment. However, other conditions are held comparable to those of individuals in the experimental group.

e. independent variable (p. 55) _____ The branch of anthropology that deals descriptively with specific cultures, especially preliterate societies.

f. dependent variables (p. 55) _____ A statistical measure of the relationship between two variables.

g. experimental group (p. 55) _____ The term used by researchers to indicate that people have agreed to participate in research after receiving information about the purposes and nature of the study, and its potential risks and benefits.

h. control group (p. 55) _____ A scientific method that seeks to confirm cause-and-effect relationships by manipulating independent variables and observing their effects on dependent variables.

i. correlation (p. 53) _____ A carefully drawn, in-depth biography of an individual or a small group of individuals that may be obtained through interviews, questionnaires, and historical records.

j. case study (p. 42) _____ A method in which organisms are observed in their natural environments.

k. informed consent (p. 57) _____ A group of study participants who receive a treatment.

Multiple-Choice Questions

(LO = Learning Objective)

1. A researcher decides to conduct a study to determine if women who have extramarital affairs are more sexually satisfied within their marriages than women who do not engage in such extramarital practices. *Sexual satisfaction* is measured by the ability to achieve orgasm with one's marital partner.
   a. The concept of sexual satisfaction has been objectively analyzed in this research project.
   b. The concept of sexual satisfaction is too vague to define.
   c. The concept of sexual satisfaction has been operationally defined for this research.
   d. The concept of sexual satisfaction is always measured by orgasmic capacity.

   p. 38   LO 3

2. In surveying the students at your school about their sexual behavior, randomly selected groups of Freshmen, Sophomores, Juniors, and Seniors in proportion to their numbers in the student body would comprise a/an
   a. population.
   b. control group.
   c. stratified random sample.
   d. target sample.

   p. 41   LO 4

3. Alfred Kinsey used (the) _____ in his study of sexual behavior.
   a. laboratory experiments
   b. correlational method
   c. survey method
   d. naturalistic observation

   p. 44   LO 6

4. In a research project, the degree to which the questionnaire measures the construct it purports to measure is a measure of its
   a. validity.
   b. reliability.
   c. sample probability.
   d. incidence.

   p. 45   LO 7

5. Kinsey compared the response of each member of married couples regarding the frequency of intercourse. If both spouses agreed on the frequency of intercourse, then Kinsey would have greater assurance that his results were
   a. valid.
   b. reliable.
   c. unbiased.
   d. interpreted correctly.
   	p. 44	LO 7

6. All of the following were findings of the Liu study of sexual behavior in China, *except*
   a. Chinese males use foreplay techniques not well known in the West.
   b. women tend to initiate the majority of divorces.
   c. Chinese youth reach sexual maturity about a year earlier than their grandparents did.
   d. about half of young Chinese people engage in premarital sex.
   	p. 49	LO 6

7. Dr. Brooks goes to a massage parlor as a potential customer and records how offers for sexual services are made. The research method used here is
   a. ethnographic observation.
   b. participant observation.
   c. obtrusive observation.
   d. naturalistic observation.
   	p. 51	LO 8

8. The work of Masters and Johnson is considered controversial because
   a. they asked people about the most private aspects of their sexual lives.
   b. deception was used to collect their data.
   c. they participated in "swinging" to collect their data.
   d. measurements were recorded during sexual activity in the laboratory.
   	pp. 51-52	LO 8

9. A psychologist documents, in detail, the sexual developmental history of a female client. He is using
   a. the case study method.
   b. the experimental method.
   c. a correlational research method.
   d. naturalistic observation.
   	p. 42	LO 8

10. If a researcher measures the degree of penile enlargement as related to the viewing of sexually explicit movie clips, the movie clips are the _____ variable, and the degree of penile enlargement is the _____ variable.
    a. independent; dependent
    b. dependent; independent
    c. treatment; independent
    d. dependent; treatment
      p. 55   LO 11

11. In an experiment to study the effects of a drug which is touted to have an aphrodisiac effect on the user, the _____ group receives the _____ of the drug, while the _____ group does not.
    a. control; treatment; experimental
    b. treatment; dependent variable; control
    c. experimental; treatment; control
    d. experimental; dependent variable; control
      p. 55   LO 11

Chapter 3

Female Sexual Anatomy and Physiology

Chapter Summary

This chapter begins with a description of the female external sex organs and the structures that underlie them. The role of the clitoris in sexual pleasure is emphasized. The incidence, procedures, and reasons for the historic and current practice of female genital mutilation are examined. The myths and rituals surrounding the hymen and virginity are presented, along with some new trends in reconstructive hymen surgery. Throughout the chapter, the authors include useful self-help health information on such topics as avoiding cystitis, exercising the P-C muscles, preventing vaginitis, getting regular pelvic exams and Pap smears, and routinely examining the breasts for abnormalities.

The female internal sex organs (the vagina, cervix, uterus, fallopian tubes, and ovaries) and their functions are described. Next, normal breast appearance and function and the incidence of breast cancer are presented. Surgical breast removal, one treatment for breast cancer, triggers varying reactions in women.

Typical hormonal changes associated with the menstrual cycle, as well as numerous historical and cross-cultural negative ideas about menstruation, are presented. The myths and facts about the changes associated with menopause are discussed.

Women commonly experience some unpleasant symptoms during the premenstrual and menstrual phases of the menstrual cycle. Problems with menstruation and the symptoms associated with dysmenorrhea, amenorrhea and PMS are identified. The chapter concludes with an examination of research on the causes of PMS and includes suggestions for reducing menstrual discomfort.

Learning Objectives

1. Recognize the lingering effects of the negative bias that has been present historically in attitudes toward female sexuality and female sexual organs.
2. Name and describe the female external sex organs.
3. Recognize that the clitoris is the only sexual organ whose only known function is pleasure.
4. Describe ritual female genital mutilation, where it is practiced, the number of women affected, and the medical complications associated with the practice.
5. Explain why the condition of the hymen cannot be used to prove or disprove virginity.
6. Name, describe, and discuss the functions of the female internal sex organs.

7. Describe the pelvic exam procedure and explain the importance of routine pelvic exams.
8. Describe normal breast appearance and function and explain the importance of breast self-examination, mammograms, and regular medical checkups.
9. Discuss the incidence of breast cancer in women, the major treatments available, survival rates and the support needed by women following breast removal.
10. Identify the four phases of the menstrual cycle and discuss the hormonal and physical changes associated with each.
11. Distinguish the myths from the facts surrounding the issue of coitus during menstruation.
12. Distinguish the myths from the facts regarding the effects of menopause on women.
13. Summarize the research regarding the cultural, social, psychological, and biological correlates of dysmenorrhea.
14. Identify the common symptoms of PMS, cite the number of women who experience symptoms, and list the possible causes of PMS and its proposed treatments.

Fill-in-the-Blanks

The external sexual structures of the female are termed the pudendum or the _____ . Covered with pubic hair, the _____ _____ consists of fatty tissue that covers the joint of the pubic bones in front of the body. The _____ _____ are large folds of skin that shield the inner portion of the female genitalia. Rich in nerve endings, the _____ _____ are hairless and located between the major lips. The _____ is the woman's most erotically charged organ. The word _____ refers to the area that contains the openings to the vagina and the urethra. Urine passes from the female's body through the _____ opening. _____ is a bladder inflammation, whose primary symptoms are burning and frequent urination. The _____ is a fold of tissue across the vaginal opening that is usually present at birth and remains at least partly intact until a woman engages in coitus. The _____ incorporates the skin and underlying tissue between the vaginal opening and the anus. Many physicians make a routine incision of this skin and tissue, an _____ , to facilitate childbirth.

Menstrual flow and babies pass through the uterus to the outer world through the _____ . The _____ is the lower end of the uterus. A

_____ _____ is a sample of cells that are examined to screen for cancer and other abnormalities. The _____ is the pear-shaped organ in which a fertilized ovum implants and develops until birth. The _____ are about 4 inches in length and extend from the upper end of the uterus. The two _____ are almond-shaped organs that are each about one and one-half inches long. _____ cancer is the second leading cause of cancer deaths among women. Nearly one in _____ women in the United States develop this cancer.

_____ is the cyclical bleeding that stems from the shedding of the uterine lining. The first phase, or _____ phase, begins with the end of menstruation and lasts about 9 or 10 days in an average ____-day cycle. During the _____ phase, the graafian follicle ruptures and releases a mature ovum near a Fallopian tube. During the _____ phase the corpus luteum begins to produce large amounts of progesterone and estrogen. If implantation does not occur the corpus luteum decomposes. The _____ phase is the sloughing off of the uterine lining.

_____ is the cessation of menstruation. _____ is pain or discomfort during menstruation. _____ is the absence of menstruation.

Short Answer Questions

(LO = Learning Objective)
1. Describe the types of female circumcision and the reasons these are sometimes performed. (LO 4 - pp. 66-67)

2. Discuss precautions women can take to help prevent cystitis. (LO 6 - pp. 66-67)

3. What is the source of the vaginal lubrication women experience during sexual arousal? Describe the process by which it is produced. (LO 6 - p. 70)

4. What are Kegels? Why should women do them? (LO 6 - p. 70)

5. What suggestions can women follow to help prevent vaginitis? (LO 6 - p. 72)

6. Approximately how many women in the U.S. have hysterectomies? Why are they usually performed? (LO 6 - p. 74)

7. Describe the procedures involved in a pelvic examination. How often should women have pelvic exams? (LO 7 - pp. 75-76)

8. Describe the methods for detection of breast cancer. How often should women do each of these? (LO 8 - pp. 79-80)

9. Why might couples abstain from coitus or engage in coitus during menstruation? (LO 11 - pp. 89-90)

10. What "symptoms" are most common among women with an estrogen deficiency due to menopause? (LO 12 - pp. 91-92)

11. Name at least four common myths about menopause. What are the facts concerning each of these myths? (LO 12 - pp. 90-91)

12. What is PMS? What are the most common symptoms? (LO 14 - pp. 94-95)

13. List at least five suggestions women can follow to reduce persistent menstrual discomfort. (LO 14 - pp. 95-96)

Matching Exercises

I. Vocabulary Exercise 1

Directions: Match each vocabulary term listed in the left-hand column with the correct definition in the right-hand column.

a.	ova (p. 62)	____	Surgical removal of the clitoris.
b.	gynecologist (p. 66)	____	Vaginal inflammation.
c.	defloration (p. 68)	____	The opening in the middle of the cervix.
d.	clitoridectomy (p. 66)	____	A capsule within an ovary that contains an ovum.
e.	pubococcygeus muscle (p. 70)	____	A condition caused by estrogen deficiency and characterized by a decline in bone density, such that bones become porous and brittle.
f.	vaginitis (p. 72)	____	The dark ring on the breast that encircles the nipple.
g.	os (p. 72)	____	Egg cells.
h.	ectopic pregnancy (p. 74)	____	The muscle that encircles the entrance to the vagina.
i.	follicle (p. 75)	____	Traits that distinguish women from men but are not directly involved in reproduction.
j.	secondary sex characteristics (p. 77)	____	A physician who treats women's diseases, especially of the reproductive tract.
k.	mammary glands (p. 77)	____	A pregnancy in which the fertilized ovum implants outside the uterus, usually in the Fallopian tube.
l.	areola (p. 77)	____	Milk-secreting glands.
m.	osteoporosis (p. 91)	____	Destruction of the hymen (especially as a cultural ritual).

II. Vocabulary Exercise 2

Directions: Match each vocabulary term listed in the left-hand column with the correct definition in the right-hand column.

a. mammography (p. 78) ____ The innermost layer of the uterus.

b. lumpectomy (p. 79) ____ Surgical removal of the uterus.

c. mastectomy (p. 79) ____ The middle, well-muscled layer of the uterus.

d. endometrium (p. 73) ____ The cessation of menstruation.

e. endometriosis (p. 73) ____ A specialized type of X-ray test that detects cancerous lumps in the breast.

f. myometrium (p. 74) ____ A combination of physical and psychological symptoms (e.g., anxiety, depression, irritability, weight gain from fluid retention, and abdominal discomfort) that regularly afflicts many women during the four- to six-day interval that precedes their menses each month.

g. perimetrium (p. 74) ____ The release of an ovum from an ovary.

h. hysterectomy (p. 74) ____ A psychological disorder of eating characterized by intense fear of putting on weight and refusal to eat enough to maintain normal body weight.

i. complete hysterectomy (p. 74) ____ Surgical removal of a lump from the breast.

j. ovulation (p. 83) ____ A substance secreted by an endocrine gland that regulates various body functions.

k. menarche (p. 83) ____ Surgical removal of the ovaries, Fallopian tubes, cervix, and uterus.

l. menopause (p. 90) ____ The first menstrual period.

m. hormone (p. 84) ____ Surgical removal of the entire breast.

n. anorexia nervosa (p. 94) ____ The outer layer of the uterus.

o. premenstrual syndrome (PMS) (p. 94) ____ A condition caused by the growth of endometrial tissue in the abdominal cavity or elsewhere outside the uterus, and characterized by menstrual pain.

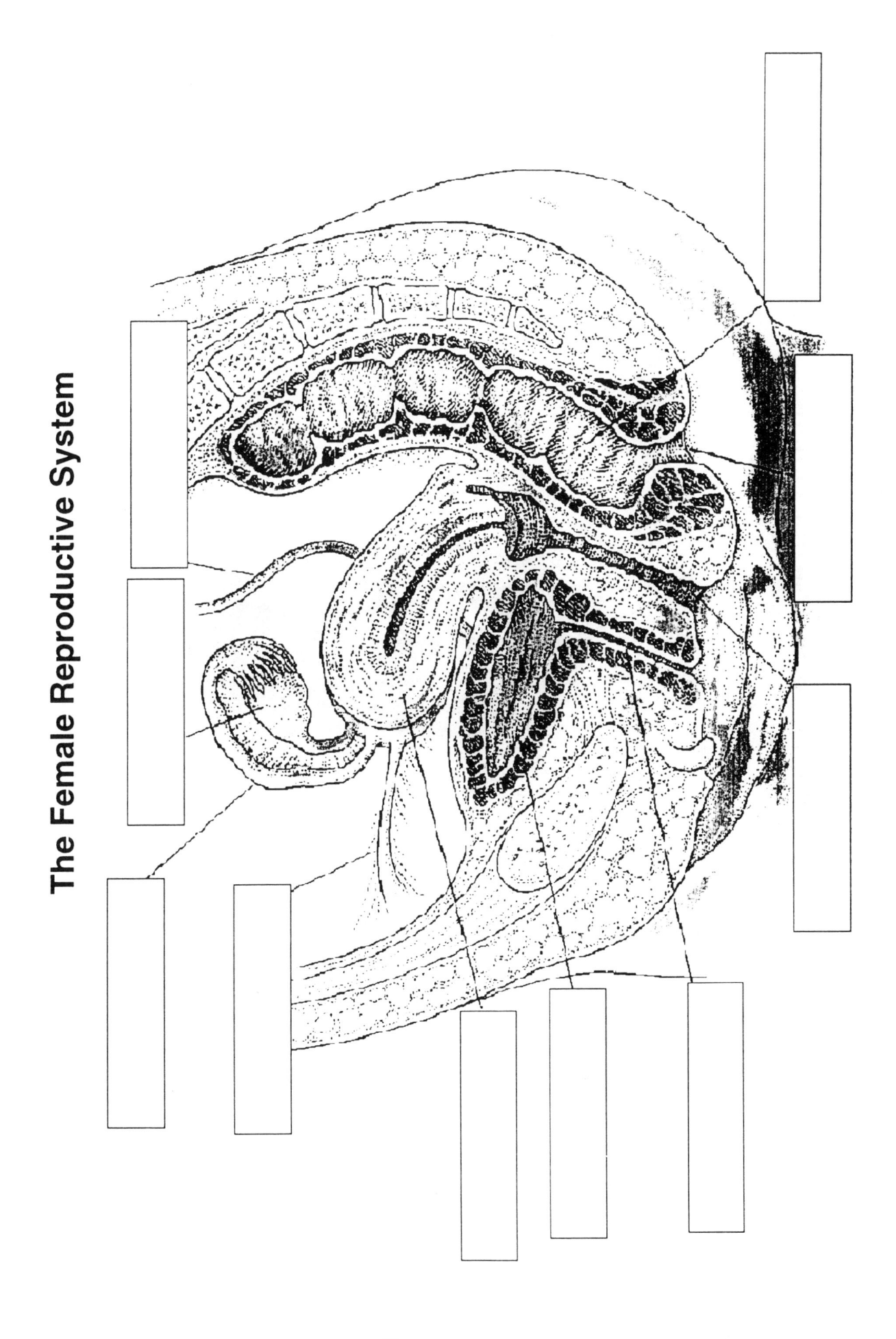

The Female Reproductive System

The External Female Sexual Organs

Internal Female Reproductive Organs

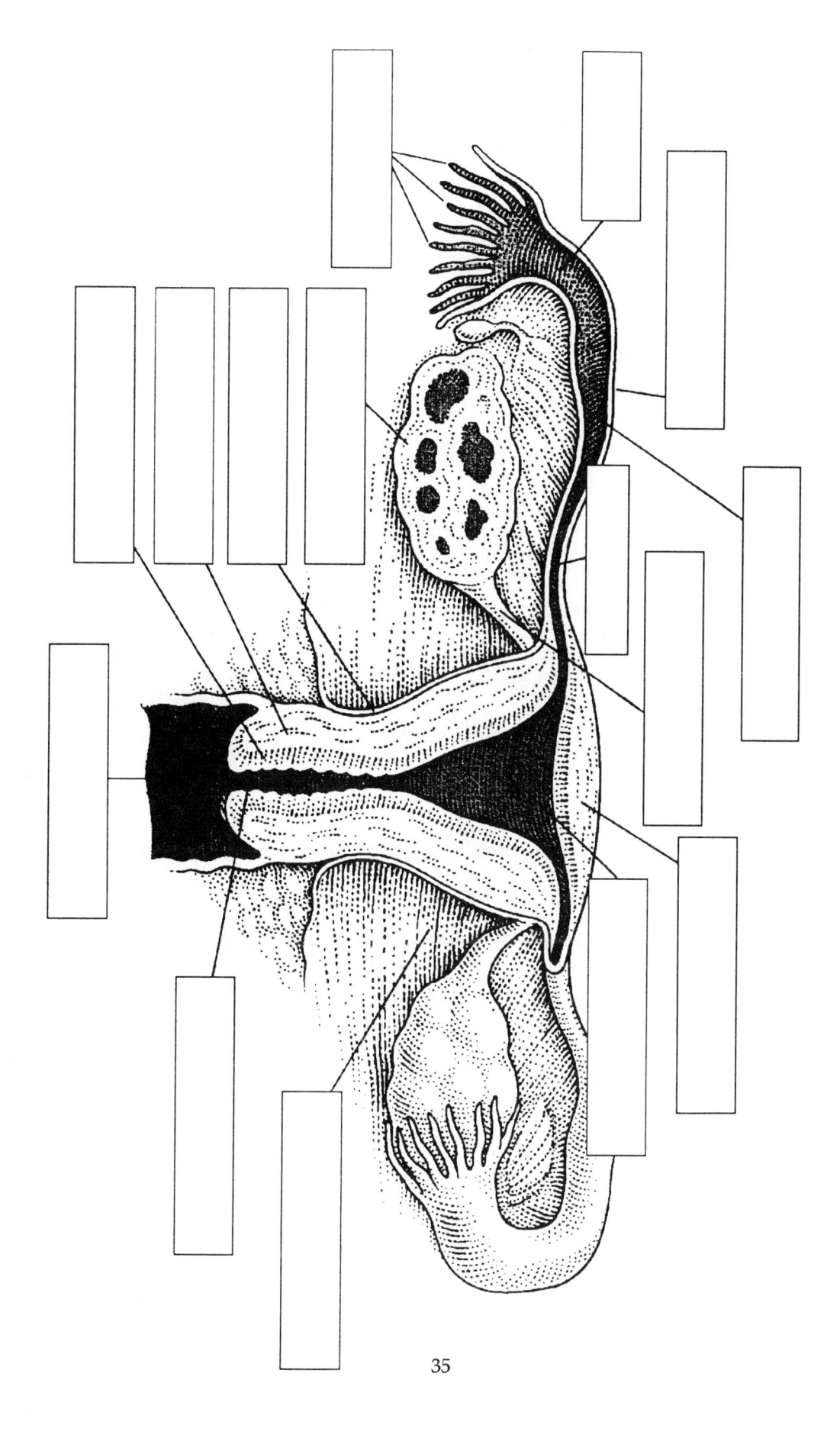

Multiple-Choice Questions

(LO = Learning Objective)

1. All of the following statements about the mons veneris are accurate, *except*
   a. it becomes covered with hair at puberty.
   b. it serves as a protective cushion during coitus.
   c. it has few nerve endings, allowing it to sustain painful thrusting.
   d. its hairy covering retains chemical secretions from the vagina.
   p. 63   LO 2

2. The clitoris serves as
   a. an essential structure in conception.
   b. a channel for urine.
   c. an organ of sexual pleasure.
   d. an organ of humility.
   p. 64   LO 3

3. Infectious organisms entering the urethral opening may cause
   a. vaginitis.
   b. cystitis.
   c. defloration.
   d. puritis.
   p. 66   LO 2

4. Genital mutilation, including clitoridectomies,
   a. is currently outlawed throughout the world.
   b. continues today in some countries of Africa and the Middle East.
   c. was a ritual social custom that disappeared at the turn of the century.
   d. is a painless procedure performed under sterile conditions in Africa.
   pp. 66-67   LO 4

5. Why is the lack of an intact hymen not a reliable indicator of whether or not a woman has engaged in coitus?
   a. Most women are born without hymen.
   b. A hymen can be torn by engaging in physical activities other than coitus.
   c. The hymen grows back, even after coitus.
   d. Clitoridectomy can be performed to replace the hymen.
   p. 68   LO 5

6. All of the following relate to the internal sexual organs of the female *except*
   a. the perineum.
   b. the vagina.
   c. the cervix.
   d. the fallopian tubes.
      pp. 69 - 74   LO 6

7. Vaginal lubrication, or "wetness," is produced by
   a. the Bartholin's glands.
   b. the vestibular bulbs.
   c. a type of sweating of the vaginal walls.
   d. fluid released by the urethral opening.
      p. 70   LO 6

8. Frequent douching may contribute to
   a. increased sexual arousal.
   b. disruption of the natural chemical balance of the vagina.
   c. excessive vasocongestion and myotonia.
   d. increased sensitivity to pain in the vagina.
      p. 72   LO 6

9. The pelvic exam procedure for women
   a. includes a Pap smear to detect cervical cancer.
   b. should only be performed after a woman is pregnant.
   c. includes a bimanual vaginal and recto-vaginal exam.
   d. both a and b.
   e. both a and c.
      pp. 75 - 76   LO 7

10. Coitus during menstruation
    a. is harmful for the female.
    b. generally does not occur because females are not sexually receptive then.
    c. is taboo cross culturally.
    d. is a matter of personal decision.
      pp. 89-90   LO 11

11. Unpleasant physical experiences accompanying menopause are caused by
    a. deficiencies in estrogen production.
    b. unstable production of FSH and LH.
    c. increased progesterone production.
    d. decreases in calcium.
      pp. 90-91   LO 12

12. Menstrual cramps are caused by excessive amounts of
    a. estrogens.
    b. anger.
    c. prostaglandins.
    d. gonadotropin releasing hormone.
            pp. 94-95   LO 13

Chapter 4

Male Sexual Anatomy and Physiology

Chapter Summary

This chapter begins by describing the penis and the structures within the penis. Research evidence about the possible benefits or drawbacks of circumcision of male infants is examined. Debunking the myths about the connection between penis size and "manliness" or sexual performance is emphasized. A description of the scrotum and its role in maintaining optimal temperature for sperm production is presented.

The authors next examine the production of sperm and testosterone by the testes. They describe the route taken by the sperm when they leave the scrotum through the vas deferens and combine with fluids from the seminal vesicles, prostate gland and Cowper's glands to produce semen.

The symptoms and treatments for urethritis and testicular cancer are described. Instructions for testicular self-examinations are given and regular medical checkups are encouraged. The symptoms of common prostate problems are described. Particular attention is given to the latest developments in detection of prostate cancer, and specific treatments are examined.

The section on male sexual functions examines the roles of reflexes, the spinal cord, the brain, and the autonomic nervous system in erection and ejaculation. Abnormalities in both functions are described briefly.

Learning Objectives

1. Describe the penis and the internal structures that make erection possible.
2. Cite the reasons people give for having male babies circumcised and the research evidence on this topic.
3. Distinguish between myths and facts derived from research on the effects of penis size on sexual performance and a partner's sexual satisfaction.
4. Describe the scrotum and its role in maintaining optimum temperature for sperm production.
5. Describe the structure of the testes and explain their functions in sperm and testosterone production.
6. Trace the route of the sperm as they leave the testes and combine with the several glandular fluids that form semen.
7. Discuss the incidence, symptoms, treatments, and survival rates associated with testicular cancer.

8. Describe the testicular self-examination procedure and the importance of self-exams and regular medical checkups for early detection of testicular and prostate cancer.
9. Identify the disorders of the prostate and their symptoms and treatments.
10. Describe the conditions under which erections can occur and explain why the process of erection is a spinal reflex.
11. Explain the effect of spinal cord injuries on erection and ejaculation.
12. Discuss the role of the brain and the autonomic nervous system in erection.
13. Describe several erectile and ejaculatory abnormalities.
14. Describe the process of ejaculation, including the roles of the spinal cord and the autonomic nervous system.

Fill-in-the-Blanks

The male external sex organs include the _____ and the _____ . _____ and _____ pass out of the penis through the urethral opening. The penis contains three cylinders of spongy material that become engorged with blood during sexual arousal, resulting in _____ . _____ is the surgical removal of the foreskin. The Academy of _____ continue to debate the health benefits of circumcision. The _____ is a pouch of loose skin that holds the testes. The testes serve two functions: they secrete _____ and they produce _____ . Structures in the lobes of the testes, the _____ _____ , produce and store hundreds of billions of sperm in a lifetime. The presence of an X or Y _____ _____ from the father determines a baby's gender.

In a sterilization operation, called a _____ , the right and left _____ _____ are severed. The _____ _____ produce a fluid rich in fructose, which nourishes sperm and helps them become active. The _____ gland produces a fluid that is alkaline; this fluid neutralizes the acidity of the vaginal tract. Fluid from the _____ glands precedes the ejaculate and often contains viable sperm. Semen is composed of sperm and fluids from the _____ _____ , the _____ _____ , and the _____ _____ .

_____ refers to bladder and urethral inflammations. _____ cancer is particularly common in the 20 - 34 year old age group. When detected early, the _____ _____ is 96 percent. Men are advised to do monthly _____ and go for regular medical checkups.

The _____ gland becomes enlarged in almost all men past the age of 50. One in eight men will develop _____ cancer. It rarely strikes men under 40, but the risk increases progressively after that age. _____ is an inflammation of the prostate gland that is usually treated with antibiotics.

Men have _____ _____ every 90 minutes or so as they sleep. Morning erections _____ (are/are not) caused by a need to urinate.

Erection and ejaculation are _____ -- automatic, unlearned responses to sexual stimulation. These responses involve the division of the nervous system called the _____ nervous system. This division of the nervous system has two branches, the _____ branch which largely governs erection, and the _____ branch, which governs ejaculation. The first stage of ejaculation, called the _____ _____, involves contractions which propel seminal fluid into the urethral bulb. The second stage, the _____ _____, involves the propulsion of the seminal fluid out of the urethral opening. In _____ _____, the ejaculate empties into the bladder rather than being expelled from the body.

Short Answer Questions

(LO = Learning Objective)
1. Evaluate the arguments made by advocates and opponents regarding routine circumcision of male infants. (LO 2 - pp. 103-104)

2. Explain the relationship, if any, between penis size and sexual performance. (LO 3 - pp. 104-105)

3. Explain why the scrotum's ability to raise and lower the testicles is important. (LO 4 - pp. 104-105)

4. Describe the process of spermatogenesis. (LO 5 - pp. 107-108)

5. What is urethritis? What preventive measures can men take to avoid getting it? (LO 8 - p. 111)

6. List the common diseases of the male reproductive system and their symptoms. (LO 7 & 9 - pp. 111-115)

7. Describe how to do testicular self-exams and the warning signs which signal that men should see their physicians. (LO 8 - pp. 113-114)

8. Which men are most likely to experience enlargement of the prostate? What symptoms might they experience? (LO 9 - p. 113)

9. Describe the complex process of erection. What accounts for the firmness of an erection? (LO 10 - pp. 115-116)

10. What are nocturnal erections? When do they occur? (LO 10 - pp. 116)

11. Describe the role of the spinal cord in the reflex that produces erection in response to tactile stimulation. (LO 10 - pp. 116-117)

12. What is a "no-hands" erection and how does it occur? (LO 12 - p. 118)

13. Describe the roles of the sympathetic and parasympathetic branches of the autonomic nervous system in erection and ejaculation.
(LO 12 & 14 - pp. 119, 121)

Matching Exercises

I. Vocabulary Exercise 1

Directions: Match each vocabulary term listed in the left-hand column with the correct definition in the right-hand column.

a. testes (p. 100)   ____ Cylinders of spongy tissue in the penis that become congested with blood and stiffen during sexual arousal.

b. penis (p. 101)   ____ The cord that suspends a testicle within the scrotum and contains a vas defers, blood vessels, nerves, and the cremaster muscle.

c. corpora cavernosa (p. 102)   ____ The sensitive strip of tissue that connects the underside of the penile glans to the shaft.

d. corpus spongiosum (p. 102)   ____ The muscle that raises and lowers the testicle in response to temperature changes and sexual stimulation.

e. corona (p. 102)   ____ The body of the penis, which expands as a result of vasocongestion.

f. frenulum (p. 102)   ____ The base of the penis, which extends into the pelvis.

g. root (p. 102)   ____ The male sex glands, suspended in the scrotum, that produce sperm cells and male sex hormones.

h. shaft (p. 102)   ____ The pouch of loose skin that contains the testes.

i. premature ejaculation (p. 121)   ____ The spongy body that runs along the bottom of the penis, contains the penile urethra, and enlarges at the tip of the penis to form the glans.

j. scrotum (p. 104)   ____ The male organ of sexual intercourse.

k. spermatic cord (p. 104)   ____ A tube that conducts sperm from the testicle to the ejaculatory duct of the penis.

l. vas deferens (p. 109)   ____ The ridge that separates the glans from the body of the penis.

m. cremaster muscle (p. 104)   ____ A sexual dysfunction in which the male persistently ejaculates too early to afford the couple adequate sexual gratification.

II. Vocabulary Exercise 2

Directions: Match each vocabulary term listed in the left-hand column with the correct definition in the right-hand column.

a. seminiferous tubules (p. 107)   ____ An inflammation of the bladder or urethra.

b. spermatogenesis (p. 107)   ____ A sterilization procedure in which the vas deferens is severed, preventing sperm from reaching the ejaculatory duct.

c. epididymis (p. 109)   ____ The second stage of ejaculation, during which muscles of the penis contract rhythmically, forcibly expelling semen.

d. vasectomy (p. 109)   ____ Structures that lie below the prostate and empty their secretions into the urethra during sexual arousal.

e. seminal vesicles (p. 109)   ____ The first phase of ejaculation, which involves contractions of the prostate gland, seminal vesicles, and the upper part of the vas deferens.

f. prostate gland (p. 110)   ____ The process by which sperm cells are produced and developed.

g. Cowper's glands (p. 110)   ____ Inflammation of the prostate gland.

h. semen (p. 111)   ____ Small glands behind the bladder that secrete fluids that combine with sperm in the ejaculatory ducts.

i. urethritis (p. 111)   ____ The enlargement and stiffening of the penis as a consequence of engorgement with blood.

j. prostatitis (p. 115)   ____ A tube that lies against the back wall of each testicle and serves as a storage facility for sperm.

k. erection (p. 115)   ____ Tiny, winding, sperm-producing tubes that are located within the lobes of the testes.

l. emission stage (p. 120)   ____ The gland that lies beneath the bladder and secretes prostatic fluid, which gives semen its characteristic odor and texture.

m. expulsion stage (p. 121)   ____ The whitish fluid that constitutes the ejaculate, consisting of sperm and secretions from the seminal vesicles, prostate, and Cowper's glands.

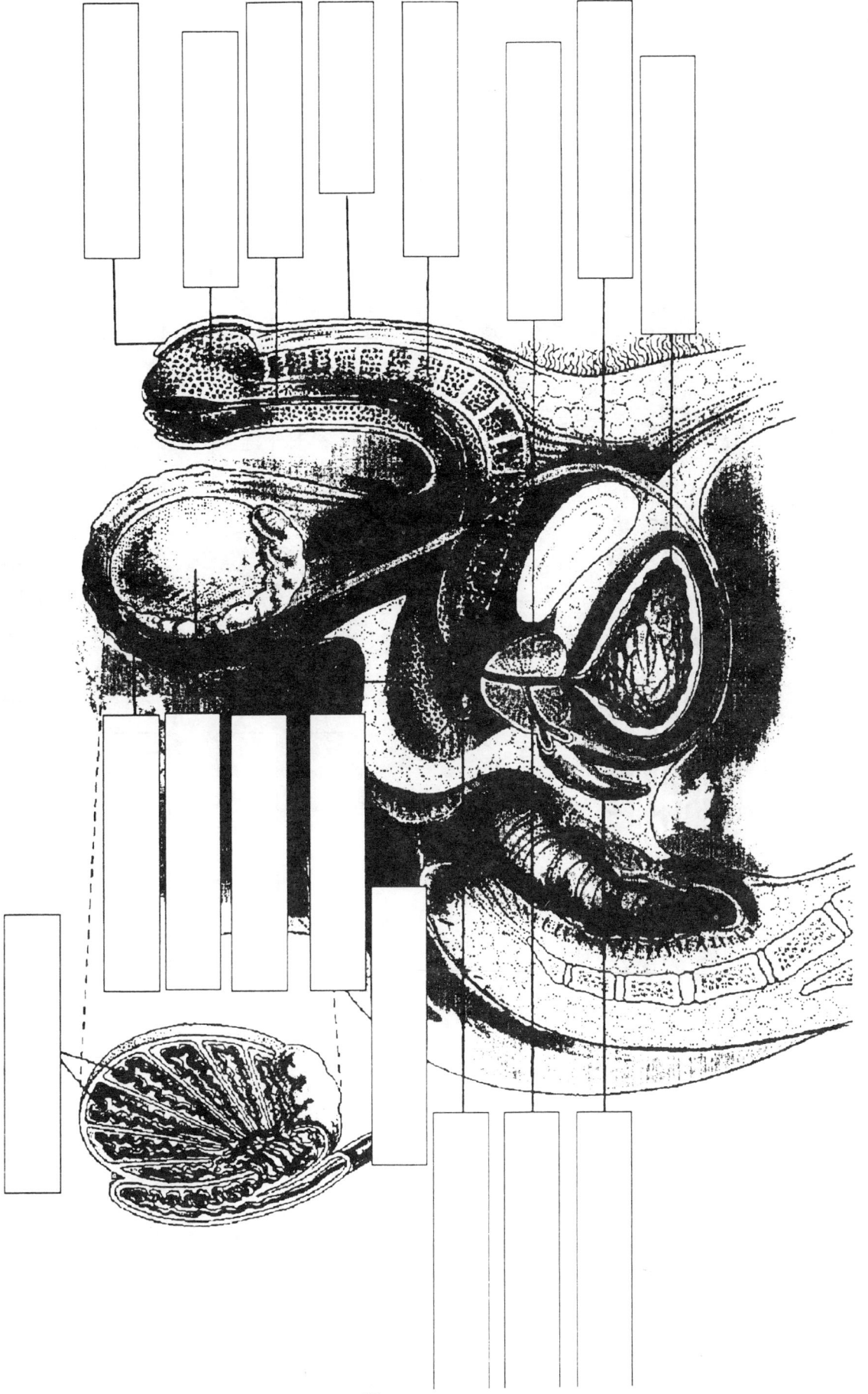

The Male Reproductive System

The Penis

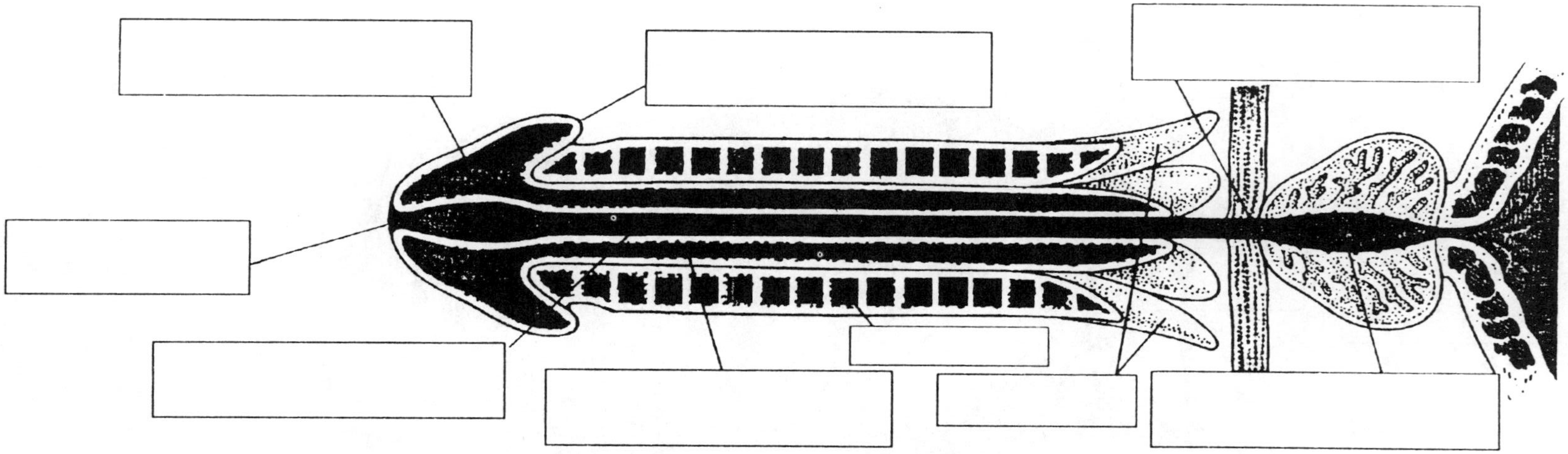

LONGITUDINAL SECTION

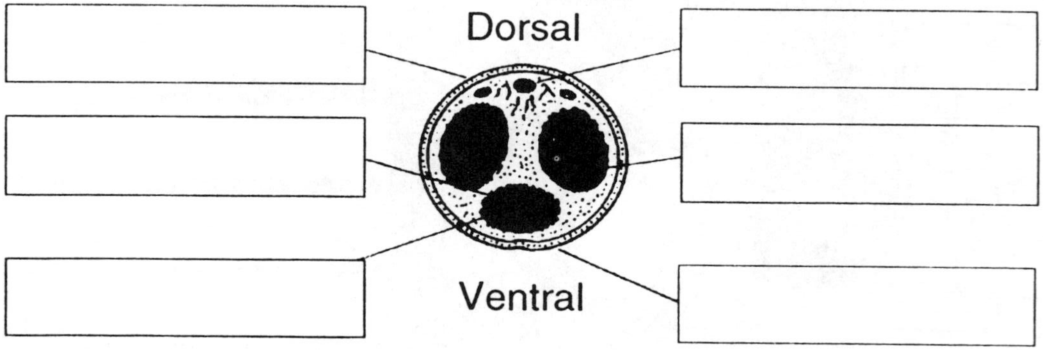

CROSS SECTION

Dorsal

Ventral

6. Spermatogenesis refers to the process in which
   a. sperm are transported through the seminiferous tubules.
   b. sperm cells are produced and stored.
   c. hormone levels in the male reproductive system are regulated.
   d. spermatocytes split.

           p. 107-108   LO 5

7. Why is enlargement of the prostate problematic?
   a. It prevents the free passage of sperm during ejaculation.
   b. It constricts the urethra causing urinary disturbances.
   c. It increases vulnerability to testicular cancer.
   d. It interferes with sexual arousal.

           pp. 112-113   LO 9

8. Prostate cancer is usually first detected by
   a. testicular self-examination.
   b. the penile strain gauge.
   c. rectal examination or a blood test.
   d. a magnetic resonance imaging examination.

           pp. 113-114   LO 9

9. Males begin to have penile erections
   a. only after the first year of life.
   b. after they have reached puberty.
   c. as soon as they are able to ejaculate.
   d. even while in the fetal environment.

           p. 116   LO 10

10. Sally and Steve are in their late 30's. She is concerned that Steve is losing interest in her because he requires more direct penile stimulation to become erect. What advice is a sex therapist likely to give?
    a. Steve is probably having an extramarital affair.
    b. You should probably seek another lover.
    c. Males take longer to achieve an erection as they age.
    d. Males in their climacteric are less sexually focused.

            pp. 118-119   LO 12

11. Sean is prepubescent.
    a. He experiences orgasm and ejaculation with sufficient sexual stimulation.
    b. He cannot achieve an erection until puberty.
    c. He experiences "dry orgasms."
    d. He experiences ejaculation without orgasm.

            p. 121   LO 14

Multiple-Choice Questions

(LO = Learning Objective)

1. The flaccid penis stiffens when
   a. the internal penile bones lock into place during sexual arousal.
   b. the penile muscles become rigid due to sexual excitement.
   c. the corpus cavernosa and corpus spongiosum sustain vasocongestion.
   d. the meatus becomes engorged with blood.
      p. 102   LO 1

2. The most sensitive part of the penis is the
   a. glans.
   b. corona.
   c. frenulum.
   d. meatus.
      p. 102   LO 1

3. The scrotum consists of
   a. the seminal vesicles.
   b. dual compartments which hold the testes.
   c. bulbourethral glands.
   d. the prostate gland.
      p. 104   LO 4

4. If a man was engaged in sexual intercourse in a very cool room, you would expect
   a. the vas deferens to lengthen and expand to allow for vasocongestion.
   b. the cremaster muscle to bring the testicles closer to the body.
   c. the dartos muscle would relax to allow the testicles to dangle farther from the body.
   d. the interstitial cells to increase production of testosterone.
      pp. 104-105   LO 4

5. Testosterone carries out all of the following functions, *except*
   a. stimulates development of secondary sex characteristics.
   b. stimulates prenatal differentiation of primary sex characteristics.
   c. stimulates sperm production.
   d. stimulates the Bartholin's gland.
      p. 106   LO 5

Chapter 5

Sexual Arousal and Response

Chapter Summary

This chapter considers factors that contribute to sexual arousal and the processes that relate to sexual response. The roles in sexual experience of vision, smell, the skin senses, taste, and hearing are examined. The effects of pheromones on humans and other animals and the role of pheromones in menstrual synchrony are presented. These effects have sparked the growth of new research and, potentially, a whole new industry.

Research on alleged aphrodisiacs is presented; these substances have not been shown to contribute to sexual arousal or response in humans. The effects on sexual functioning of psychoactive drugs (including alcohol, marijuana, amphetamines, and cocaine) are explored.

The brain plays a central role in sexual functioning. The authors examine the roles played by the cerebral cortex, the limbic system, and the female and male sex hormones in sexual behavior. The role of testosterone in female and male sexual behavior is emphasized.

Masters and Johnson's sexual response cycle identifies the physiological changes associated with sexual arousal and response; the similarities between the physiological responses of men and women are emphasized. The four phases of the cycle are: excitement, plateau, orgasmic, and resolution. Kaplan has proposed an alternate model of sexual response consisting of three stages: desire, excitement, and orgasm.

Finally, the authors present research evidence that addresses the orgasm controversies: the question of multiple orgasms in women and men, the debate over types of orgasms in women, and the existence of the G-spot.

Learning Objectives

1. Describe the role of vision in sexual arousal.
2. Describe the role of smell in sexual arousal and discuss the research on the influence of pheromones on human and other animal behavior.
3. Define erogenous zones and identify their locations.
4. Describe the roles of taste and hearing in sexual arousal.
5. Summarize the research on substances that have aphrodisiac or anaphrodisiac properties.
6. Identify the major psychoactive drugs and explain their psychological and physical effects on sexual arousal.
7. Identify the parts of the cerebral cortex and the limbic system that play roles in sexual arousal and sexual behavior.

8. Summarize the research on the role of sex hormones in sexual orientation and interest in male and female humans and other animals.
9. Name the four phases and describe the changes associated with each phase of the sexual response cycle proposed by Masters and Johnson.
10. Compare Kaplan's three-stage model of sexual arousal with Masters and Johnson's four-phase model.
11. Summarize the research on the female and male capacity for multiple orgasms.
12. Evaluate the research concerning the types of orgasms women experience.
13. Evaluate the evidence concerning the existence of the Grafenberg spot in women.

Fill-in-the-Blanks

Each of the senses plays a role in the sexual experiences of humans, but _____ usually plays the largest role. More directly involved in the sexual behavior of "lower" mammals is the sense of _____ . _____ are odorless chemical secretions which trigger sexual behavior in many organisms. The extent of their effect on humans is not yet known. In one study women exposed to underarm secretions from other women experienced _____ _____ . _____ _____ are parts of the body that are especially sensitive to strokes and caresses. Taste plays only a minor role in sexual arousal and response, but, as evidenced by the telephone sex industry, _____ plays a larger role.

An _____ is a substance that is sexually arousing or capable of increasing one's capacity for sexual pleasure or response. _____ drugs are widely believed to have these effects. However, alcohol is a central nervous system _____ and biochemically _____ sexual arousal. Although users of hallucinogenics and stimulants report various effects on sexual response, _____ of these drugs has a consistent aphrodisiac effect on all users.

Various parts of the brain, particularly the _____ _____ and the _____ _____ play important roles in sexual functioning. Research on animals and a few people seemingly located "_____ _____" in or near the hypothalamus. Rats will repeatedly press controls to receive bursts of electricity in these areas.

_____ are chemical substances that are secreted by endocrine glands and discharged directly into the bloodstream. _____ is

52

the major male sex hormone, and _____ and _____ are the major female sex hormones. Sex hormones released at puberty cause the flowering of _____ _____ _____ , such as growth of facial and pubic hair and breast development. Men who are castrated usually exhibit a gradual loss of _____ _____ and the capacity to attain _____ and to _____ . Female sex hormones _____ (do/do not) appear to play a direct role in determining sexual motivation or response in human females. In most other mammals, females are sexually receptive only during _____ . Research suggests that _____ play a more prominent role than ovarian hormones in women's sex drives.

_____ and _____ studied the physiological responses of men and women to sexual stimulation. These researchers proposed four phases of the _____ _____ _____ : _____ , _____ , _____ , and _____ . Early in this cycle, both males and females experience _____ (swelling of genital tissues with blood) and _____ (muscle tension).

_____ _____ _____ developed a model of sexual response in which the three stages are _____ , _____ , and _____ . Her clinical experience with people with _____ _____ formed the basis for her model.

According to Masters and Johnson, most women are capable of experiencing _____ orgasms; evidence for this in men is limited to a relatively few cases. Sigmund Freud believed that women have two types of orgasm: _____ orgasms and _____ orgasms; Masters and Johnson, however, were only able to find one type. The _____ _____ is a bean-shaped area within the anterior wall of the vagina, which may have special erotic significance. Its existence remains debatable.

Short Answer Questions

(LO = Learning Objective)
1. Explain why the menstrual cycles of women who live together tend to become synchronized. (LO 2 - p. 127)

2. Define primary and secondary erogenous zones. List several primary erogenous zones. (LO 3 - p. 128)

3. What effect do anaphrodisiacs have? Name several chemicals that act as anaphrodisiacs. (LO 5 - pp. 130-131)

4. Explain the effects of alcohol on sexual behavior. (LO 6 - p. 132)

5. Define the difference between the organizing effects and the activating effects of sex hormones. (LO 8 - p. 137)

6. What does research indicate about the effects of androgens on male and female sexual interest? (LO 8 - pp. 138 - 139)

7. Name and describe the two major phenomena experienced by both males and females early in the sexual response cycle. (LO 9 - p. 140)

8. Explain the male/female differences in the resolution phase of the Sexual Response Cycle. (LO 9 - p. 144)

9. Describe the variations in patterns of sexual response for males and females described by Masters and Johnson. (LO 9 - pp. 140-144)

10. In what significant ways is Kaplan's model of sexual response different from Masters and Johnson's model? Explain. (LO 10 - pp. 144-145)

11. Are men capable of multiple orgasms? (LO 11 - p. 146)

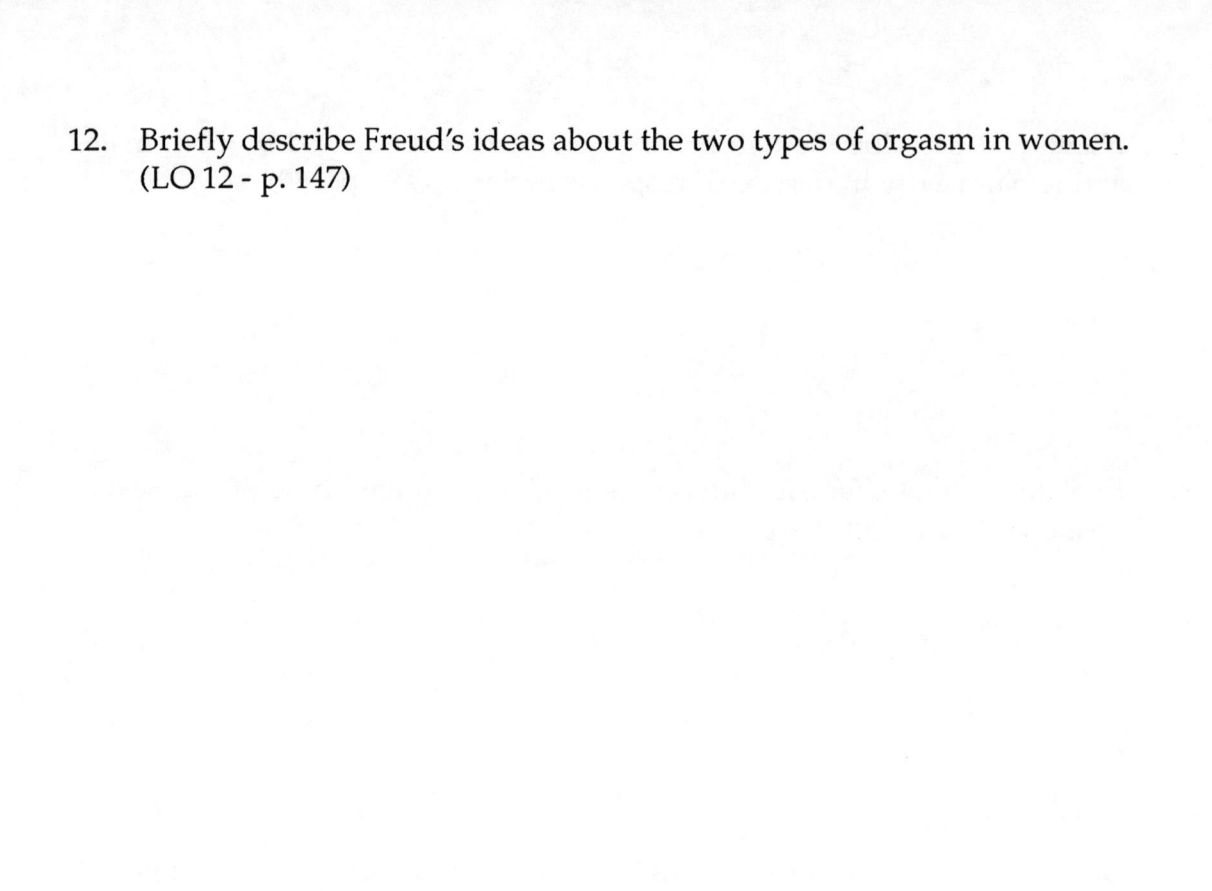

12. Briefly describe Freud's ideas about the two types of orgasm in women. (LO 12 - p. 147)

Matching Exercises

I. Vocabulary Exercise 1

Directions: Match each vocabulary term listed in the left-hand column with the correct definition in the right-hand column.

a. aphrodisiac (p. 126) ____ Parts of the body that are especially sensitive to tactile sexual stimulation.

b. pheromones (p. 127) ____ A substance that decreases the levels of androgens in the bloodstream.

c. erogenous zones (p. 128) ____ Erogenous zones that are particularly sensitive because they are richly endowed with nerve endings.

d. primary erogenous zones (p. 128) ____ Surgical removal of the ovaries.

e. secondary erogenous zones (p. 128) ____ Any drug or other agent that is sexually arousing or increases sexual desire.

f. anaphrodisiacs (p. 130) ____ An abnormal condition marked by abnormally low levels of testosterone production.

g. antiandrogen (p. 131) ____ The wrinkled surface area (gray matter) of the cerebrum.

h. limbic system (p. 134) ____ A person with a gender-identity disorder in which he or she feels that he or she is really a member of the other gender and trapped in a body of the wrong gender.

i. cerebral cortex (p. 134) ____ Drugs or other agents whose effects are antagonistic to sexual arousal or sexual desire.

j. transsexual (p. 137) ____ A group of structures active in memory, motivation, and emotion; the structures that are part of this system form a fringe along the inner edge of the cerebrum.

k. hypogonadism (p. 139) ____ Chemical substances secreted externally by certain animals which convey information to, or produce specific responses in, other members of the same species.

l. ovariectomy (p. 140) ____ Parts of the body that become erotically sensitized through experience.

II. Vocabulary Exercise 2

Directions: Match each vocabulary term listed in the left-hand column with the correct definition in the right-hand column.

a. sexual response cycle (SRC) (p. 140)　　____ A reddish rash that appears on the chest or breasts late in the excitement phase of the sexual response cycle.

b. vasocongestion (p. 140)　　____ Thickening of the walls of the outer third of the vagina that occurs during the plateau phase of the sexual response cycle.

c. myotonia (p. 140)　　____ Masters and Johnson's model of sexual response, which consists of four phases.

d. excitement phase (p. 141)　　____ A period of time following a response (e.g., orgasm) during which an individual is no longer responsive to stimulation (e.g., sexual stimulation).

e. sex flush (p. 141)　　____ The first phase of the sexual response cycle, which is characterized by erection in the male, vaginal lubrication in the female, and muscle tension and increases in heart rate in both males and females.

f. plateau phase (p. 141)　　____ The fourth phase of the sexual response cycle, during which the body gradually returns to its prearoused state.

g. orgasmic platform (p. 142)　　____ One or more additional orgasms following the first, which occur within a short period of time and before the body has returned to a pre-plateau level of arousal.

h. sex skin (p. 142)　　____ Swelling of the genital tissues with blood, causing erection of the penis and engorgement of the area surrounding the vaginal opening.

i. resolution phase (p. 144)　　____ Part of the anterior wall of the vagina, whose prolonged stimulation causes particularly intense orgasms and a female ejaculation.

j. refractory period (p. 144)　　____ Reddening of the labia minora that occurs during the plateau phase.

k. multiple orgasm (p. 146)　　____ Muscle tension.

l. Grafenberg spot (G-spot) (p. 149)　　____ The second phase of the sexual response cycle, which is characterized by increases in vasocongestion, muscle tension, heart rate, and blood pressure in preparation for orgasm.

Multiple-Choice Questions

(LO = Learning Objective)

1. If Kim and Susan are roommates, what is likely to happen?
   a. Their PMS symptoms will become almost identical.
   b. Pheromones will help them to bond emotionally.
   c. They will become sexually attracted to one another because of the effects of pheromones.
   d. Their menstrual cycles will become synchronized.
         p. 127   LO 2

2. Any substance that increases sexual arousal or desire is called a/an
   a. pheromone.
   b. antiandrogen.
   c. hypogonadal agent.
   d. aphrodisiac.
         p. 126   LO 2

3. Anaphrodisiacs
   a. can dampen sexual drive.
   b. enhance erectile response.
   c. elevate mood which increases our capacity for orgasm.
   d. have no effect upon our sexual capacity.
         p. 130   LO 5

4. All of the following help explain why alcohol is so strongly associated with sexual enjoyment, *except*
   a. alcohol induces some feelings of euphoria.
   b. it impairs information processing and therefore judgment.
   c. its vasodilating effects increase sexual arousal and prolong orgasm.
   d. intoxication serves as a convenient reason for socially deviant behavior.
         p. 132   LO 6

5. Your memories of your first romantic kiss, your ability to recreate your favorite sexual fantasy, and your learned association between silk and sexual arousal are all contained in your
   a. limbic system.
   b. cerebral cortex.
   c. cerebellum.
   d. thalamus.
         p. 134   LO 7

6. Ultimately, the secretion of sex hormones by the ovaries and testes is regulated by the
   a. hypothalamus and pituitary gland.
   b. pituitary and adrenal glands.
   c. limbic system and Bartholin's gland.
   d. medulla and pons.
   p. 136   LO 8

7. It is generally accepted that testosterone affects the frequency and intensity of sexual interest in both men and women. In other words, this hormone has a/an _____ effect.
   a. organizing
   b. activating
   c. developmental
   d. cyclical
   p. 137   LO 8

8. Following orgasm Tom is incapable of experiencing another orgasm or ejaculation. He is worried that he is suffering from a sexual dysfunction. What would you tell him?
   a. He should visit a urologist to determine if he has testicular cancer.
   b. This is normal and is called the refractory period.
   c. He should relax more and the problem will disappear.
   d. This is normal and is called the retraction period.
   p. 144   LO 9

9. The stages of Kaplan's model of sexual response include all of the following *except*
   a. orgasm
   b. excitement
   c. resolution
   d. desire
   pp. 144-145   LO 10

10. A major gender difference in sexual response is
    a. men's greater levels of physical arousal and subsequent pleasure.
    b. men's higher level of myotonia and vasocongestion.
    c. women's greater capacity for multiple orgasms.
    d. women's extended plateau period.
    pp. 146-147   LO 11

11. According to Masters and Johnson,
    a. women may experience either a clitoral or vaginal orgasm.
    b. three types of orgasm occur in women.
    c. stimulation of the G-spot produces an intense orgasm.
    d. there is only one kind of orgasm.
             pp. 146-147   LO 12

12. The Grafenberg spot (G-spot) is most directly stimulated in all of the following ways, *except*
    a. male-superior position
    b. female-superior position
    c. rear entry position
    d. stimulation with one's finger
             pp. 148-149   LO 13

Other Activities

I. Sexual Response Cycle

Directions: In the following chart, list the physical changes in men and in women associated with each of the four stages of Masters and Johnson's Sexual Response Cycle.

PHASES	PHYSICAL CHANGES IN MALES	PHYSICAL CHANGES IN FEMALES
Excitement		
Plateau		
Orgasm		
Resolution		

Chapter 6

Gender Identity and Gender Roles

Chapter Summary

This chapter discusses the biological, psychological, and sociocultural aspects of gender. It begins by describing prenatal sexual differentiation; sexual differentiation of the embryonic structures begins at about the seventh week after conception. Testosterone plays a significant role in sexual differentiation. The development of the testes and ovaries and the descent of the testes into the scrotal sac are described. The effects of sex chromosomal abnormalities on sexual characteristics, physical health, and psychological development are presented.

The influence of nature and nurture on gender identity is explored. Gender identity is almost always consistent with anatomic gender. In rare cases, prenatal hormonal errors result in mixed indicators of gender. Gender assignment and rearing of hermaphrodites and pseudohermaphrodites are discussed. Transsexualism is a gender-identity disorder in which people have the anatomic sex of one gender but feel they are members of the other gender. The efficacy of hormone treatment and gender-reassignment surgery is examined.

Gender roles are broad cultural expectations about men and women that can result in stereotyping. Examples of sexism and its effects are presented. Research that examines male-female differences in cognitive abilities and personality is discussed, as well as a new consideration of male and female athletic abilities.

Gender typing is examined from biological, cross-cultural, and psychological perspectives. Within the psychological perspective, the psychoanalytic, social-learning, cognitive-developmental, and gender-schema theories of gender typing are presented.

Finally, the authors examine how stereotypical gender-role expectations affect dating practices and sexual behavior. Masculine or androgynous males and females tend to be better adjusted psychologically than those who are feminine or undifferentiated.

Learning Objectives

1. Trace the influences of sex chromosomes and hormones on sexual differentiation during the embryonic and fetal stages.
2. Discuss the research relevant to the nature-nurture debate about determination of gender identity.

3. Define transsexualism, discuss the theoretical perspectives on transsexualism, and describe the techniques and limitations of gender-reassignment surgery.
4. Define sexism, give examples, and discuss its effects on women and men.
5. Summarize the research on male-female differences in cognitive abilities, personality traits, and communication styles.
6. Summarize the biological and sociobiological perspectives on gender typing.
7. Summarize the cross-cultural evidence on gender typing.
8. Explain the psychological perspectives on gender typing.
9. Examine the influence of stereotypical gender roles on sexual behavior and relationships.
10. Define psychological androgyny and examine its influence on self-esteem, adjustment, and sexual behavior.

Fill-in-the-Blanks

When a sperm cell fertilizes an ovum, ____ chromosomes from the male parent combine with ____ chromosomes from the female parent. An ovum carries an ____ sex chromosome, and a sperm carries an _____ chromosome. The _____ determines the sex of the child. The basic blueprint of the human embryo is _____ ; for males, the genetic instructions in the ____ sex chromosome lead to sexual differentiation beginning about the _____ week after conception. _____ syndrome in males is caused by an extra X chromosome. _____ syndrome in females is caused by the loss of some X chromosome material.

Our _____ _____ is our awareness of being male or female. It is almost always consistent with chromosomal gender. _____ possess the gonads of one gender but external genitalia that are ambiguous or typical of the other gender. Some receive a male and some a female _____ _____ at birth. True _____ , people born with both ovarian and testicular tissue, are quite rare.

_____ are people who feel trapped in a body of the wrong gender. These individuals show cross-gender preferences, usually beginning in _____ _____. One option for treatment is _____ _____ _____ , an irreversible process accompanied by a lifetime of hormone treatments. Postoperative adjustment is more favorable for _____ - to - _____ than for _____ - to - _____ .

_____ _____ are broad cultural expectations about the ways in which males and females are to behave. Measured cognitive differences between males and females are _____ (small/large) and may largely reflect _____ influences. In almost all cultures, it is _____ who are more aggressive.

_____ attribute social behaviors, such as aggression and gender roles, to heredity. Other theorists argue that _____ _____ _____ masculinize or feminize the brain and create predispositions consistent with gender-role stereotypes. Anthropologists believe that differences in gender roles can be explained in terms of differing _____ _____ .

Sigmund Freud explained gender typing in terms of _____ . _____ - _____ theorists explain gender-typed behavior in terms of such processes as _____ learning, identification and _____ . According to cognitive-developmental theory, children form concepts or _____ about gender and conform their behavior to these gender concepts. Gender-schema theory proposes that children develop a _____ _____ and then begin to judge themselves according to traits considered relevant to their gender.

One cultural stereotype about gender roles and sexual behavior is that men are sexually _____ and women are sexually _____ . Men are expected to _____ sexual encounters and then take the lead in determining sexual behaviors. Another stereotype is that women do not have spontaneous sexual desires. According to this stereotype, men are generally _____ and women are generally _____ .

People who are _____ _____ tend to have higher self-esteem and to be better adjusted psychologically than people who are feminine or undifferentiated. These people have a combination of stereotypical _____ and _____ behavior patterns.

Short Answer Questions

(LO = Learning Objective)

1. Describe what triggers the process of prenatal sexual differentiation. (LO 1 - pp. 154-155)

2. Define the difference between hermaphrodites and pseudohermaphrodites. (LO 2 - pp. 158-159)

3. What do most scientists today conclude about the acquisition of gender identity? (LO 2 - p. 160)

4. Summarize the research on the postoperative adjustment of transsexuals who have had gender-reassignment surgery. (LO 3 - pp. 163-164)

5. Summarize the research surrounding the common belief that boys are better at math than girls. (LO 5 - pp. 170-171)

6. Summarize the sociobiological explanation of gender typing. (LO 6 - pp. 173-174)

7. How do anthropologists explain the differences in gender roles across cultures? (LO 7 - pp. 174-175)

8. Define socialization and identify some of the primary instruments of socialization of gender roles in the United States. (LO 8 - pp. 176-177)

9. What does research indicate about sexism in America's schools. (LO 8 - p. 177)

10. Describe a typical dating experience and identify the gender role influences.
    (LO 9 - p. 180)

11. What does research show about comparisons between people who are categorized as masculine, androgynous, feminine, or undifferentiated?
    (LO 10 - pp. 181-183)

Matching Exercises

I. Vocabulary Exercise 1

Directions: Match each vocabulary term listed in the left-hand column with the correct definition in the right-hand column.

a. sexual differentiation (p. 154) ____ The labeling of a newborn as a male or female.

b. chromosome (p. 154) ____ The condition defined by undescended testes.

c. zygote (p. 154) ____ A sex-chromosomal disorder caused by an extra X sex chromosome.

d. embryo (p. 154) ____ The process by which males and females develop distinct reproductive anatomy.

e. androgens (p. 155) ____ People who possess both ovarian and testicular tissue.

f. testosterone (p. 155) ____ The male sex hormone that fosters the development of male sex characteristics and is connected with the sex drive.

g. inguinal canal (p. 157) ____ Male sex hormones.

h. cryptorchidism (p. 157) ____ One of the rodlike structures found in the nuclei of every living cell that carry the genetic code in the form of genes.

i. Klinefelter's syndrome (p. 157) ____ People who possess the gonads of one gender but external genitalia that are ambiguous or typical of the opposite gender.

j. gender identity (p. 157) ____ A fertilized ovum (egg cell).

k. gender assignment (p. 157) ____ The psychological sense of being male or female.

l. pseudohermaphrodites (p. 158) ____ A fetal canal that connects the scrotum and the testes, allowing their descent.

m. hermaphrodites (p. 158) ____ The stage of prenatal development that begins with implantation of a fertilized ovum in the uterus and concludes with development of the major organ systems at about two months after conception.

II. Vocabulary Exercise 2

Directions: Match each vocabulary term listed in the left-hand column with the correct definition in the right-hand column.

a. transsexuals (p. 161)   ____ A coital position in which the woman is on top.

b. stereotype (p. 166)   ____ A conflict of the phallic stage in which the boy wishes to possess his mother sexually and perceives his father as a rival in love.

c. gender roles (p. 166)   ____ The concept that people retain their genders for a lifetime.

d. sexism (p. 168)   ____ Possession of stereotypical masculine traits, such as assertiveness and instrumental skills, along with stereotypical feminine traits, such as nurturance, expressiveness, and cooperation.

e. gender typing (p. 173)   ____ The process of guiding people into socially acceptable behavior patterns by means of information, rewards, and punishments.

f. Oedipus complex (p. 176)   ____ A cluster of mental representations about male and female physical qualities, behaviors, and personality traits.

g. socialization (p. 176)   ____ A fixed, conventional idea about a group of people.

h. gender stability (p. 178)   ____ A coital position in which the man is on top.

i. gender constancy (p. 178)   ____ The prejudgment that, because of gender, a person will possess negative traits.

j. gender schema (p. 179)   ____ People who have a gender-identity disorder in which they feel trapped in the body of the wrong gender.

k. female-superior position (p. 180)   ____ The process by which children acquire behavior that is deemed appropriate to their gender.

l. male-superior position (p. 180)   ____ Complex clusters of ways in which males and females are expected to behave.

m. psychological androgyny (p.181)   ____ The concept that people's genders do not change, even if they alter their dress or behavior.

Multiple-Choice Questions

(LO = Learning Objective)

1. For unknown reasons, an XY embryo fails to produce any androgens. What will happen to the embryo?
    a. It will be attracted to people of the same sex as an adult.
    b. It will become an anatomical male.
    c. It will become an anatomical female.
    d. It will become a transsexual.
            p. 155   LO 1

2. After gender-reassignment surgery, a transsexual can do all of the following, *except*
    a. engage in sexual activity.
    b. experience orgasm.
    c. impregnate or become pregnant.
    d. live socially as a member of the other gender.
            p. 163   LO 3

3. Julie is considered to be "pushy" because she does not hesitate to make her position clear. Jerry is considered to be assertive because everyone always knows where he stands on issues. This is an example of
    a. gender differentiation.
    b. sexism.
    c. androgyny.
    d. acculturation.
            p. 181   LO 4

4. All of the following statements about gender differences are accurate, *except*
    a. boys are slower to develop language skills.
    b. boys have a slight advantage in visual-spatial skills.
    c. girls have greater computational skills in elementary school.
    d. in adolescence, girls have greater problem-solving abilities.
            pp. 170-171   LO 5

5. If a group of men and women were having a discussion, research would lead you to predict all of the following, *except*
    a. men would interrupt more.
    b. men would dominate the conversation.
    c. women would express more personal feelings.
    d. women would initiate more topics of conversation.
            p. 171   LO 5

6. Anthropologists propose that cultural differences in gender roles reflect
   a. patriarchal attitudes towards masculine and feminine behaviors.
   b. cultural adaptations to social and natural environments.
   c. biological imprinting in the chromosomes of females and males.
   d. survival strategies inherited through the process of natural selection.
   pp. 174-175   LO 7

7. Which perspective would assert that females are genetically predisposed to empathize and nurture in order to perpetuate the survival of the species?
   a. biological perspective
   b. sociobiological perspective
   c. psychoanalytic perspective
   d. behavioral perspective
   pp. 173-174   LO 6

8. Freud believed children have an incestuous wish for their parent of the opposite gender. This
   a. is called the Oedipus complex for males.
   b. is called the Electra complex for females.
   c. occurs during the phallic period of psychosexual development.
   d. all of the above.
   e. none of the above.
   p. 176   LO 8

9. According to social learning theorists, gender differences in aggression are largely influenced by
   a. testosterone levels.
   b. modeling and reinforcement.
   c. parental identification.
   d. sexual preferences.
   p. 176   LO 8

10. According to _____ theory, children form schemas about gender and then conform their behavior to their gender concepts.
    a. sociobiological
    b. psychoanalytic
    c. cognitive-developmental
    d. social-learning
    p. 178   LO 8

11. On a psychological test, you scored high on androgyny. According to research cited in your text, most likely you
    a. have a stronger sex drive than others of your gender.
    b. better adjusted psychologically than people who are feminine or undifferentiated.
    c. are a rare type among college students.
    d. will have greater difficulty than others in finding a satisfying partner.
        pp. 182-183   LO 10

12. Jesse is cooperative, science-oriented, assertive, moderately interested in sex, and emotionally expressive. He is
    a. experiencing low levels of testosterone.
    b. stereotypically male.
    c. considered androgynous.
    d. a transsexual.
        pp. 181-183   LO 10

> Other Activities

I. Perspectives on Gender Typing

Directions: Read the text section on the perspectives on gender typing. Complete the chart below, listing the explanations offered by each perspective.

PERSPECTIVES	EXPLANATIONS FOR GENDER TYPING
BIOLOGICAL 　Sociobiology 　Prenatal Brain 　Organization	
CROSS-CULTURAL	
PSYCHOLOGICAL 　Psychoanalytic Theory 　Social-Learning Theory 　Cognitive-Developmental 　Theory 　Gender-Schema Theory	

Chapter 7

Attraction and Love

Chapter Summary

Attraction is determined by a number of factors. Physical attractiveness is a major determinant of interpersonal and sexual attraction. In our culture, slenderness, especially for women, is highly valued. Both genders consider smiling faces more attractive. Women place relatively greater emphasis on traits like status and earning potential, whereas men give relatively more consideration to physical attractiveness. Women and men are also influenced by the images of the ideal people they see on the internet – "cyberbabes" and "cyberhunks." Some sociobiologists believe that evolutionary forces favor the continuation of such gender differences in preferred traits because certain preferred traits provide reproductive advantages.

According to the matching hypothesis, people tend to develop romantic relationships with people who are similar to themselves in attractiveness. The matching hypothesis also applies to race/ethnicity, age, level of education, and age. Similarity in attitudes and views is a strong contributor to attraction, friendships, and love relationships. Reciprocation of positive words and actions is also a potent contributor to feelings of attraction.

The Greeks had four concepts related to the modern meanings of love: *storge, agape, philia,* and *eros*. Western culture has a long tradition of idealizing the concept of romantic love. A vast majority of people in the United States see romantic love as prerequisite for marriage. Early in a relationship, infatuation and more enduring forms of romantic love may be indistinguishable.

Berscheid and Hatfield define romantic love in terms of intense physiological arousal and cognitive appraisal of that arousal as love. Hendrick and Hendrick suggest that there are six styles of love among college students: romantic love, game-playing love, friendship, logical love, possessive love, and selfless love. Sternberg suggests that there are three distinct components of love: intimacy, passion, and decision/commitment. Romantic love is characterized by the combination of passion and intimacy, but it lacks commitment. Companionate love, characterized by intimacy and commitment, is typical of long-term friendships and some long-term marriages. A balance of all three components typifies what is, for many people, an ideal marriage.

Learning Objectives

1. Summarize the research on the role of physical attractiveness in attraction.
2. Identify the characteristics men and women look for in a potential partner for a long-term relationship.

3. Discuss the sociobiological view of the different characteristics men and women desire in their mates.
4. Analyze how the "matching hypothesis" accounts for partner choice.
5. Describe the influence of attitudinal similarity on attraction and on relationships.
6. Define *reciprocity* and describe its effect on attraction and on maintaining relationships.
7. Discuss the four Greek concepts of love: *storge, agape, philia,* and *eros.*
8. Identify the characteristics of and male-female differences in romantic love.
9. Discuss three contemporary models of love and the associated explanations of the origins of love.

Fill-in-the-Blanks

_____ _____ is a major determinant of sexual attraction. Most of the world's societies consider _____ (thinness/ plumpness) in women to be desirable. Generally, men across cultures place greater emphasis on the _____ _____ and _____ _____ of partners, while women place greater emphasis on the _____ _____ of partners. However, even greater emphasis was placed on the characteristics _____, _____ and _____ by both men and women from 37 cultures. In a study done in the United States, college students chose _____ as the most highly desired quality in long-term partners.

The _____ _____ proposes that people tend to develop romantic relationships with people who are similar to themselves in physical attractiveness. Similarity in _____ also contributes to initial attraction. _____, a mutual exchange of positive words and actions, is also a powerful determinant of attraction.

In our culture, we idealize the concept of _____ _____. It is considered by most to be a prerequisite for marriage. Although we use only one term, the Greeks had four concepts related to the modern meanings of love: _____, _____, _____, and _____. _____ is defined as a state of intense absorption in or focusing on another person.

Social psychologists Berscheid and Hatfield define romantic love in terms of a state of _____ _____ _____ and a _____ _____ of this as love. The Hendricks speak of the six styles of love: _____ love, _____ love, _____, _____

love, _____ love, and _____ love. Psychologist Sternberg proposes a _____ theory of love; the three distinct components of love are _____ , _____ , and _____ .

Short Answer Questions

(LO = Learning Objective)

1. Describe how college men and women feel about body shape and size for themselves and their partners. (LO 1 - pp. 190-191)

2. Summarize the findings in the Buss review of gender differences in preferences in mates. (LO 2 - p. 196)

3. How do sociobiologists view gender differences in perceptions of attractiveness and in mate preferences? (LO 3 - pp. 196-197)

4. How does the matching hypothesis explain our choices of people with whom we develop romantic relationships? (LO 4 - p. 197)

5. According to researchers, what is the relationship between attraction and attitude similarity? (LO 5 - pp. 197-198)

6. What is the relationship between reciprocity and attraction? (LO 6 - p. 198)

7. In the United States, how do the majority of people view the relationship between romantic love and marriage? (LO 8 - pp. 199-200)

8. List the characteristics of infatuation. (LO 8 - p. 202)

9. What gender differences in styles of love did the Hendricks find? (LO 9 - p. 203)

10. How is the balance among Sternberg's three components of love likely to change during the course of a long-term relationship? (LO 9 - pp. 203-204)

11. How would Sternberg describe incompatibility according to the Triangular Theory of Love? (LO 9 - pp. 204-205)

Matching Exercises

I. Vocabulary Exercise 1

Directions: Match each vocabulary term listed in the left-hand column with the correct definition in the right-hand column.

a. anorexia nervosa (p. 190)

b. matching hypothesis (p. 197)

c. reciprocity (p. 198)

d. *storge* (p. 199)

e. *agape* (p. 199)

f. *philia* (p. 199)

g. *eros* (p. 199)

h. infatuation (p. 202)

i. romantic love (p. 207)

____ The kind of love that is closest in meaning to the modern-day concept of passion.

____ A state of intense absorption in or focus on another person, which is usually accompanied by sexual desire, elation, and general physiological arousal or excitement; passion.

____ The concept that people tend to develop romantic relationships with people who are similar to themselves in attractiveness.

____ A kind of love characterized by feelings of passion and intimacy.

____ Loving attachment and nonsexual affection; the type of emotion that binds parents to children.

____ A potentially life-threatening eating disorder characterized by refusal to maintain a healthful body weight, intense fear of being overweight, a distorted body image, and, in females, lack of menstruation (amenorrhea).

____ Selfless love; a kind of loving that is similar to generosity and charity.

____ Mutual exchange.

____ Friendship love, which is based on liking and respect rather than sexual desire.

Multiple-Choice Questions

(LO = Learning Objective)

1. Roger examines his physique in the mirror. If he is typical of college men, he will conclude
    a. he is flabbier than the ideal man.
    b. he could stand to lose a little weight to be more appealing to women.
    c. he is close to ideal and rather appealing.
    d. he is more muscular than what most females find appealing.
          p. 191   LO 1

2. In a meaningful relationship, _____ was rated as the most valued characteristic by college students.
    a. warmth
    b. honesty
    c. tenderness
    d. personality
          p. 193   LO 2

3. Across cultures, the two features more highly valued by men in prospective mates are
    a. physical attractiveness and fidelity.
    b. domestic skills and reputation.
    c. sexual interest and relative youthfulness.
    d. physical attractiveness and relative youthfulness.
          p. 195   LO 2

4. If you believe that clear eyes, a good complexion, firm muscle tone, and a younger age in our choice of a sexual partner are inherited preferences, then you are in agreement with
    a. the love theorists.
    b. sociobiologists.
    c. cognitive-developmental theorists.
    d. cross-cultural researchers.
          p. 196   LO 3

5. Couples in romantic relationships tend to be similar in physical attractiveness. This supports
   a. the coupling hypothesis.
   b. the concept of gender matching.
   c. the matching hypothesis.
   d. the sociocultural hypothesis.
   p. 197   LO 4

6. Reciprocity is
   a. mutual exchange of positive feelings between two people.
   b. defined as our tendency to be attracted to people who are similar to us in physical attractiveness.
   c. a potent determinant of attraction.
   d. a and c
   e. b and c
   p. 198   LO 6

7. Although she makes only a moderate salary as an elementary school teacher, Carol donates 10% of her salary to the "Save the Children Foundation." Her love for children is best described as
   a. storge.
   b. agape.
   c. philia.
   d. eros.
   p. 199   LO 7

8. Kay and Sharon talk on the phone almost every day. They often attend functions together and can depend on one another during times of crises. They like and respect one another. This relationship reflects the Greek concept of
   a. eros.
   b. storge.
   c. philia.
   d. agape.
   p. 199   LO 7

9. Labeling our attraction to another as "love" rather than "lust" allows us to
   a. discuss our romantic relationships even at the family dinner table.
   b. ennoble attraction and sexual arousal to both ourselves and society.
   c. be viewed as less primitive or animalistic.
   d. all of the above.
   e. none of the above.
   pp. 199-200   LO 8

10. Kim can hardly wait to see Jason, whom she met while riding in a helicopter over a live volcano. It is possible that the degree of attraction she feels is due to
    a. her physiological arousal from the exciting helicopter ride.
    b. the emotional state induced by her hormonal levels.
    c. her cognitive appraisal of her physiological arousal.
    d. both a and c.
    e. both b and c.
        p. 202   LO 9

Other Activities

I. Models of Love

Directions: Read the text section on the models of love. Complete the chart below by summarizing each model in the left-hand column and listing the components of each model in the right-hand column.

Theorists	Components
Berscheid & Hatfield	Three Simultaneous Events 1. 2. 3.
C. & S. Hendrick	Six Styles of Love 1. 2. 3. 4. 5. 6.
Sternberg (Triangular Theory of Love)	Three Components of Love 1. 2. 3. Eight Types of Love 1. 2. 3. 4. 5. 6. 7. 8.

Chapter 8

Relationships, Intimacy, and Communication

Chapter Summary

Romantic relationships undergo five stages of development: attraction, building, continuation, deterioration, and ending. Similarity in the level of physical attractiveness, similarity in attitudes, and mutual liking motivate people to build relationships. Partners frequently use small talk and gradual mutual self-disclosure to do so. Modern technology allows people to meet, "date," and establish an intimate relationship online. Factors such as variety, caring, positive evaluations, lack of jealousy, perceived fairness in the relationship, and mutual feelings of satisfaction encourage continuation of relationships. Factors that foster deterioration include failure to invest time and energy in the relationship, deciding to put an end to it, or simply permitting deterioration to proceed unchecked. Relationships tend to end when the partners find little satisfaction in the affiliation, alternative partners are available, couples are not committed to preserving the relationship, or they expect the relationship to falter.

Loneliness is a state of painful isolation, of feeling cut off from others. The causes of loneliness include a lack of social skills and a lack of relationship skills, among others. Suggestions for coping with loneliness are presented.

Intimacy involves feelings of emotional closeness with another person and the desire to share each other's inmost thoughts and feelings. The core features of building and maintaining intimate relationships are knowing and liking yourself, trusting and caring, being honest, committing oneself to the relationship, maintaining one's individuality within the relationship, and communicating well, both verbally and nonverbally.

Communication skills for enhancing relationships and sexual relations are explained in detail. These skills involve challenging irrational beliefs, getting communication started, listening to a partner, learning about a partner's needs, providing information to a partner, making requests, and delivering and receiving criticism. When good communication skills are not enough to resolve an impasse, partners may need to take a break, agree to tolerate difference, or agree to disagree on some issues.

Learning Objectives

1. Cite the five stages of development characteristic of romantic relationships.
2. Describe the process of building a relationship from initial conversation through mutual and increasing self-disclosure.
3. Identify the factors that generally lead to continuation of a relationship.

4. Explain the effects of jealousy in a relationship and identify characteristics of a jealous person.
5. Examine passive and active responses that will determine whether a deteriorating relationship ends or is renewed.
6. Summarize the causes of loneliness and suggest ways of coping with loneliness.
7. Identify the characteristics of intimate relationships and the skills necessary for building and maintaining an intimate relationship.
8. Explain the importance of good communication, both verbal and nonverbal, in an intimate relationship.
9. Examine the irrational beliefs and fears about sexual communication that can cause difficulties in intimate relationships.
10. Give examples of ways to begin a conversation about your sexual relationship and examples of specific listening skills that will encourage the continuation of communication.
11. Identify the skills associated with giving and receiving information and requests in an intimate sexual relationship.
12. Explain the skills involved in giving and receiving criticism.
13. Give examples of how partners can handle disagreements that may not be resolved even with good communication skills.

Fill-in-the-Blanks

According to Levinger, _____ relationships undergo five stages of development: _____ , _____ , _____ , _____ , and _____ . During the second stage, _____ allows an exchange of information but stresses the breadth of topic coverage rather than in-depth discussion. Early _____-_____ , the revelation of intimate information, is viewed negatively. If this second stage goes well, a couple may develop _____ , in which two individuals come to view themselves as "we" instead of two "I's."

In the third stage of this ABCDE model, the _____ stage, factors either encourage or discourage the further development of a relationship. _____ _____ is aroused when we suspect that an intimate relationship is threatened by a rival. In the fourth stage, the _____ stage, couples may respond in either active or passive ways. _____ is the fifth stage of the relationship.

_____ is a state of painful isolation, of feeling cut off from others. By contrast, _____ involves feelings of emotional closeness and connectedness with another person. It is characterized by attitudes of mutual _____, _____, and _____.

Good _____ is an essential element of an intimate relationship; it involves sending and receiving messages accurately. _____ _____ includes tone of voice, gestures, body posture, and facial expression. Women are more apt than men to _____ the people with whom they interact. Direct _____ _____ makes people appear to be self-assertive, direct, and candid.

Many people have _____ beliefs about relationships and sex; one is that our partners can read our minds about what types of sexual stimulation we desire. Obviously, people cannot read minds and we must learn to communicate and to listen effectively. One listening skill is _____, which means restating the speaker's words to confirm your comprehension. When requesting changes in your partner's behavior, you must be _____. Even when differences cannot be resolved, relationships can continue if couples learn to _____ differences and _____ to disagree.

Short Answer Questions

(LO = Learning Objective)
1. Describe the role of small talk in building a relationship. (LO 2 - p. 213)

2. What factors lead to the building of a relationship? (LO 2 - pp. 213-217)

3. How are "early self-disclosers" viewed? (LO 2 - pp. 216-217)

4. How does jealousy affect a relationship? (LO 4 - pp. 218-219)

5. What factors contribute to the deterioration of a relationship? (LO 5 - pp. 219-220)

6. Name several characteristics of lonely people. (LO 6 - p. 221)

7. What suggestions do the authors give for coping with loneliness? (LO 6 - pp. 221-222)

8. What is the relationship between emotional and sexual intimacy? (LO 7 - p. 223)

9. Name several channels of nonverbal communication. Do people place more weight on verbal or nonverbal communication? (LO 8 - pp. 225-226)

10. List some skills one should learn to be able to communicate effectively with one's partner about sex. (LO 8 - pp. 226-233)

11. Describe the exercises suggested by the authors for using nonverbal methods to communicate sexual likes and dislikes. (LO 11 - p. 230)

12. When partners who are communicating effectively reach an impasse, what approaches can they take? (LO 13 - pp. 233-234)

Matching Exercises

I. Vocabulary Exercise 1

Directions: Match each vocabulary term listed in the left-hand column with the correct definition in the right-hand column.

a. ABCDE model (p. 213) ____ Feelings of closeness and connectedness that are marked by sharing of inmost thoughts and feelings.

b. social-exchange theory (p. 212) ____ A phase in building a relationship in which a couple come to regard themselves as "we," no longer two "I's" who happen to be in the same place at the same time.

c. surface contact (p. 213) ____ The view that the development of a relationship reflects the unfolding of social exchanges—that is, the rewards and costs of maintaining the relationship as opposed to ending it.

d. small talk (p. 213) ____ Levinger's view, which approaches romantic relationships in terms of five stages: attraction, building, continuation, deterioration, and ending.

e. self-disclosure (p. 216) ____ A probing phase of building a relationship in which people seek common ground and check out feelings of attraction.

f. mutuality (p. 217) ____ The revelation of personal, perhaps intimate, information.

g. intimacy (p. 223) ____ A superficial kind of conversation that allows exchange of information, but stresses breadth of topic coverage rather than in-depth discussion.

Multiple-Choice Questions

(LO = Learning Objective)

1. Levinger's ABCDE model describes the stages of romantic relationships. This acronym represents
   a. attraction, building, commitment, deterioration, and ending.
   b. affiliation, building, continuation, determination, and ending.
   c. attraction, building, continuation, deterioration, and ending.
   d. affiliation, budding, continuation, deterioration, and ending.

   p. 213   LO 1

2. The purpose of "small talk" in a relationship is to
   a. uncover personality flaws and weaknesses.
   b. reveal the more intimate aspects of each others' lives.
   c. allow each person to try the other out for the possibility of friendship.
   d. begin the process of reciprocal self-disclosure of deep feelings.

   p. 213   LO 2

3. According to Wortman and her colleagues, a person who shares intimate information early in a conversation is
   a. perceived as genuine and honest.
   b. perceived as less mature, less secure, and less well adjusted.
   c. more likely to get dates.
   d. perceived as bold, assertive and independent.

   p. 218   LO 3

4. Extreme cases of jealousy are associated with
   a. commitment and devotion.
   b. depression and violence.
   c. companionate and consummate love.
   d. sexual passion and romance.

   p. 219   LO 4

5. All of the following have been found to facilitate the ending of romantic relationships, *except*
   a. availability of other partners.
   b. little or no commitment to the relationship.
   c. low expectations about the likelihood of any relationship lasting.
   d. belief that problems can be overcome.

   p. 220   LO 5

6. When a relationship is perceived to be "falling apart,"
   a. go with the flow and see what happens.
   b. practicing improved communication skills is an active response.
   c. doing nothing is a passive response.
   d. abandon the relationship because if you are perfectly matched no effort needs to be invested.
   e. both b and c.
   pp. 219-220   LO 5

7. _____ is when we feel emotional closeness and connectedness with another person, sharing our innermost thoughts and feelings.
   a. Mutuality
   b. Intimacy
   c. Companionship
   d. Commitment
   p. 223   LO 7

8. Although _____ is a core feature of intimacy, intimate relationships involve a balance in which some things are revealed and others are not.
   a. strength
   b. silence
   c. mutual diagnosis
   d. honesty
   p. 224   LO 7

9. In healthy relationships, couples who have a strong sense of togetherness
   a. have given up their individuality.
   b. attempt to dominate each others' lives.
   c. maintain individual interests, likes, and dislikes.
   d. have mutually decided to do everything together.
   p. 224   LO 7

10. To communicate effectively about sexual matters, couples
    a. need to agree on their choices of language when talking about sex.
    b. should share their experiences about previous sexual encounters with others.
    c. need to agree that they can be verbally abusive if angry.
    d. must decide who will dominate the conversation.
    pp. 224-225   LO 9

11. If you tell your partner, "It was really hard to talk about, but I'm glad that you told me how you feel about oral sex," this statement
    a. reinforces your partner for communicating about sex.
    b. illustrates how to deliver criticism in a timely manner.
    c. shows your partner that you are upset.
    d. is an example of active listening.
       p. 229   LO 10

12. When delivering criticism to your partner
    a. use "you" statements to make your point clear.
    b. speak your mind as soon as you can.
    c. frame your displeasure in terms of your own feelings.
    d. it is not necessary to be too specific.
       pp. 231-232   LO 12

Other Activities

I. ABCDE Model of Romantic Relationships

Directions: Complete the following chart by supplying the missing information.

STAGE	DESCRIPTION OF THE STAGE	BEHAVIORS OF THE PARTNERS
ATTRACTION		
BUILDING		Surface Contact Small Talk Gradually Increasing Self-Disclosure Attaining Mutuality
CONTINUATION		
DETERIORATION	When one or more partners see the relationship as less rewarding than it has been.	
ENDING		

95

Chapter 9

Sexual Techniques and Behavior Patterns

Chapter Summary

This chapter explores sexual techniques and behaviors people engage in alone and with partners. Masturbation may be practiced by means of manual stimulation of the genitals, perhaps with the aid of an electric vibrator. Until recent years, masturbation was thought to be physically and mentally harmful, but no research evidence supports this view. Surveys indicate that most people have masturbated at some point in their lives. Most men report that they masturbate by manual manipulation of the penis. Most women masturbate by massaging the mons, labia minora, and clitoral region with circular or back-and-forth motions.

Sexual fantasies often accompany masturbation or sex with another person. Although one of the most common fantasies is sex with one's partner, many people fantasize about sexual activities in which they would not engage. Multimedia interactivity, such as CD-ROM programs and virtual sex interaction, has opened new possibilities for fantasy and sexual outlets.

The pattern and duration of foreplay varies widely within and across cultures. Women usually desire longer periods of foreplay than men do. Couples kiss for enjoyment or as a prelude to intercourse. Kissing may also be affectionate and without erotic significance. Touching or caressing erogenous zones can be highly arousing. Men typically prefer direct stroking of their genitals by their partners early in lovemaking. Women, however, tend to prefer that their partners caress their genitals after a period of general body contact. Most women enjoy breast stimulation. The hands and the mouth can be used to stimulate the breasts. The popularity of oral-genital stimulation has increased dramatically since Kinsey's day.

Couples today use a greater variety of coital positions than in Kinsey's time. The five most commonly used positions are the male-superior position, the female-superior position, the lateral-entry position, the rear-entry position, and anal intercourse. Each position has advantages and disadvantages for a couple. The male-superior position is the most commonly used, but the female-superior position allows the woman greater freedom of movement and may also help the male control ejaculation.

Learning Objectives

1. Summarize historical and religious views on masturbation.
2. Cite the incidence of masturbation and describe the common techniques used by males and females.

3. Describe the common sexual fantasies of males and females and the role fantasy plays in arousal and masturbation.
4. Describe common foreplay techniques, such as kissing and breast and genital stimulation.
5. Describe fellatio and cunnilingus techniques and state how widely they are practiced among specific populations.
6. List the four basic intercourse positions and the advantages and disadvantages of each.
7. Compare the myths and facts about African-American sexual behavior.
8. Describe the incidence and frequency of fantasy during coitus and the effects of fantasy on relationships.
9. Discuss who engages in anal intercourse and the necessary precautions to take.

Fill-in-the-Blanks

_____ involves self-stimulation of the genitals. Until recent years, it was thought to be _____ and _____ harmful. Across surveys, _____ report a higher frequency of masturbation than _____ .

Most men report that they masturbate by _____ _____.Most women stimulate the _____ , _____ _____, and the _____; very few women masturbate by _____ _____ .

A _____ _____ is a private mental experience involving thoughts and images that are sexually arousing to the individual. In the *Playboy* (Hunt) survey, the most commonly reported fantasy by both men and women was "_____."

_____ involves various forms of noncoital sex, such as cuddling, kissing, petting, and oral-genital contact. Generally, women want _____ periods of these behaviors than do men. Although _____ is almost universal in our culture, it occurs less often among the world's cultures than manual or oral stimulation of the genitals. Most women enjoy _____ stimulation, but many men are uncomfortable when receiving this stimulation.

Although the popularity of _____ and _____ (two forms of oral-genital stimulation) has increased dramatically since Kinsey's day, _____ Americans remain less likely than _____ Americans to engage in oral sex. The "69" position allows two people to experience _____ _____ stimulation.

_____, or sexual intercourse, is sexual activity in which the penis in inserted into the vagina. The male-superior position is sometimes referred to as the _____ position. One of the advantages of the female-superior position for a man is that it can help him control _____ .

Survey results comparing the responses of African Americans and White Americans has _____ (continued to/failed to) support the idea that African Americans are more sexually permissive. If age of first coitus is used as the criterion for permissiveness, _____ _____ _____ are more permissive. If masturbating, performing fellatio, or masturbating one's partner are used as the criteria for permissiveness, _____ _____ _____ and _____ would be deemed more permissive.

_____ intercourse is the major act that comes under the legal definition of sodomy. Recent surveys show that in the United States about _____-_____% of men and women, respectively, engage in this behavior at least occasionally. Kissing or licking the anus is termed _____ and it carries a serious health risk.

Short Answer Questions

(LO = Learning Objective)
1. Historically, what has been the Judeo-Christian view of masturbation? (LO 1 - pp. 238-239)

2. What conclusions have been reached through scientific research on masturbation? (LO 2 - pp. 240-243)

3. What is the relationship between sexual fantasies and acting out those fantasies? (LO 3 - pp. 246-247)

4. Summarize the gender differences in fantasy themes. (LO 3 - p. 246)

5. Describe the cross-cultural and gender differences in foreplay. (LO 4 - pp. 248-250)

6. How common is oral-genital stimulation in the United States? (LO 5 - p. 251)

7. Describe any racial differences in the incidence of oral-genital sexual activity. (LO 5 - pp. 252-253)

8. Cite some stereotypes about African-American sexual behavior and then cite the research findings. (LO 7 - p. 260)

9. Describe the role of fantasy during coitus. (LO 8 - pp. 260-261)

10. What greater precautions should couples who engage in anal sex take? (LO 9 - p. 263)

11. Cite survey results indicating how many men and women engage in anal sex. What factors seem to influence people's decisions? (LO 9 - p. 262)

Matching Exercises

I. Vocabulary Exercise 1

Directions: Match each vocabulary term listed in the left-hand column with the correct definition in the right-hand column.

a. masturbation (p. 238)   ____ Recurrent difficulty in achieving or sustaining an erection sufficient to successfully engage in sexual intercourse.

b. dildo (p. 238)   ____ Physical interactions that are sexually stimulating and set the stage for intercourse.

c. coitus interruptus (p. 239)   ____ Oral stimulation of the anus.

d. impotence (male erectile disorder or erectile dysfunction) (p. 240)   ____ Oral stimulation of the male genitals.

e. foreplay (p. 247)   ____ A penis-shaped object used in sexual activity.

f. fellatio (p. 251)   ____ The coital position in which the man is on top. Also termed the *male-superior position*.

g. cunnilingus (p. 251)   ____ Oral stimulation of the female genitals.

h. missionary position (p. 255)   ____ Sexual self-stimulation.

i. anilingus (p. 262)   ____ The practice of withdrawing the penis prior to ejaculation during sexual intercourse.

Multiple-Choice Questions

(LO = Learning Objective)

1. Masturbation has been condemned by Judeo-Christian tradition in part because it
   a. is more pleasurable than intercourse.
   b. spreads disease more easily.
   c. is not a form of procreative sex.
   d. debilitated those who engaged in it frequently.
         pp. 238-239   LO 1

2. If you were a 19th century parent who was concerned that your teenager masturbated, you would be likely to do all of the following, *except*
   a. prepare a daily bowl of corn flakes for him/her.
   b. introduce the teenager to strong coffee and tea.
   c. serve graham crackers and whole wheat bread frequently.
   d. purchase a medically approved device that would prevent masturbation.
         pp. 239-240   LO 1

3. How can masturbation help females who are preorgasmic?
   a. It encourages physical self-exploration and increases self-knowledge.
   b. It increases a sense of control as they reject their usual sexual partners.
   c. It increases muscle tone in the pubococcygeus muscle.
   d. It allows partners freedom from responsibility for pleasing them .
         p. 242   LO 2

4. Among women, research has shown that there is an association between
   a. early masturbation and later sexual promiscuity later in life.
   b. negative attitudes toward masturbation and difficulty experiencing orgasm.
   c. positive attitudes towards masturbation and multiple sex partners.
   d. masturbation after marriage and marital dissatisfaction.
         p. 242   LO 2

5. Who engages in sexual fantasies?
   a. men and women without regular sexual partners
   b. individuals who find it difficult to become aroused with tactile and visual stimulation
   c. individuals who are reluctant to masturbate
   d. a vast majority of both men and women, especially during masturbation
         p. 246   LO 3

6. Foreplay
   a. may be a prelude to coitus.
   b. may be engaged in without coitus in mind.
   c. in some form, is engaged in by virtually all species of mammals.
   d. all of the above.
   e. none of the above.
      pp. 247-248   LO 4

7. All of the following are accurate statements about breast stimulation, *except*
   a. some women report achieving orgasm from breast stimulation alone.
   b. the nipples are erotically sensitive in both genders.
   c. female breast size is related to the amount of arousal experienced from stimulation.
   d. the type of breast stimulation desired varies among individuals.
      p. 251   LO 4

8. Fellatio refers to
   a. oral stimulation of the clitoris.
   b. anal stimulation with the tongue.
   c. anal intercourse.
   d. oral stimulation of the male genitals.
      p. 251   LO 5

9. Cunnilingus refers to
   a. a type of venereal disease.
   b. oral stimulation of the female genitals.
   c. sexually deviant behavior with animals.
   d. oral stimulation of the penis.
      p. 251   LO 5

10. Which statement most accurately describes racial differences found in the prevalence of oral-genital stimulation?
    a. A large majority of African American men surveyed had engaged in cunnilingus.
    b. Relatively few White women engage in fellatio.
    c. Only a small number of White men engaged in cunnilingus.
    d. In general, more Whites engage in this activity than do African Americans.
       p. 252   LO 5

11. All of the following are advantages of the male-superior position, *except*
    a. it can be highly arousing for the man.
    b. kissing can continue.
    c. the woman can control the amount of clitoral stimulation she receives.
    d. the male's buttocks and scrotum can be stimulated more easily.
       pp. 255-256   LO 6

12. Recent research indicates that
    a. African American women were more likely to have had 10 or more sexual partners than White women.
    b. White women were more likely to have had 10 or more sexual partners than African American women.
    c. overall, African Americans are more sexually permissive than whites.
    d. there were no differences found.
       p. 260   LO 7

Other Activities

I. SEXUAL INTERCOURSE POSITIONS

Directions: Complete the following chart by describing each sexual intercourse position and then identifying the advantages and disadvantages of each position.

POSITIONS (Descriptions)	ADVANTAGES AND DISADVANTAGES
Male-Superior Position	
Female-Superior Position	
Lateral-Entry Position	
Rear-Entry Position	
Anal Intercourse	

Chapter 10

Sexual Orientation

Chapter Summary

Sexual orientation describes the directionality of one's sexual interests, but one's sexual behavior may not always be consistent with one's sexual orientation. Kinsey and his colleagues found evidence of degrees of gay and heterosexual orientations, with bisexuality representing a midpoint between the two. Storms suggests gay and heterosexual orientations may be independent dimensions rather than polar opposites. Bisexual people are attracted to males and females.

Throughout much of Western history, male-male and female-female sexual behaviors were deemed sinful and criminal. Information from the cross-cultural perspective concludes that male-male sexual behavior is practiced by at least some members of most societies. Little is known about female-female sexual behavior in non-Western cultures. The conclusion from the cross-species perspective is that many animals engage in behaviors that resemble human male-male or female-female sexual behaviors, but the motivation is not clear. The attitudes of the majority of people in our society toward gay people are negative, but during the past generation gay people have organized effective political groups to fight discrimination and combat the AIDS epidemic. The biological perspective indicates increasing evidence of genetic and brain structure contributions to gay sexual orientation. Within the psychological perspective, psychoanalytic theory connects gay orientation to improper resolution of the Oedipus or Electra complex, and learning theory focuses on the role of reinforcement of early sexual behavior. Gay men and lesbians are more likely than heterosexuals to report childhood behavior stereotypical of the other gender.

Evidence has failed to show that gay men and lesbians are more emotionally unstable or more subject to psychological disorders than heterosexuals. Few wish to change their sexual orientation. Coming out is a two-pronged process: coming out to oneself and coming out to others. The gay community can also use the internet as a way to meet people and find support, through websites such as Planet Out.

Gay couples generally express themselves sexually through as wide a range of activities as heterosexuals. However, gay males and lesbians spend more time caressing their partners' bodies before approaching the genitals. Gay males living with partners are more likely to engage in extracurricular sexual activity than are lesbians. However, many gay men have changed their sexual behaviors since the advent of AIDS. The varied lifestyles of gay men and lesbians have been studied and classified.

Learning Objectives

1. Define sexual orientation and distinguish between sexual orientation, gender identity, and sexual behavior.
2. Compare and contrast the Kinsey continuum and Storm's two-dimensional model of sexual orientation.
3. Discuss the incidence, the various definitions, and the societal views of bisexuality.
4. Examine Western culture's historical and religious perspectives on gay male and lesbian sexual orientations.
5. Describe the incidence of and societal reaction to gay male and lesbian sexual orientations and behaviors across cultures and ethnicities.
6. Summarize the information on same-gender sexual behavior in other species.
7. Discuss contemporary attitudes toward gay male and lesbian sexual orientations, including the topics of homophobia, gay bashing, gay activism, and stereotyping.
8. Discuss the influence of genetics, sex hormone levels in adults, prenatal hormonal effects, and brain structure differences on adult sexual orientation.
9. Summarize the psychoanalytic and learning theories of the reasons for gay male and lesbian sexual orientations.
10. Examine the link between early gender nonconformity and later gay male and lesbian sexual orientations.
11. Summarize the research about the adjustment of gay men and lesbians, the number who wish to change their orientation, and the success of these attempts.
12. Explain the "coming out" process.
13. Compare the sexual techniques of gay male, lesbian, and heterosexual partners.
14. Examine the variations in the lifestyles of gay men and lesbians.

Fill-in-the-Blanks

_____ _____ refers to an erotic attraction to, and preference for developing romantic relationships with, members of the other gender. _____ _____ refers to an erotic attraction to members of one's own gender. _____ refers to erotic attraction to both males and females. Kinsey and his colleagues proposed a ____ - point _____ of sexual orientation rather than two opposite poles. Male-male and female-female sexual experiences during adolescence are common and _____ (do/do not) mean one will develop a gay male or lesbian sexual orientation. _____ does not accept the Kinsey model of sexual orientation; he argues that gay and heterosexual orientations may be _____ _____.

Historically, most religious denominations have _____ same-gender sexual behaviors, as well as other nonprocreative sexual activities such as _____, _____ _____, and _____ _____. Cross-cultural research indicates that some societies _____ male-male sexual activity, often as part of an initiation rite into manhood for young men. Little is known about _____ sexual activity in non-Western cultures. Most people in the U.S. view gay sexual orientations negatively. Research indicates that more than 90% of cases of child molestation involve _____ male assailants. There is _____ (clear/no) evidence that children reared by gay parents are more likely to be gay themselves.

_____ involves intense negative feelings toward gay people. People who have a strong stake in maintaining _____ _____ _____ may feel more threatened by gay people. _____ _____ are less tolerant of gay people than are _____ _____. Many states have sodomy laws that prohibit both heterosexuals and gay people from engaging in _____ _____, _____ _____, and _____ _____. Many other countries have _____ male-male and female-female sexual activity. Many people presume there is a link between gender role and gender orientation; this leads to the stereotypes of _____ gay men and _____ lesbians.

Biological research has failed to connect sexual orientation with reliable differences in adult levels of _____ _____. In adulthood, administering testosterone increases the intensity of sexual _____, but does not change sexual _____. A recent study by the National Cancer Institute supports the role of a _____ factor in sexual orientation. Research by LeVay suggests there are _____ _____ between the brains of heterosexual and gay men.

In Freud's view, a gay male sexual orientation results from failure to resolve the _____ _____ by successfully identifying with the parent of the same gender. _____

_____ (in males) and _____ _____ (in females) also play a role, according to Freud.

Gay men and lesbians report a greater incidence of _____-_____ behavior as children than do heterosexuals. Evidence _____ (clearly shows/has failed to show) that gay people are more emotionally unstable or more subject to psychological disorders than heterosexuals.

_____ _____ is a two-pronged process: recognizing and accepting one's gay orientation and declaring oneself to the world. During sexual behaviors, _____ and _____ spend more time caressing their partner's bodies before approaching the genitals. More _____ (gay males/lesbians) are involved in committed relationships.

Short Answer Questions

(LO = Learning Objective)

1. In what way are people with a gay male or lesbian sexual orientation different from transsexuals? (LO 1 - p. 268)

2. What is the relationship between people's sexual orientation and their sexual behavior? (LO 1 - pp. 268-269)

3. Name several factors to consider when interpreting survey data about the percentages of people who are gay males or lesbians. (LO 1 - p. 271)

4. Why is less known about lesbians than about gay males historically and cross-culturally? (LO 4 & 5 - pp. 274-276)

5. What can you conclude from the information that various animal species engage in same-gender sexual behaviors? (LO 6 - p. 277)

6. Summarize the attitudes toward gay people as reported in recent surveys. (LO 7 - pp. 278-279)

7. What myths and stereotypes do many people believe about gay men and lesbians? (LO 7 - pp. 281-282)

8. What conclusions can be reached from a review of the research on the genetic influences on sexual orientation? (LO 8 - pp. 282-284)

9. According to Freud, what causes a gay sexual orientation? (LO 9 - pp. 284-285)

10. What, if any, relationship exists between childhood gender nonconformity and adult sexual orientation? (LO 10 - pp. 287-288)

11. Summarize the research findings on the psychological adjustment of gay men and lesbians. (LO 11 - pp. 288-289)

12. Describe some of the lifestyle differences between gay men and lesbians. (LO 14 - pp. 295-296)

Matching Exercises

I. Vocabulary Exercise 1

Directions: Match each vocabulary term listed in the left-hand column with the correct definition in the right-hand column.

a. sexual orientation (p. 266)   ____ Violence against homosexuals.

b. heterosexual orientation (p. 266)   ____ The revelation of the identities of gay people by other gay people. The method is intended to combat discrimination against gay people by forcing individuals out of the closet and into the fray.

c. homosexual orientation (p. 267)   ____ The directionality of one's sexual interests—toward members of the same gender, the other gender, or both genders.

d. gay males (p. 267)   ____ A lesbian who assumes a traditional masculine gender role.

e. lesbians (p. 267)   ____ Of an erotic nature and involving members of the other gender.

f. bisexuality (p. 267)   ____ A cluster of negative attitudes and feelings toward gay people, including intolerance, hatred, and fear.

g. heteroerotic (p. 269)   ____ A lesbian who assumes a traditional feminine gender role.

h. homoerotic (p. 269)   ____ Females who are erotically attracted to and desire to form romantic relationships with other females.

i. outing (p. 281)   ____ Of an erotic nature and involving members of one's own gender.

j. homophobia (p. 279)   ____ Erotic attraction to, and interest in developing romantic relationships with, males and females.

k. gay bashing (p. 279)   ____ Erotic attraction to, and preference for developing romantic relationships with, members of one's own gender.

l. butch (p. 282)   ____ Males who are erotically attracted to and Desire to form romantic relationships with other males.

m. femme (p. 282)   ____ Erotic attraction to, and preference for developing romantic relationships with, members of the other gender.

II. Vocabulary Exercise 2

Directions: Match each vocabulary term listed in the left-hand column with the correct definition in the right-hand column.

a. activating effects (p. 283)   ____ Bell and Weinberg's term for gays who live alone and have sexual, social, or psycho-logical problems.

b. polymorphously perverse (p. 284)   ____ In psychoanalytic theory, the most basic defense mechanism through which threatening ideas and impulses are ejected from conscious awareness.

c. displacement (p. 284)   ____ The name homosexuals give to searching for a sex partner.

d. castration anxiety (p. 284)   ____ Bell and Weinberg's term for gays who live alone and have few sexual contacts.

e. penis envy (p. 285)   ____ Those effects of sex hormones that influence the level of the sex drive but not sexual orientation.

f. repression (p. 285)   ____ Bell and Weinberg's term for gays who live alone, have adapted well to a swinging lifestyle, and are sociable and well adjusted.

g. cruising (p. 295)   ____ In psychoanalytic theory, a man's fear that his genitals will be removed. This is an element of the Oedipus complex and is implicated in the directionality of erotic interests.

h. close couples (p. 296)   ____ In psychoanalytic theory, a defense mechanism that allows one to transfer unacceptable wishes or desires onto more appropriate or less threatening objects.

i. open couples (p. 296)   ____ Bell and Weinberg's term for gay couples who live together but engage in secret affairs.

j. functionals (p. 296)   ____ In psychoanalytic theory, the girl's wish to have a penis.

k. dysfunctionals (p. 296)   ____ In psychoanalytic theory, being receptive to all forms of sexual stimulation.

l. asexuals (p. 296)   ____ Bell and Weinberg's term for gay couples whose relationships resemble marriage in their depth of commitment and exclusiveness.

Multiple-Choice Questions

(LO = Learning Objective)

1. Which statement is accurate?
    a. Heterosexuals do not have sexual fantasies about erotic encounters with people of the same sex.
    b. Gays and lesbians do not have sexual fantasies about erotic encounters with partners of the other sex.
    c. One's sexual orientation is not always expressed in sexual behavior.
    d. People who perceive themselves as gay or lesbian are heterosexual until they have had a same sex encounter.
    p. 268   LO 1

2. The term *bisexual* refers to
    a. a person with sex organs of both genders.
    b. someone who is not erotically attracted to either gender.
    c. a person who enjoys both coitus and anal intercourse.
    d. someone who responds sexually to both genders.
    p. 273   LO 3

3. Cross-culturally, societies that highly value female virginity before marriage and segregate young men and women
    a. have more female-female sexual behaviors among adults.
    b. have more male-male sexual behaviors among adults.
    c. are more warlike and encouraging of all types of sexual expression.
    d. are less tolerant of sexual activities among children and adolescents.
    p. 275   LO 5

4. Negative attitudes towards gays have led to all of the following, *except*
    a. denying custody or visitation rights to gays after a divorce.
    b. preventing gays from adopting children.
    c. barring open homosexuals from serving in the military.
    d. preventing open homosexuals from running for elected office.
    pp. 278, 294   LO 7

5. According to research, homophobia is linked to all of the following, *except*
    a. being exclusively heterosexual.
    b. a belief in male dominance.
    c. support of stereotypical gender roles.
    d. a belief in the naturalness of female subservience.
    pp. 279-280   LO 7

6. A local gay rights activist gives a speech in which she states that she is in favor of "outing". This means this leader supports
   a. gay organizations openly contributing to the political campaigns.
   b. throwing out laws that discriminate against gay people.
   c. outlawing any form of gay bashing.
   d. revealing the identity of closeted gays who are in important positions.
   p. 281   LO 7

7. According to LeVay, gay men have a _____ compared to heterosexual men.
   a. larger more complex cerebral cortex
   b. less developed sperm producing apparatus
   c. cluster of cells in the anterior hypothalamus which is smaller
   d. smaller connecting fiber between the hypothalamus and the pituitary gland
   pp. 283-284   LO 8

8. Learning theories
   a. are similar to Freudian concepts of the Oedipus Complex.
   b. emphasize the resolution of intrapsychic conflicts.
   c. believe there is a genetic component to our sexual orientation.
   d. focus on the role of reinforcement of early patterns of sexual behavior.
   pp. 286-287   LO 9

9. Which is *not* accurate regarding gays and lesbians?
   a. They follow a variety of lifestyles.
   b. They are more highly educated than Americans in general.
   c. They report similar levels of satisfaction with their relationships as do heterosexual couples.
   d. They are primarily from lower socioeconomic levels.
   pp. 288-289   LO 11

10. What have researchers concluded about family determinants of sexual orientation?
    a. The role of the father is more critical than that of the mother.
    b. A person's relationship with his or her siblings may be more predictive than parental relationships.
    c. There is great variation in the family dynamics of gay men and women.
    d. The families of lesbians are more disturbed than those of gay men.
    p. 286   LO 9

11. To "come out" to others usually involves
    a. wearing the clothing of the opposite gender.
    b. fears of rejection and loss of love from family and friends.
    c. retaliation against those who have created the situation.
    d. changing one's name and identity to gain anonymity.
       p. 292   LO 12

12. How do gay men and women differ from heterosexuals in their sexual techniques?
    a. Gays never alternate the dominant and submissive roles.
    b. Gays spend more time than heterosexuals holding, kissing, and caressing each other before approaching the breasts and genitals.
    c. Heterosexuals are more adept at foreplay techniques.
    d. There were no differences found.
       pp. 293-294   LO 13

Other Activities

I. Perspectives on Homosexuality

Directions: Complete the chart below by supplying a summary of the theories and the support for each of the following perspectives on homosexuality.

Perspective	Description and Supporting Evidence
Historical	
Cross-Cultural	
Cross-Species	

Biological
 	
    Genetics
 	
    Hormonal Influences
 	
    Brain Structure	

Psychological
 	
    Psychoanalytic
 	
    Learning Theories	

Chapter 11

Conception, Pregnancy, and Childbirth

Chapter Summary

Fertilization normally occurs in a Fallopian tube. Optimizing the chances of conception involves engaging in coitus around the time of ovulation. As we enter the new millennium, bearing children is no longer restricted to young adults, and many women are choosing to remain childfree. A couple who wishes to conceive a child of a particular gender may use one of several available sperm-separation procedures, none of which is perfectly reliable. Sperm and egg donation is becoming more sophisticated, and prospective customers can even go to websites and browse through lists of donor characteristics.

The causes of infertility in males and females are explained. The methods for overcoming infertility include artificial insemination with the father's or a donor's sperm, in vitro fertilization, GIFT, ZIFT, donor IVF, embryonic transfer, intracytoplasmic injection, and surrogate motherhood.

The early signs and effects of pregnancy are described, and the possible causes of spontaneous abortion are discussed. Generally, coitus during a normal pregnancy is safe until the start of labor. Psychological responses to pregnancy reflect whether the woman or couple wanted to be pregnant, the woman's physical changes, and attitudes toward the woman's physical changes.

Prenatal development can be divided into three periods. The germinal stage is the period from conception to implantation. The embryonic stage begins with implantation and extends to about the eighth week of development; it is characterized by differentiation of major organ systems. The fetal stage (characterized by continued maturation of the organ systems and dramatic increases in size) begins by the ninth week and continues until birth. Factors that affect prenatal development include maternal diet, maternal diseases and disorders, drugs, maternal malnutrition, and exposure to teratogens. Chromosomal and genetic abnormalities can lead to particular defects and syndromes.

In the first stage of childbirth uterine contractions efface and dilate the cervix. The second stage begins when the baby first appears at the opening of the birth canal and ends with the birth of the baby. During the third stage, the placenta is expelled. Contemporary methods of childbirth are explained. Some parents may choose to deliver at a birth center or at home instead of at a hospital. Prenatal anoxia, preterm delivery, and low-birthweight are significant birth problems.

The postpartum period involves possible mood changes or depression, decisions about breast-feeding or bottle-feeding, delaying coitus for about six weeks, and resumption of ovulation and menstruation.

Learning Objectives

1. Describe the process of conception.
2. Identify the various methods of increasing the chances of conception and their success rates.
3. Describe various gender selection techniques and their success rates.
4. Describe the causes of infertility in males and females.
5. List and describe alternative ways of becoming parents.
6. Examine the biological and psychological effects of pregnancy on women.
7. Trace prenatal development through the germinal, embryonic, and fetal stages.
8. Describe the effects on the embryo and fetus of maternal diet, maternal diseases and disorders, maternal and paternal use of drugs, and other environmental influences.
9. Discuss possible chromosomal and genetic abnormalities in the fetus and the tests used to detect them.
10. Describe the physical changes associated with the three stages of childbirth.
11. Discuss historical and current methods of childbirth, including the use of anesthesia, preparation for childbirth, and the need for and frequency of Cesarean sections.
12. Compare hospitals and alternative locations for giving birth.
13. Explain the causes, the effects at birth, and the effects later in a child's life of anoxia, preterm delivery, and low-birthweight.
14. Explain the emotional and physical changes that women may experience during the postpartum period.
15. Discuss the advantages and disadvantages of breast-feeding and bottle-feeding.

Fill-in-the-Blanks

_____ is the union of a sperm cell and an ovum. _____ carry X sex chromosomes; _____ carry either X or Y sex chromosomes. About _____ to _____ boys are conceived for every 100 girls. Male fetuses are more likely to be lost in a _____ _____.

Fertilization usually occurs in a _____ _____. Sperm reach the fallopian tubes _____ to _____ minutes after ejaculation. The ovum can be fertilized for about _____ to _____ hours after ovulation.

Assuming a woman's cycle is fairly regular, she can learn to predict the day of ovulation by measuring her BBT (_____ _____ _____). Two additional methods for predicting ovulation are tracking the thickness of the _____ _____ and analyzing the _____ for _____ _____.

One method for selecting the gender of a child is _____ approach, which is based on the fact that Y sperm are faster swimmers and X sperm are more durable. Another method is _____ _____ .

The term _____ is usually not applied until the failure to conceive has persisted for more than a year. The most common cause of male infertility is _____ _____ _____ . For these men, the sperm from multiple ejaculations can be injected into a partner's uterus at the time of ovulation. This describes one variation of _____ _____ . Infertility in women can be caused by a variety of conditions. A number of alternative ways of becoming parents are now available, including conceiving via _____ _____ _____ ; the product of this is commonly called a "test-tube baby".

The first sign of pregnancy for many women is a _____ _____ . Other early effects of pregnancy include _____ _____ , _____ _____ , and _____ _____ . Pregnancy tests detect _____ in a woman's urine or blood. Three-fourths of _____ (spontaneous abortions) occur during the first _____ weeks of pregnancy.

Most health professionals concur that coitus is safe _____ _____ , providing the pregnancy is normal and the woman has no history of miscarriages. If one dates pregnancy from the date fertilization is assumed to have taken place, the normal gestation period is _____ days. The great majority of babies are born during the _____ - day period that spans the due date.

The seven or eight day period from conception to implantation in the uterine wall is termed the _____ stage. The period from implantation to about the eighth week of development is called the _____ stage. Development of the embryo follows two general trends: _____ , (from the head downward) and

_____ (from the center of the body outward). The embryo (or fetus) is suspended within the _____ sac in the _____ fluid.

Nutrients and waste products are exchanged between mother and embryo (or fetus) through the _____. The fetus is connected to this organ by the _____ cord. The _____ passes from the woman's body after delivery, and is also called the "afterbirth".

The _____ stage begins about the ninth week and continues until the birth. During the second trimester, the fetus increases its weight from _____ to _____. Usually the mother can feel movement by the middle of the _____ month. Near the end of the second trimester, the fetus approaches the _____ __ _____. However, only a _____ of babies born at the end of the second trimester who weigh under two pounds will survive.

Environmental influences or agents that can harm the embryo or fetus are called _____. These include drugs taken by the mother, substances produced by the mother's body, and disease-causing organisms. For example, nearly 40% of children whose mothers drank heavily during pregnancy develop _____ _____ _____. Babies whose mothers _____ during pregnancy weigh less on the average at birth. These babies are also more likely to experience asthma and a variety of other problems. _____ and CVS (_____ _____ _____) are two tests used to detect chromosomal and genetic abnormalities in the fetus.

Most women will experience _____ - _____ contractions, or "false labor". "Real" contractions become increasingly more regular, stronger, and closer together. In the first stage of childbirth, contractions _____ and _____ the cervix to about four inches in diameter. _____ to _____ hours of labor is considered average for a first birth. _____ usually lasts about 30 minutes and occurs when the cervix is nearly fully dilated and the baby's head begins to move into the vagina. The second stage begins when the _____ is fully dilated and ends with the _____. It lasts a few minutes to a few hours. An incision in the perineum, an _____, may be performed. During the third stage, the _____ is expelled.

The _____ method, or prepared childbirth, emphasizes education, physical fitness, and techniques for relaxation and breathing. In a _____ _____, the baby is delivered through an incision in the abdomen and the uterus.

In the United States most births occur in hospitals. An alternative location is a _____ _____, which has some medical equipment available and is usually located near a hospital. Another alternative is _____ _____, which some argue exposes the mother and baby to unnecessary risks.

One birth problem is prenatal _____, or oxygen deprivation. Another is prematurity, if the baby is born prior to _____ weeks of gestation. Prematurity is often linked to low-birthweight. A baby is considered to have a low-birthweight if it weighs less than _____ pounds.

Following birth, some mothers experience persistent and severe mood changes, called _____ _____. _____-_____ has several benefits to mother and baby, but it may be difficult or impossible if the mother must return to work shortly after birth or has many other responsibilities. Physicians usually advise a couple to wait _____ weeks after delivery to resume intercourse.

Short Answer Questions

(LO = Learning Objective)

1. Describe the process of fertilization. (LO 1 - p. 301)

2. What can a couple do to optimize their chances of conception? (LO 2 pp. 301-306)

3. What methods could a couple use to select the gender of their child? (LO 3 - p. 304)

4. List and briefly describe several alternative ways of becoming parents. (LO 5 - pp. 306-311)

5. What are the functions of the amniotic sac and the amniotic fluid? (LO 7 - p. 318)

6. Approximately how much weight should a woman gain during pregnancy? Why? (LO 8 - p. 320)

7. What does Rh incompatibility mean? (LO 8 - p. 322)

8. What are the characteristics of babies born with FAS? (LO 8 - p. 323)

9. What medical procedures are used to detect the presence of biochemical and chromosomal abnormalities? (LO 9 - p. 327)

10. Describe the Lamaze method, or prepared childbirth, and its advantages. (LO 11 - p. 331)

11. Describe the advantages and disadvantages of breast-feeding.
    (LO 15 - p. 336-337)

Matching Exercises

I. Vocabulary Exercise 1

Directions: Match each vocabulary term listed in the left-hand column with the correct definition in the right-hand column.

a. zygote (p. 300)   ____ A method of conception in which mature ova are surgically removed from an ovary and placed in a laboratory dish along with sperm.

b. amniocentesis (p. 300)   ____ The introduction of sperm in the reproductive tract through means other than sexual intercourse.

____ A fertilized ovum.

c. Down syndrome (p. 300)

d. spontaneous abortion (p. 300)   ____ A method of conception in which an ovum is fertilized in a laboratory dish and then placed in a Fallopian tube.

e. infertility (p. 306)   ____ The production of antibodies that attack naturally occurring substances that are (incorrectly) recognized as being foreign or harmful.

f. auto-immune response (p. 307)   ____ A chromosomal abnormality that leads to mental retardation, caused by an extra chromosome on the twenty-first pair.

____ A method of conception in which sperm and ova are inserted into a Fallopian tube to encourage conception.

g. artificial insemination (p. 307)

h. laparoscopy (p. 308)   ____ The sudden, involuntary expulsion of the embryo or fetus from the uterus before it is capable of independent life.

i. in vitro fertilization (p. 309)   ____ A variation of in vitro fertilization in which the ovum is taken from one woman, fertilized, and then injected into the uterus or Fallopian tube of another woman.

j. gamete intrafallopian transfer (GIFT) (p. 309)   ____ A procedure for drawing off and examining fetal cells in the amniotic fluid to determine the presence of various disorders in the fetus.

____ A medical procedure in which a long, narrow tube (laparoscope) is inserted through an incision in the navel, permitting the visual inspection of organs in the pelvic cavity.

k. zygote intrafallopian transfer (ZIFT) (p. 309)

l. donor IVF (p. 309)   ____ Inability to conceive a child.

II. Vocabulary Exercise 2

Directions: Match each vocabulary term listed in the left-hand column with the correct definition in the right-hand column.

a. embryonic transfer (p. 310) ____ From the head downward.

b. surrogate mother (p. 310) ____ A spontaneous abortion.

c. human chorionic gonadotropin (p. 313) ____ The birth of a dead fetus.

d. Hegar's sign (p. 313) ____ A stage within the germinal stage of prenatal development, when the embryo is a sphere of cells surrounding a cavity of fluid.

e. morning sickness (p. 313) ____ From the central axis of the body outward.

f. miscarriage (p. 313) ____ The period of prenatal development prior to implantation in the uterus.

g. sympathetic pregnancy (p. 315) ____ A hormone produced by women shortly after conception, which stimulates the corpus luteum to continue to produce progesterone. Its presence in a woman's urine indicates that she is pregnant.

h. germinal stage (p. 316) ____ The stage of prenatal development that lasts from implantation through the eighth week, and which is characterized by the differentiation of the major organ systems.

i. blastocyst (p. 316) ____ The experiencing of a number of signs of pregnancy by the father.

j. stillbirth (p. 321) ____ Softness of a section of the uterus between the uterine body and the cervix, which indicates that a woman is pregnant.

____ A method of conception in which a woman volunteer is artificially inseminated by the male partner of the intended mother, after which the embryo is removed from the volunteer and inserted within the uterus of the intended mother.

k. embryonic stage (p. 317)

____ Symptoms of pregnancy, including nausea, aversions to specific foods, and vomiting.

l. cephalocaudal (p. 317)

____ A woman who is impregnated through artificial insemination, with the sperm of a prospective father, carries the embryo and fetus to term, and then gives the child to the prospective parents.

m. proximodistal (p. 317)

III. Vocabulary Exercise 3

Directions: Match each vocabulary term listed in the left-hand column with the correct definition in the right-hand column.

a. amniotic sac (p. 318) _____ A condition in which antibodies produced by a pregnant woman are transmitted to the fetus and may cause brain damage or death.

b. amniotic fluid (p. 318) _____ A life-threatening condition that is characterized by high blood pressure.

c. placenta (p. 319) _____ An estrogen that was once given to women at risk for miscarriage to help maintain pregnancy.

d. umbilical cord (p. 319) _____ Environmental influences or agents that can damage an embryo or fetus.

e. age of viability (p. 319) _____ Following birth.

f. cephalic presentation (p. 319) _____ A pregnancy in which the fertilized ovum implants someplace other than the uterus.

g. breech presentation (p. 319) _____ The sac containing the fetus.

h. teratogens (p. 320) _____ A cluster of symptoms caused by maternal drinking in which the child shows develop-mental lags and characteristic facial features, such as an underdeveloped upper jaw, flattened nose and widely spaced eyes.

i. critical period of vulnerability (p. 320) _____ A tube that connects the fetus to the placenta.

j. toxemia (p. 321) _____ Emergence of the baby feet first from the womb.

k. ectopic pregnancy (p. 321) _____ Fluid within the amniotic sac that suspends and protects the fetus.

l. Rh incompatibility (p. 321) _____ A period of time during which an embryo or fetus is vulnerable to the effects of a teratogen.

m. DES (diethylstilbestrol) (p. 323) _____ An organ connected to the fetus by the umbilical cord. It serves as a relay station between mother and fetus, allowing the exchange of nutrients and wastes.

n. fetal alcohol syndrome (p. 323) _____ Emergence of the baby headfirst from the womb.

o. postpartum (p. 335) _____ The age at which a fetus can sustain independent life.

IV. Vocabulary Exercise 4

Directions: Match each vocabulary term listed in the left-hand column with the correct definition in the right-hand column.

a. Braxton-Hicks contractions (p. 328) ____ Production of milk by the mammary glands.

b. efface (p. 328) ____ A childbirth method in which women learn about childbirth, learn to relax and to breathe in patterns that conserve energy and lessen pain, and have a coach present at childbirth. Also termed *prepared childbirth*.

c. dilate (p. 328) ____ Anesthesia that eliminates pain in a specific area of the body, as during childbirth.

d. transition (p. 328) ____ A reddish vaginal discharge that may persist for a month after delivery.

e. episiotomy (p. 328) ____ A method of childbirth in which the fetus is delivered through a surgical incision in the abdomen.

f. general anesthesia (p. 330) ____ So-called false labor contractions that are relatively painless.

g. local anesthesia (p. 331) ____ Born prior to 37 weeks of gestation.

h. natural childbirth (p. 331) ____ A method of childbirth in which women use no anesthesia but are given other strategies for coping with discomfort and are educated about childbirth.

i. Lamaze method (p. 331) ____ The process during which the cervix becomes nearly fully dilated and the head of the fetus begins to move into the birth canal.

j. cesarean section (p. 331) ____ Oxygen deprivation.

k. transverse position (p. 332) ____ A surgical incision in the perineum that widens the birth canal, preventing random tearing during childbirth.

l. anoxia (p. 333) ____ To become thin.

m. preterm (p. 334) ____ The use of drugs to put people to sleep and eliminate pain, as during childbirth.

n. lactation (p. 336) ____ To open or widen.

o. lochia (p. 337) ____ A crosswise birth position.

Multiple-Choice Questions

(LO = Learning Objective)

1. A fertilized ovum is called a/an
   a. embryo.
   b. fetus.
   c. follicle.
   d. zygote.
           p. 300   LO 1

2. Basal body temperature charting allows for
   a. identification of the optimal time for conception.
   b. predicting the time of ovulation.
   c. both of the above.
   d. none of the above.
           pp. 303-304   LO 2

3. Y-bearing sperm are _____ while X-bearing sperm are _____ .
   a. bigger; faster
   b. smaller and faster; more durable
   c. bigger and faster; more abundant
   d. smaller and faster; more aggressive
           p. 304   LO 3

4. The major causes of infertility in females include all of the following *except*
   a. inability to orgasm during coitus thus lowering acidity levels in the vagina.
   b. failure to ovulate.
   c. obstructions of the reproductive tract.
   d. endometriosis.
           p. 308   LO 4

5. Rosalia missed her period about three weeks ago and asks her physician for a pregnancy test. She is confirmed as pregnant if there is _____ in her urine.
   a. follicle stimulating hormone
   b. hyaluronidase
   c. luteinizing hormone
   d. human chorionic gonadotropin
           p. 313   LO 6

6. In the developing fetus, arm buds appear before hands and fingers. This is in keeping with
   a. the cephalocaudal principle.
   b. the proximodistal principle.
   c. Nagele's Rule.
   d. the concept of critical period.
   	p. 318		LO 7

7. The correct order of the stages of prenatal development is
   a. trophoblast stage, embryonic stage, fetal stage.
   b. germinal stage, embryonic stage, fetal stage.
   c. blastocyst stage, embryonic stage, fetal stage.
   d. embryonic stage, germinal stage, fetal stage.
   	p. 315		LO 7

8. At which stage of development are the major organ systems considered most vulnerable to the effects of teratogens?
   a. germinal stage
   b. embryonic stage
   c. fetal stage
   d. teratogenic stage
   	p. 317		LO 8

9. Debra is concerned about the possibility that her fetus has inherited a familial disease. To check for this genetic problem, she will undergo
   a. basal body temperature testing.
   b. Shettles' procedure.
   c. amniocentesis.
   d. urine analysis.
   	p. 327		LO 9

10. The second stage of childbirth ends with
    a. the transition period.
    b. birth of the baby.
    c. crowning.
    d. episiotomy.
    	p. 328		LO 10

11. Gestation lasts for approximately
    a. 37 weeks.
    b. 48 weeks.
    c. 57 weeks.
    d. 40 weeks.
          p. 334   LO 13

12. The term postpartum refers to the time
    a. following the midpoint of pregnancy.
    b. following birth.
    c. following conception.
    d. when a mother first feels her fetus move.
          p. 335   LO 14

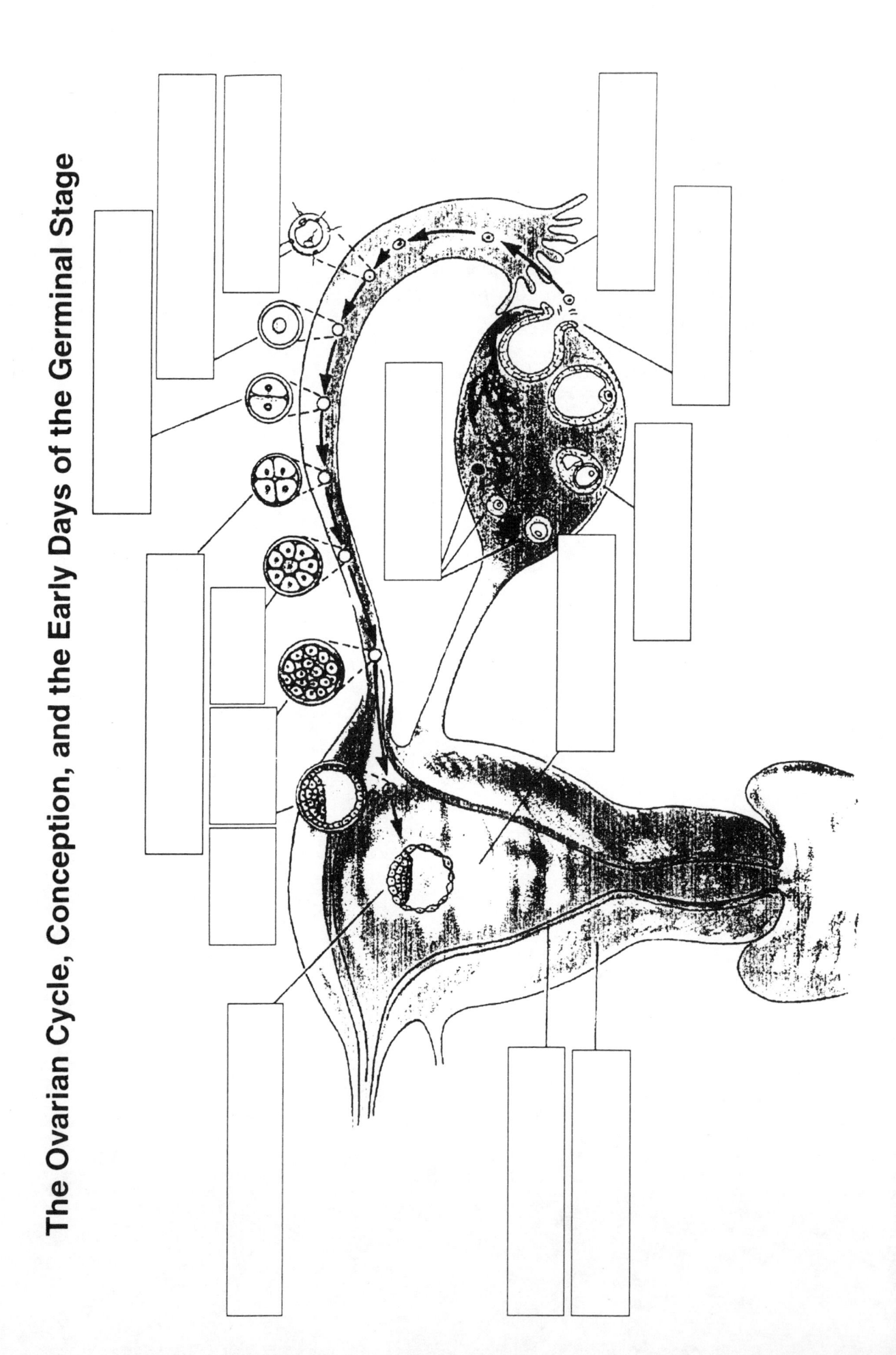

The Ovarian Cycle, Conception, and the Early Days of the Germinal Stage

The Three Stages of Labor

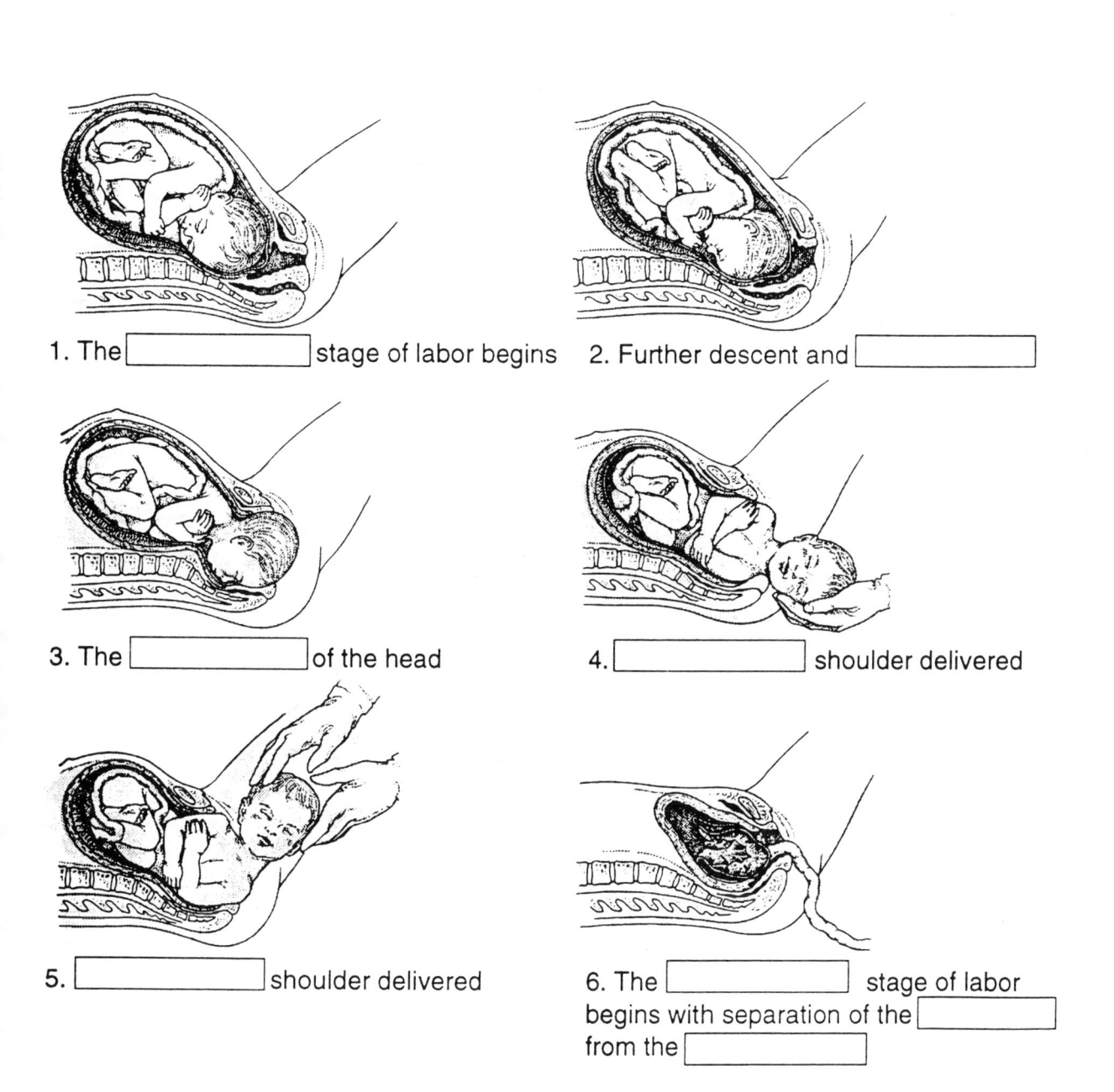

1. The [first] stage of labor begins

2. Further descent and [rotation]

3. The [crowning] of the head

4. [Anterior] shoulder delivered

5. [Posterior] shoulder delivered

6. The [third] stage of labor begins with separation of the [placenta] from the [uterus]

Other Activities

I. Stages of Childbirth

Directions: Complete the chart below by supplying information about the events that take place during the three stages of childbirth.

Stage	Events Taking Place and Average Length of Stage
FIRST STAGE Transition	
SECOND STAGE	
THIRD STAGE	

Chapter 12

Contraception and Abortion

Chapter Summary

The legal history of contraception in the United States includes the Comstock law of 1873, which prohibited sending contraceptive information or devices through the mail. In 1918 the courts ruled that physicians could disseminate such information to aid in the cure and prevention of disease. In 1965 the Supreme Court struck down the last impediment to sale and use of contraception.

Birth-control pills include combination pills and minipills. Oral contraception is nearly 100 percent effective. The main drawbacks are side effects and potential health risks. Norplant, with its extremely low failure rate, involves implantation of six small tubes of progestin in a woman's upper arm. The IUD (intrauterine device) is highly effective but has possible troublesome side effects and the potential for serious health complications.

The diaphragm, when used correctly and with a spermicidal cream or jelly, is highly reliable and safe, because together they block the passage of sperm and kill sperm. The typical failure rate is high, but spermicides that contain nonoxynol-9 may also provide some protection against STIs. The cervical cap, which also has a high failure rate, is also intended to be used with a spermicide. Latex condoms have a high failure rate when used alone, but when used with spermicides, their effectiveness rivals that of birth-control pills. They also afford protection against STIs. Douching and withdrawal should not be considered methods of contraception. Rhythms methods have a high failure rate, but they appeal to some for religious reasons and because they are a natural method. Sterilization has a very low failure rate, but it should be considered irreversible. In recent years, the female condom and Depo-Provera have become available.

Other new contraceptives are being researched. It does appear that new advances will be made in mechanical and chemical barrier methods, hormone-delivery systems, intrauterine devices (IUDs), and methods for men.

Historically, abortions were legal until "quickening" occurred. Around the time of the Civil War, during the last half of the 1800s, all states passed laws outlawing abortion. Abortion was, in effect, legalized in 1973; however, recent Supreme Court decisions have allowed states to adopt greater restrictions than those set forth in *Roe v. Wade*.

Abortion methods in use today in the United States include vacuum aspiration, D & C, D & E, induction of labor by intra-amniotic infusion, and hysterotomy. Choosing to have an abortion is typically a painful decision, but women generally show positive psychological adjustment after an abortion.

Learning Objectives

1. Define contraception and trace the history of methods of contraception.
2. Discuss the history of contraception law in the United States.
3. List eight issues to consider when choosing a contraceptive.
4. Describe how oral contraceptives work and discuss their effectiveness, reversibility, advantages, and disadvantages.
5. Describe how Norplant works, and discuss its effectiveness, reversibility, advantages, and disadvantages.
6. Describe how IUDs work and discuss their effectiveness, reversibility, advantages, and disadvantages.
7. Describe the diaphragm, and discuss how it works, its effectiveness, reversibility, advantages, and disadvantages.
8. Identify the types of spermicides and discuss their use alone or with other methods, their effectiveness, reversibility, advantages and disadvantages.
9. Describe the cervical cap and discuss how it works, its effectiveness, reversibility, advantages, and disadvantages.
10. Describe how condoms are used, and discuss their effectiveness, reversibility, advantages, and disadvantages.
11. Describe douching and withdrawal and explain why both are considered non-methods of contraception.
12. Name and explain the four fertility awareness techniques and discuss their effectiveness, advantages, and disadvantages.
13. Explain the procedures used in male and female sterilization and discuss the effectiveness, advantages, and disadvantages of the procedures.
14. Describe the advantages and disadvantages of the female condom and Depo-Provera, and discuss possible future developments in contraception.
15. Summarize the history of abortion, the changing abortion laws in the United States, and attitudes toward abortion.
16. Describe the six methods of abortion, including RU-486, the possible complications associated with each, and the time period during pregnancy in which each can be performed.
17. Describe the findings from the research on psychological consequences of abortion in the United States and Japan.

Fill-in-the-Blanks

Oral contraceptives are commonly referred to as _____ _____ _____ . There are two types: _____ _____ , which contain synthetic forms of estrogen and progestin, and _____ , which contain only progestin. Pills containing both synthetic hormones work by _____ _____ . Pills with only progestin work by _____ and _____ . "_____ - _____" pills are for one-time emergency protection.

One contraceptive device, _____ , involves implanting six tubes containing progestin under the skin of a woman's upper arm. It works by suppressing _____ and thickening the _____ _____ . Its contraceptive effect occurs within ___ _____ after insertion and lasts for about _____ _____ . The failure rate is less than _____ percent.

IUD is the abbreviation for _____ _____ . It is a small device that is inserted into the _____ . Although researchers do not know exactly how IUDs work, they probably prevent _____ .

A _____ is a shallow rubber dome, which is available only by prescription and must be fitted by a health professional. It is unreliable as a barrier alone and should be used with a _____ _____ or _____ . It should not be inserted more than ____ hours prior to coitus and should be left in place at least ____ hours after coitus.

_____ are chemical agents that kill sperm. They should be left in place in the vagina (no douching) for at least ____ to ____ hours after coitus. The main disadvantage is their high _____ _____ .

The _____ _____ is made of latex or plastic and fits snugly over the cervical opening. Like the diaphragm, this device should be used with a _____. It should be left in place at least ___ hours after intercourse.

Most _____ are made of latex. When used with a _____ , their effectiveness rivals that of birth control pills. They also offer protection against _____ that is unparalleled among contraceptive devices.

_____ after coitus should be considered a "non-method" of contraception because of its high failure rate. _____ also has a high failure rate, partly because active sperm may be present in the pre-ejaculatory fluid from the Cowper's glands.

Rhythm methods (_____ _____ methods) are the only contraceptive methods that are acceptable to the Roman Catholic church. They work by predicting _____ so the couple can _____ coitus when the woman is fertile. One rhythm method, the _____ method, assumes that ovulation occurs 14 days prior to menstruation. Most women who use this method need to abstain for about _____ days during the middle of each cycle. Another rhythm method, the _____ _____ _____ _____ , is based on predicting ovulation by charting a woman's body temperature on awakening in the morning. The _____ _____ method relies on tracking changes in the viscosity of the cervical mucus. _____ - _____ kits allow women to test their urine daily for the presence of luteinizing hormone.

_____ is the most widely used form of birth control among married couples aged 30 and above in the United States. The male sterilization procedure is termed the _____ ; it is nearly 100% effective. Although an operation to reverse male sterilization (_____) is available, successful reversal is not guaranteed and sterilization should be considered permanent.

Although several different procedures are used in female sterilization, all prevent ova and sperm from passing through the _____ _____ . These procedures are nearly _____ percent effective. Generally, _____ (women/men) incur significantly more medical complications from sterilization procedures, usually resulting from the use of anesthesia.

A relatively new device, the _____ _____ , is a polyurethane sheath that is put in the vagina and held in place by plastic rings fitted over the vaginal opening and against the cervix. _____ - _____ is an injectable long-acting drug, which is administered once every three months.

More than _____ million abortions are performed in the United States each year. The majority of the women having legal abortions are in their _____ (teens, 20s, 30s, 40s). About ninety percent of the abortions in the United States occur within the _____ _____ of pregnancy. _____ v _____ was the 1973 Supreme Court decision that legalized abortion nationwide.

_____ _____ is the safest and most common method of abortion and it is used in more than 90% of abortions in the United States. It can only be performed during the _____ trimester.

The D & C (_____ and _____) and the D & E (_____ and _____) are generally used during the _____ trimester. They are done in a hospital, usually under _____ anesthesia.

_____ - _____ _____ is an abortion method that involves injecting a saline or prostaglandin solution into the amniotic sac to induce premature labor. A _____ involves incisions in the abdomen and uterus to remove the fetus and the uterine contents. It is major surgery and very rarely performed.

Two different methods of drug-induced abortion are being researched: _____ - _____ , which is approved and available in France and other countries, and a combination of _____ and _____ .

Short Answer Questions

(LO = Learning Objective)

1. Briefly describe the history of contraception in the United States. (LO 2 - pp. 343-345)

2. Name eight issues a couple might consider when choosing a contraceptive. (LO 3 - pp. 345-347)

3. How might one's belief about when life begins influence one's choice of birth control? (LO 3 - p. 345)

4. What are "morning-after" pills? (LO 4 - p. 351)

5. Why should people use latex condoms instead of those made of animal intestines? (LO 10 - p. 360)

6. For whom might fertility awareness methods be an appropriate form of contraception? (LO 12 - pp. 363-366)

7. Briefly describe the history of abortion in the United States. (LO 15 - pp. 374-375)

8. Summarize the *Roe v. Wade* decision. (LO 15 - p. 374)

9. During what part of pregnancy are most abortions in the United States done? How safe are abortions? (LO 16 - pp. 377-378)

10. Briefly describe the psychological consequences of induced abortion. (LO 17 - p. 380)

Matching Exercises

I. Vocabulary Exercise 1

Directions: Match each vocabulary term listed in the left-hand column with the correct definition in the right-hand column.

a.	coitus interruptus (p. 343)	_____	To rinse or wash the vaginal canal by inserting a liquid and allowing it to drain out.
b.	condom (p. 359)	_____	A birth-control pill that contains synthetic progesterone but no estrogen.
c.	oral contraceptive (p. 348)	_____	A fertility awareness method of contraception that relies on prediction of ovulation by tracking the viscosity of the cervical mucus.
d.	combination pill (p. 348)	_____	A method of contraception in which the penis is withdrawn from the vagina prior to ejaculation. Also referred to as the *withdrawal method*.
e.	minipill (p. 348)	_____	An agent that protects against disease.
f.	intrauterine device (p. 353)	_____	A contraceptive, consisting of sex hormones, which is taken by mouth.
g.	diaphragm (p. 355)	_____	A fertility awareness (rhythm) method of contraception that relies on prediction of ovulation by tracking menstrual cycles, typically for a 10- to 12-month period, and assuming that ovulation occurs 14 days prior to menstruation.
h.	prophylactic (p. 359)	_____	A small object that is inserted into the uterus and left in place to prevent conception.
i.	douche (p. 363)	_____	The days during the menstrual cycle during which a woman is most likely to be fertile.
j.	calendar method (p. 364)	_____	A sheath made of animal membrane or latex that covers the penis during coitus and serves as a barrier to sperm following ejaculation.
k.	basal body temperature (BBT) method (p. 364)	_____	A fertility awareness method of contraception that relies on prediction of ovulation by tracking the woman's temperature during the course of the menstrual cycle.
l.	ovulation method (p. 365)	_____	A birth control pill that contains synthetic estrogen and progesterone.
m.	peak days (p. 365)	_____	A shallow rubber cup or dome, fitted to the contour of a woman's vagina, that is coated with a spermicide and inserted prior to coitus to prevent conception.

II. Vocabulary Exercise 2

Directions: Match each vocabulary term listed in the left-hand column with the correct definition in the right-hand column.

a.	vasectomy (p. 366)	____	Surgical removal of the uterus. (*Not* appropriate as a method of sterilization.)
b.	vasovasotomy (p. 367)	____	The surgical method of reversing vasectomy in which the cut or cauterized ends of the vas deferens are sewn together.
c.	tubal sterilization (p. 370)	____	Abbreviation for *dilation and curettage*, an operation in which the cervix is dilated and uterine contents are then gently scraped away.
d.	minilaparotomy (p. 370)	____	A kind of tubal sterilization in which a small incision is made in the abdomen to provide access to the Fallopian tubes.
e.	laparoscopy (p. 370)	____	The surgical method of male sterilization in which sperm are prevented from reaching the urethra by cutting each vas deferens and tying it back or cauterizing it.
f.	culpotomy (p. 370)	____	An abortion method in which the fetus is removed by Cesarean section.
g.	hysterectomy (p. 370)	____	An abortion method in which a substance is injected into the amniotic sac to induce premature labor. Also called *instillation*.
h.	vacuum aspiration (p. 377)	____	The most common method of female sterilization, in which the Fallopian tubes are surgically blocked to prevent the meeting of the sperm and ova. Also called *tubal ligation*.
i.	D & C (p. 377)	____	Tubal sterilization by means of a laparoscope, which is inserted through a small incision just below the navel and used to cauterize, cut, or clamp the Fallopian tubes. Sometimes referred to as "belly button surgery."
j.	D & E (p. 378)	____	Removal of the uterine contents by suction. An abortion method used early in pregnancy.
k.	intra-amniotic infusion (p. 378)	____	Abbreviation for *dilation and evacuation*, an abortion method in which the cervix is dilated prior to vacuum aspiration.
l.	hysterotomy (p. 378)	____	A kind of tubal sterilization in which the Fallopian tubes are approached through an incision in the back wall of the vagina.

Multiple-Choice Questions

(LO = Learning Objective)

1. The 1960s were important in the history of contraception because
   a. sending contraceptive information through the mail became legal.
   b. the last law preventing the free sale of contraceptives was defeated and and oral contraceptives became available.
   c. women won the right to terminate a pregnancy.
   d. condoms were developed and mass marketed.
           p. 345   LO 2

2. The issue of _____ refers to the effect a contraceptive method will have upon the ability to conceive in the future.
   a. shared responsibility
   b. moral acceptability
   c. reversibility
   d. safety
           p. 346   LO 3

3. Oral contraceptives work most directly by
   a. interfering with penetration of the ova by the sperm.
   b. thickening the uterine mucosa, thus preventing passage of sperm.
   c. suppressing follicle maturation and ovulation.
   d. preventing attachment of the fertilized egg to the wall of the uterus.
           p. 349   LO 4

4. All of the following are true regarding Norplant, *except*
   a. it is a contraceptive implant.
   b. it consists of six match stick-sized silicone tubes.
   c. it releases small, steady doses of progestin.
   d. it must be removed in two years.
           p. 352   LO 5

5. The IUD's effectiveness appears to be due to its ability to
   a. suppress ovulation.
   b. kill sperm or reduce their motility.
   c. prevent uterine implantation.
   d. decrease the sperm's ability to penetrate the zona pellucida.
           p. 354   LO 6

6. A diaphragm and condom are similar in each respect, *except*
   a. both act to prevent implantation of the fertilized ovum.
   b. both are more effective in combating STIs when used with a spermicide containing nonoxynol-9.
   c. both act as barriers between sperm and ova.
   d. both are made of a latex rubber material.
        pp. 356-361   LO 7

7. The cervical cap
   a. fits inside the uterus to prevent conception.
   b. is a 2-inch spermicidal film used to cap the cervix.
   c. forms a barrier between sperm and ova.
   d. is a type of female condom.
        p. 359   LO 9

8. All of the following are guidelines from your text regarding condom usage, *except*
   a. use only water-based lubricants with condoms.
   b. unroll the condom all the way to the bottom of the penis.
   c. use only oil-based lubricants with condoms.
   d. check condoms for tears and cracks.
        pp. 361-362   LO 10

9. A vasectomy is performed by
   a. severing the epididymis.
   b. removal of the prostate gland.
   c. cauterizing a small section of the urethra.
   d. severing the two vas deferens.
        pp. 366-367   LO 13

10. The most common technique of female sterilization is
    a. culpotomy.
    b. tubal ligation.
    c. laparoscopy.
    d. minilaparotomy.
        p. 370   LO 13

11. According to national public opinion polls taken since *Roe v. Wade*, the attitude toward legalized abortion is
    a. shifting from year to year.
    b. antagonistic, except when the mother's life is in danger.
    c. supportive under all circumstances.
    d. supportive under some circumstances.
        p. 375   LO 15

12. In the United States, the most commonly used method of inducing abortion is
    a. dilation and curettage.
    b. dilation and evacuation.
    c. vacuum aspiration.
    d. intra-amniotic infusion.
            p. 377   LO 16

Other Activities

I. Weighing the Alternatives

Directions: Complete the chart below by listing the variations within each method and the advantages and disadvantages of using each method.

Methods	Advantages	Disadvantages
Birth Control Pills		
Norplant		
IUD		
Diaphragm		
Spermicides		
Cervical Cap		
Condoms		
Rhythm methods		
Sterilization		

Chapter 13

Sexuality in Childhood and Adolescence

Chapter Summary

Human beings show sexual responsiveness even prior to birth; male fetuses have been found to have erections. Stimulation of the genitals in infancy may produce sensations of pleasure, and pelvic thrusting has been observed in humans as early as 8 to 10 months of age. Masturbation may begin as early as 6 to 12 months. Some infants seem capable of sexual responses that closely resemble orgasm. Children in the United States typically do not engage in genital play with others until about the age of two.

Studying sexual behavior in early childhood is difficult, and therefore the statistics concerning the incidence of masturbation at ages 3 to 8 are speculative. In early childhood, children show curiosity about the genitals and may play "doctor." Same-gender sex play during this period may be more common than heterosexual play and does not presage adult sexual orientation.

Preadolescents tend to become self-conscious about their bodies. Masturbation is apparently the primary means of achieving orgasm for both genders. Preadolescent sex play often involves mutual display of the genitals, with or without touching. Group dating and mixed-gender parties often provide preadolescents with their first exposure to heterosexual activities. Much preadolescent same-gender sexual behavior involves sexual exploration and is short-lived. Despite the increased availability of sex education programs, peers apparently remain the major source of sexual information. Despite a lack of research demonstrating a link between sex education and early sexual experimentation, most school sex education continues to be limited to biological information about puberty and conception.

Adolescence begins with the advent of puberty and the appearance of secondary sex characteristics. Once it begins, most major changes in primary sex characteristics occur within three years in girls and within four years in boys. Masturbation is a major sexual outlet during adolescence. Adolescents today date earlier than in past generations and most engage in petting as a way of achieving sexual gratification. First intercourse occurs at younger ages than in the past, and there are many reasons for this. As a result, programs that encourage teens to resist sexual pressure without jeopardizing their relationships with peers have been developed.

For most adolescents, same-gender sexual encounters are transitory. However, coming to terms with adolescence is often more intense for gay and lesbian teens. The incidence of premarital intercourse, especially for females, has increased dramatically since Kinsey's day. Sexually active teenagers use contraception inconsistently, if at all, and almost one million teenage girls in the United States become pregnant each year. The risk of medical complications for the teens and their children is quite high. These young mothers face an uphill struggle because many are undereducated, unskilled, and overburdened with responsibility. The debate continues over the best methods or programs to decrease the rate of teen sex and pregnancy.

Learning Objectives

1. Summarize the information on infants' capacity for sexual response, including the information on masturbation and genital play.
2. Discuss masturbation in early childhood and suggest how parents might react if they discover their children masturbating.
3. Describe typical male-female, male-male, and female-female sexual behavior among children ages three to eight.
4. Discuss the incidence of masturbation and of male-female, male-male, and female-female sexual behaviors among preadolescents.
5. List the main sources of sexual information for male and female preadolescents.
6. Identify the physical changes associated with puberty in females and males and the averages ages at which these changes occur.
7. Discuss the ages at which males and females typically begin masturbating to orgasm and the incidence of masturbation among teenagers.
8. Describe the changes since the Kinsey studies in the average age at which males and females begin dating and petting and the incidence of oral sex among dating teens.
9. Cite the average age of first intercourse, the incidence of premarital intercourse, and the motives and factors that influence when teens will engage in intercourse.
10. Describe the incidence of male-male and female-female sexual behavior among teenagers and the additional stresses experienced by gay and lesbian teenagers.
11. Discuss ethnic and cross-cultural differences in premarital intercourse, use of contraception, teenage pregnancy, and resolution of unwanted pregnancies.
12. Describe the physical effects of first intercourse and males' and females' psychological reactions to the experience.
13. Discuss the issues surrounding teen pregnancy, including the impact on the teenage mother's life, the impact on the children of teenage mothers, and the role of teen fathers.
14. Discuss contraception use and the factors that determine contraception use among sexually active teens.
15. List and evaluate the suggested strategies for combating teenage pregnancy.

Fill-in-the-Blanks

Most boys have _____ during the first few weeks after birth or may even be born with them. _____ _____ can be observed in humans around eight to ten months of age and seems to be an expression of affection rather than sexual interest. _____ is typical for infants and young children and _____ may occur in some children as early as the second year of life. Generally, children in the United States do not engage in _____ _____ with others until age two or later.

Statistics on childhood sex play are very difficult to collect, but there are indications that _____ (heterosexual/same-gender sexual) play may be more common than _____ (heterosexual/same-gender sexual) play. Games like "show" and "playing doctor" may begin earlier but are common in children between the ages of _____ and _____ . Preadolescents (ages 9 to 13) typically have "best friends" of the _____ (same/other) gender. A 1995 *Nightline* poll showed that _____ are the main source of sexual information for both genders in this age group. Most school sex education programs emphasize the biological aspects of _____ and _____ . Some people question the effect of sex education on sexual experimentation. Research _____ (has demonstrated/has failed to demonstrate) that exposure to sex education increases early sexual experimentation.

Adolescence begins at _____ and ends with the ability to _____ _____ . Puberty begins with the appearance of _____ _____ _____ and ends when the long bones make no further gains in length. The first appearance of _____ _____ is often the first visible sign of puberty. Toward the end of puberty, reproduction becomes possible. The two principal markers of reproductive potential are _____ in girls and first _____ in boys. In the United States, the average of first menstruation is between _____ and _____ years. _____ is the hormone which has major effects on the pubertal development of girls. Reproductive capacity *may* lag behind menarche by as much as _____ _____ .

Boys typically experience their first ejaculation by age _____ or _____ . About a year after first ejaculation, boys may also begin _____ _____ , which are also called "wet dreams." Only half of boys in the

United States shave (of necessity) by age _____. Nearly half of boys experience temporary enlargement of the breasts, or _____ .

In Coles and Stokes's 1985 study of teenagers, nearly _____ of the males and about _____ of the females reported masturbating. Teens who date earlier are more likely to engage in _____ . Teens who initiate sex earlier are _____ (more/less) likely to use contraception and _____ (more/less) likely to incur an unwanted pregnancy. If a young woman keeps her baby, she is _____ (more/less) likely to leave school early. _____ is an almost universally practiced behavior among adolescents in the United States.

The incidence of _____ _____ has increased greatly since Kinsey's time. In a 1982 study of 16-year-old high school students, more students had engaged in _____ _____ than in coitus. The average person in the United States today engages in sexual intercourse for the first time between ____ and ____ years of age. In a 1985 study, about ____ percent of adolescents reported same-gender sexual experiences. Over 90 percent of these experiences were with _____ (peers/adults).

Nearly _____ _____ teenage girls in the U.S. become pregnant each year; this is _____ in every 10 girls between the ages of 15 and 19. About _____ percent of these pregnancies end in abortion; about _____ produce live births. The largest number become pregnant because of _____ about reproduction and contraception. Sexually active teenagers use contraception _____ , or not at all.

Short Answer Questions

(LO = Learning Objective)
1. At what age do boys begin having erections? (LO 1 - p. 386)

2. What is the earliest age children begin having orgasms? (LO 1 - p. 387)

3. Contrast sexually permissive societies with sexually restrictive societies in terms of childhood sexual behaviors which are allowed. (LO 3 - p. 388)

4. Describe typical male-female behavior among children ages three to eight. (LO 3 - pp. 390-391)

5. What is the connection between sex education and early sexual experimentation? (LO 5 - pp. 393-394)

6. Cite two reasons the age of menarche has been decreasing. (LO 6 - pp. 396-397)

7. What effects does estrogen have on pubertal development of girls? (LO 6 - p. 398)

8. What effects does testosterone have on pubertal development of boys? (LO 6 – p. 398)

9. What motives seem to prompt adolescents to have their first sexual intercourse experience? (LO 9 - pp. 403-404)

10. What factors increase the chances that adolescents will engage in early intercourse? (LO 9 - pp. 406-407)

11. What percentage of adolescents report same-gender sexual experiences? With whom? (LO 10 - p. 408)

12. Compare African American, Hispanic American, and White American teenagers in terms of premarital intercourse, use of contraception, and resolution of unwanted pregnancies. (LO 11 – pp. 404-405)

13. Compare the feelings of males and females about first intercourse. (LO 12 – p. 406)

14. What are the consequences of unplanned teenage pregnancy to teen mothers and their children? (LO 13 - pp. 408-410)

Matching Exercises

I. Vocabulary Exercise 1

Directions: Match each vocabulary term listed in the left-hand column with the correct definition in the right-hand column.

a. puberty (p. 395)   ____ Physical characteristics that differentiate males and females and are directly involved in reproduction, such as the sex organs.

b. secondary sex characteristics (p. 395)   ____ A structure of muscle and cartilage at the upper end of the trachea that contains the vocal cords; the voice box.

c. primary sex characteristics (p. 396)   ____ Without ovulation.

d. menarche (p. 396)   ____ The stage of development during which reproduction first becomes possible. It begins with the appearance of *secondary sex characteristics* and ends when the long bones make no further gains in length.

e. anovulatory (p. 398)   ____ Involuntary ejaculation of seminal fluid while asleep. Also referred to as a "wet dream," although the individual need not be dreaming about sex, or dreaming at all, at the time.

f. nocturnal emission (p. 399)   ____ Physical characteristics that differentiate males and females and that usually appear at puberty but are not directly involved in reproduction, such as the bodily distribution of hair and fat, development of the muscle mass, or deepening of the voice.

g. larynx (p. 399)   ____ Overdevelopment of a male's breasts.

h. gynecomastia (p. 399)   ____ The onset of menstruation; first menstruation.

Multiple-Choice Questions

(LO = Learning Objective)

1. Regarding childhood masturbation, sex educators suggest that parents
   a. temporarily withdraw love, rather than punish such behavior.
   b. use guilt rather than shame in response to such behavior.
   c. acknowledge the pleasure felt, but instruct them to do this in private.
   d. use phrases such as "Don't touch yourself down there!" or pull the child's hand away and distract him/her.

   p. 390   LO 2

2. David and Jerry, both nine-year-olds, are best friends who often confide in each other. They have displayed their genitals to one another and have engaged in mutual masturbation. Their behavior
   a. indicates that they have been sexually molested.
   b. is a definite sign that they are gay.
   c. is fairly typical of boys their age.
   d. points to future problems in heterosexual relationships.

   pp. 392-393   LO 4

3. What is the major source of information about sex for preadolescents?
   a. Reading
   b. Sex education in schools
   c. Peers
   e. None of the above

   p. 393   LO 5

4. At puberty, the male genitals begin to grow, facial and body hair appears, and the voice deepens. These changes are mainly due to the action of
   a. testosterone.
   b. follicle stimulating hormones.
   c. luteinizing hormones.
   d. human chorionic gonadotropin.

   pp. 398-399   LO 6

5. If you observe 12- to 13-year-old adolescent girls and boys,
   a. overall, the girls will be more physically mature compared to the boys.
   b. overall, the boys will be more physically mature compared to the girls.
   c. about the same number of boys and girls will have reached puberty.
   d. most of them will still have child-like physical characteristics.

   p. 399   LO 6

6. All of the following statements about contemporary adolescent sexual behavior are true, *except*
   a. oral sex has become more common.
   b. petting has become almost universal.
   c. masturbation is a major sexual outlet for boys and girls.
   d. there is still a wide gender gap in terms of premarital sex.
   p. 403   LO 8

7. Teenagers who initiate sexual intercourse earlier are
   a. less likely to use contraception.
   b. more likely to use contraception.
   c. have clear educational goals and want to marry upon completion of their high school education.
   d. experience strong attraction to both genders.
   p. 410   LO 9

8. Teenagers who engaged in male-male or female-female sexual behavior
   a. were usually seduced or forced by an older adult.
   b. typically did so with peers.
   c. were usually male and engaged in unprotected anal sex.
   d. always developed a homosexual orientation as an adult.
   p. 393   LO 10

9. Which statement is true when comparing Hispanic American, African American, and White American teenagers?
   a. There are more adolescent abortions among Hispanic Americans.
   b. There are more adolescent abortions among African Americans.
   c. More African American and Hispanic American teens carry their pregnancies to term.
   d. There are no significant differences among the groups.
   p. 405   LO 1

10. In the United States, approximately how many adolescent girls become pregnant each year?
    a. 100,000
    b. 500,000
    c. 1,000,000
    d. 2,000,000
    p. 408   LO 11

11. How do most female adolescents feel after their first intercourse?
    a. glad
    b. afraid
    c. guilty
    d. ambivalent
            p. 406   LO 11

12. Approximately 200,000 teenage pregnancies each year
    a. are false alarms.
    b. end in live births.
    c. end in miscarriages.
    d. end in abortions.
            p. 4   LO 12

Other Activities

I. Examining Issues

Directions: Sex education and the distribution of contraceptives in schools are both controversial issues. In the space below, summarize the current state of sex education and of contraceptive distribution in schools. Then, summarize the arguments for and against sex education and contraceptive distribution. Finally, draw your own conclusions about what should be done.

Sex Education in Schools:

    Current Situation:

    Pros:

    Cons:

    My Position:

Contraceptive Distribution:

    Current Situation:

    Pros:

    Cons:

    My Position:

Chapter 14

Sexuality in Adulthood

Chapter Summary

Singlehood increased sharply in recent years. The reasons include postponement of marriage, lessened stigma attached to remaining single, increased prevalence of divorce, and, particularly for women, the desire to become established in a career. Some couples choose cohabitation because of the lack of the legal and economic entanglements of marriage or because of the economic advantages of sharing household expenses.

Throughout Western history, marriages have legitimized sexual relations, sanctioned the permanence of relationships, provided for the orderly transmission of wealth, and provided a setting for child rearing. In Greek, Roman, and Christian traditions, marriages were patriarchal. Today, romantic love is seen as an essential aspect. The major types of marriage are monogamy and polygamy. People in the United States tend to marry within their geographical area, race/ethnic background, educational level, religion, and social class. They tend to marry people similar in physical attractiveness, with similar attitudes, and who seem likely to meet their material, sexual, and psychological needs.

Married couples today engage in coitus more frequently and for longer durations of time, report higher levels of sexual satisfaction, and engage in a greater variety of sexual activities than in Kinsey's day. A large majority disapproves of extramarital sex, but, for a variety of reasons, some people engage in it. A spouse's discovery of infidelity often damages the marriage. A tiny minority of married couples engages in swinging. Alternative marital styles, such as open marriages, permit intimate relationships outside the marriage.

Domestic violence is present at all levels of our society. Such violence is often triggered by criticism or rejection by one's partner. Feminist theorists consider domestic violence a product of the power relationship between men and women in society.

The reasons about half the marriages in the United States end in divorce include relaxed restrictions on divorce, greater financial independence of women, and the expectation that marriages should be happy. Divorce is often associated with financial and emotional problems, feelings of failure and depression, and difficulties in raising children.

Myths about sexuality among older people abound. Although physical changes can impair sexual activity, potential problems can usually be averted. Sexual activity tends to decline with age and the length of the relationship.

People with disabilities are often seen as sexless. Although disabilities may require adjustments by both partners, disabled people have the same needs, feelings, and desires as people without disabilities.

Learning Objectives

1. Discuss the increasing number of singles in the United States, why some people remain single, and the problems experienced by singles.
2. Identify the people most likely to cohabit, the reasons they give for cohabiting, and the relationship between cohabitation and later marriage.
3. Summarize the history of marriage, and cite the percentage of people who marry.
4. Discuss why people marry and the types of marriages people have.
5. Describe the factors that influence mate selection in the United States.
6. Describe the changes since the Kinsey studies in marital foreplay; the frequency, techniques, and duration of marital sex; and the satisfaction husbands and wives express about marital sex.
7. Discuss the patterns of extramarital sex, attitudes toward it, and its effects.
8. Cite the percentage of marriages that end in divorce, and discuss the costs of divorce for children, women, and men.
9. Describe open marriage and group marriage and the effects of each on those involved.
10. Examine the physical changes associated with aging in females and males and the patterns of sexual activity among older people.
11. Discuss the myths about and the societal reactions to the sexuality of disabled people.
12. Describe the challenges associated with sexual relations between people with various disabilities and their partners.

Fill-in-the-Blanks

_____ is the most common life-style among people in their early twenties. By the early 1990s, about one in _____ people age 18 and older in the United States had never married. Most singles are _____ and _____. Most singles are sexually active, and many practice _____ _____, or one exclusive relationship after another. Some practice _____, or complete sexual abstinence.

_____ is the U.S. Bureau of Census' abbreviation for cohabitation. The number of cohabiting couples _____ (doubled/ remained about the same) between 1980 and the early 1990s. Cohabitors are generally _____ (more/less) well-educated and _____ (more/less) affluent. The likelihood of divorce within ten years of marriage is nearly _____ as great among those who cohabited before marriage.

The institution of _____ is found in all human societies and is the most common life-style. In the United States, about ____ percent of adult men and ____ percent of adult women are married and living with their spouses. The average age of marriage today is _____ for men and _____ for women.

Among the ancient Hebrews, Greeks, and Romans, and in traditional Christianity, men dominated all the important aspects of life, a system called _____ . Women were viewed as little more than _____ , or moveable pieces of property. As late as the nineteenth century, sex in marriage was viewed as a husband's _____ and a wife's _____. Until the nineteenth century, _____ was not considered to be a basis for marriage.

There are two major types of marriage: _____ and _____ . Among the world's societies, _____ is by far the most prevalent form of polygamy; _____ is practiced only rarely.

The concept of "like marrying like" is termed _____ . We tend to marry others who are "like" us in _____ _____ , _____ _____ , _____ , and _____ _____. Interracial marriages account for fewer than ____ in every 100 marriages in the United States.

The _____ _____ of the 60s and 70s led to increases in the _____ of marital sex and the _____ of coital positions. The frequency of coitus tends to decrease with _____ and with _____ _____ _____ . The duration of both _____ and _____ has increased since Kinsey's time.

One measure of marital sexual satisfaction is _____ _____; nearly all men report this, but lower numbers of women do. Another measure of marital sexual satisfaction is how _____ satisfying the sexual relations are. Women who take an active role during sex are _____ (more/less) satisfied than those who assume the traditional passive female role.

Extramarital sex can be divided into two types: _____ _____ (clandestine affairs) and _____ _____ (relationships conducted openly with the knowledge and consent of the partner). In the NHSLS study, _____ % of married women and _____ % of married men reported remaining loyal to their spouses. The majority of people in the United States _____ (disapproves/is accepting) of extra-marital affairs. _____ , or "mate swapping," is a form of consensual adultery.

At least one woman in eight is subjected to violence at the hands of her _____ each year. About _____ die from this violence.

Nearly _____ of all marriages in the United States end in divorce. About _____ of children under 18 live in single-parent households. Fewer _____ (men/women) than _____ (men/women) remarry. The divorce rate in remarriages is _____ (higher/lower) than that of first marriages.

Most older people _____ (retain/lose) their capacity to respond sexually. Age-related changes tend to occur more gradually in _____ than in _____ . One study showed _____ (no/moderate) differences between younger and older men in level of sexual satisfaction or enjoyment. The most important determinant of continued sexual activity may be _____ _____ .

_____ _____ , a muscular disorder caused by central nervous system damage, does not generally impair sexual interest, capacity for orgasm, or fertility. Some _____ - _____ _____ cause a loss of sensation in the parts of the body that lie beneath the site of injury. Most women with this type of disability can become _____ . _____ _____ do not directly affect genital responsiveness, but people with these disabilities may require special sex-education curricula and help in developing self-confidence and social skills. Despite the negative stereotypes about people with _____ _____ , most are capable of learning the basics of reproduction and the social rules for responsible expression of their sexuality.

Short Answer Questions

(LO = Learning Objective)
1. What factors have contributed to the increasing proportion of singles? (LO 1 - p. 418)

2. Explain why *selection factors* may account for the results of some studies which show that couples who cohabit prior to marriage have higher divorce rates. (LO 2 - p. 420)

3. Briefly describe the history of marriage in Western culture. (LO 3 - pp. 421-423)

4. Whom are we most likely to marry? (LO 5 - p. 424)

5. What influences played a role in the changes in marital sexuality since Kinsey's time? (LO 6 - pp. 426-427)

6. What factors help account for a U.S. divorce rate that increased steadily through the twentieth century until it leveled off in the 1980s?
(LO 8 - pp. 435-436)

7. Briefly describe the emotional and financial "costs" of divorce for the husband and wife. (LO 8 - pp. 436-437)

8. List some of the physical changes associated with aging in females and males. (LO 10 - pp. 439-441)

9. Briefly describe the current patterns of sexual activity among older people. (LO 10 - pp. 441-442)

10. List some factors that contribute to the myths and stereotypes about sex among the disabled. (LO 11 - p. 443)

Matching Exercises

I. Vocabulary Exercise 1

Directions: Match each vocabulary term listed in the left-hand column with the correct definition in the right-hand column.

a. serial monogamy (p. 418) ____ Living together as though married but without legal sanction.

b. celibacy (p. 418) ____ A movable piece of personal property, such as furniture or livestock.

c. cohabitation (p. 418) ____ A pattern of involvement in one exclusive relationship after another, as opposed to engaging in multiple sexual relationships at the same time.

d. patriarchy (p. 421) ____ Simultaneous marriage to more than one person.

e. chattel (p. 422) ____ Complete sexual abstinence. (Sometimes used to describe the state of being unmarried, especially in the case of people who take vows to remain single.)

f. monogamy (p. 425) ____ A form of social organization in which the father or eldest male runs the group or family; government, rule, or domination by men.

g. polygamy (p. 424) ____ Marriage to one person.

II. Vocabulary Exercise 2

Directions: Match each vocabulary term listed in the left-hand column with the correct definition in the right-hand column.

a. polygyny (p. 424)   ____ A form of consensual adultery in which both spouses share extramarital sexual experiences. Also referred to as *mate swapping*.

b. polyandry (p. 424)   ____ A progressive disease that is characterized by inflammation or pain in the joints.

c. homogamy (p. 424)   ____ The tendency for women to "marry up" (in social or economic status) and for men to "marry down."

d. mating gradient (p. 425)   ____ A muscular disorder that is caused by dam-age to the central nervous system (usually prior to or during birth) and characterized by spastic paralysis.

e. extramarital sex (p. 431)   ____ Extramarital sex that is engaged in openly with the knowledge and consent of one's spouse.

f. conventional adultery (p. 431)   ____ The practice of marrying people who are similar in social background and standing.

g. consensual adultery (p. 431)   ____ Sexual relations between a married person and someone other than his or her spouse.

h. swinging (p. 432)   ____ Swinging; mate swapping.

i. comarital sex (p. 433)   ____ A marriage that is characterized by the personal privacy of the spouses and the agreed-upon liberty of each spouse to form intimate relationships, which may include sexually intimate relationships, with people other than the spouse.

j. open marriage (p. 438)   ____ A form of marriage in which a woman is married to more than one man at the same time.

k. group marriage (p. 438)   ____ A form of marriage in which a man is married to more than one woman at the same time.

l. cerebral palsy (p. 444)   ____ A social arrangement in which three or more people share an intimate relationship. Group marriages are illegal in the United States.

m. arthritis (p. 445)   ____ Extramarital sex that is kept clandestine (hidden) from one's spouse.

Multiple-Choice Questions

(LO = Learning Objective)

1. People who have a series of exclusive sexual relationships are practicing
   a. serial sexuality.
   b. multiple partnering.
   c. serial monogamy.
   d. serial polygamy.
          p. 418   LO 1

2. The term POSSLQ was introduced by the census bureau and refers to
   a. cohabiting couples.
   b. singles living alone who practice serial monogamy.
   c. singles living together who are celibate.
   d. married couples living together who do not have a sexual relationship.
          p. 418   LO 2

3. Researchers generally find that couples who cohabit prior to marriage are more likely to
   a. have a successful marriage.
   b. have extramarital affairs.
   c. get divorced.
   d. have children in the first year of marriage.
          p. 420   LO 2

4. As a "well-adjusted" nineteenth century woman, your attitude toward sex with your husband would most likely be
   a. a duty and method of producing children.
   b. a shared intimacy carried out in a loving and considerate context.
   c. an exchange of sexual favors for economic gain, such as control of property.
   d. a spiritual act, dedicated to a loving God.
          p. 422   LO 3

5. The term "mating gradient" refers to the tendency for
   a. males to seek more affluent, older women as mates.
   b. females to seek marriage partners who are at least two years younger.
   c. females to marry more affluent males.
   d. males to seek partners with more economic potential than their own.
          p. 425   LO 5

6. One of the most significant changes to result from the "sexual revolution" was
   a. more egalitarian marital sexual expression.
   b. increased infidelity among both men and women.
   c. a growing interest in rare and bizarre sexual expression.
   d. increased bisexuality among young adults.
   pp. 426-427   LO 6

7. If the marriages of those in your Human Sexuality class are typical, how many are likely to end in divorce?
   a. approximately 10%.
   b. approximately 33%.
   c. approximately 50%.
   d. approximately 80%.
   p. 435   LO 8

8. Children of divorce adjust much better when
   a. their parents are able to cooperate to be actively involved in their children's lives.
   b. the divorce happens during middle childhood.
   c. the noncustodial parent defers to the custodial parent in all decisions affecting the children.
   d. there are several siblings able to support each other emotionally.
   p. 437   LO 8

9. Which statement is accurate regarding remarriages?
   a. They are more fulfilling than first marriages.
   b. They tend to be more stable.
   c. They are more likely to end in divorce.
   d. The reasons for remarriage are economically motivated.
   p. 437   LO 8

10. The physical changes in the female genitalia that occur for menopausal females are due to
    a. lack of use.
    b. a decline in estrogen production.
    c. partners whose sexual functioning is also changing.
    d. the psychological changes that accompany menopause.
    p. 439   LO 10

11. All of the following generally decline with advancing age, *except*
    a. sexual satisfaction.
    b. coital frequency.
    c. masturbation.
    d. availability of an interested and supportive partner.
    pp. 441-442   LO 11

12. Paula is disabled and physically dependent upon her parents. Paula is likely to experience
    a. a lack of sexual interest or feelings.
    b. a lack of a clear sexual orientation.
    c. exploitation by those who are not disabled.
    d. overprotective and infantilizing parents.
    pp. 443-445   LO 11

Other Activities

I. Adult Lifestyle Choices

Directions: Adult lifestyle choices include singlehood, cohabitation, and marriage. In the chart below, write in what you consider to be the advantages and disadvantages of each.

Lifestyle Choice	Advantages	Disadvantages
SINGLEHOOD		
COHABITATION		
MARRIAGE		

Chapter 15

Sexual Dysfunctions

Chapter Summary

Sexual desire disorders are characterized by a lack of sexual desire or an aversion to genital sexual contact. Sexual arousal disorders involve difficulty achieving or sustaining erections, or failing to become sufficiently lubricated. Among the orgasmic disorders, women most often experience difficulty reaching orgasm, whereas men are more likely to experience premature ejaculation. Sexual pain disorders include dyspareunia and vaginismus.

Some sexual dysfunctions involve organic factors. Fatigue can lead to erectile disorder and orgasmic disorder in men and to orgasmic disorder and inadequate lubrication in women. Painful coitus may reflect underlying infections. Various medical conditions, medications, and other drugs may also impair sexual functioning.

Psychosocial factors connected with sexual dysfunctions include cultural influences, psychosexual trauma, sexual orientation, ineffective sexual techniques, relationship problems, psychological conflicts, lack of sexual skills, irrational beliefs, and performance anxiety.

Sex therapy involves changing self-defeating beliefs and attitudes, teaching sexual skills and knowledge, improving sexual communication, and reducing performance anxiety. Masters and Johnson pioneered the direct, behavioral approach to treating sexual dysfunctions. Kaplan's psychosexual therapy combines behavioral and psychoanalytic methods.

For hypoactive sexual desire, therapists may prescribe self-stimulation exercises, sensate focus exercises, and increasing the couple's sexual skills. People with impaired sexual arousal learn to receive sexual stimulation from their partners under relaxed circumstances to relieve anxiety. Masters and Johnson's couples-oriented approach and nondemand genital play or a program of directed masturbation is used in treating anorgasmic women. Premature ejaculation is usually treated with the squeeze technique or the stop-start method, dyspareunia with medical intervention, and vaginismus with plastic vaginal dilators of increasing size. The success of sex therapy varies with the type of sexual dysfunction treated and the quality of the relationship. Biological treatments for erectile dysfunction include penile implants, vascular surgery, hormone treatments, penile injection, and the vacuum constriction device.

Suggestions are given for organizations to contact and questions to ask when trying to locate a qualified sex therapist.

Learning Objectives

1. Name and describe the two sexual desire disorders, and discuss factors that may contribute to their development.
2. Name the sexual arousal disorders in males and females, and discuss factors that may contribute to their development.
3. Describe the three disorders of the orgasm phase, and discuss factors that may contribute to their development.
4. Describe the sexual pain disorders, and discuss factors that may contribute to their development.
5. Discuss the possible organic causes of various sexual dysfunctions, including hormonal, vascular, neurological, and chemical causes.
6. Discuss the numerous psychosocial contributors to sexual dysfunction.
7. Identify the commonalities among most sex therapies.
8. Compare the Masters-and-Johnson approach to sex therapy to Helen Singer Kaplan's approach.
9. Discuss specific approaches used to treat the various sexual dysfunctions.
10. Evaluate various sex therapies in terms of their success rates in treating specific sexual dysfunctions.
11. Describe the biomedical treatments available for erectile dysfunction, the success rates, and the satisfaction rates expressed by the men who receive these treatments.
12. Discuss the organizations people could contact and the questions they could ask to help them locate a qualified sex therapist.

Fill-in-the-Blanks

Most sexual dysfunctions can be grouped into four categories: 1) _____ _____ disorders, 2) _____ _____ disorders, 3) _____ disorders, and 4) _____ _____ disorders.

_____ _____ _____ is one of the most commonly diagnosed sexual dysfunctions. Abrupt changes in sexual desire can often be explained by psychological and interpersonal factors, such as _____ , _____ _____ , and problems in the _____ . People with _____ _____ disorder find sex disgusting or aversive, and they avoid genital contact.

Sexual arousal disorders have, in the past, been labeled with the pejorative terms of _____ in the male and _____ in the female. Perhaps 10 to 15 million men in the United States suffer from

_____ _____, or persistent difficulty in achieving or maintaining an erection.

In _____ _____, a person experiences a delay in reaching or a failure to reach orgasm. This disorder is more common in _____ than in _____. Women who have never achieved orgasm are sometimes labeled _____, or _____. The most common male sexual dysfunction is _____ _____.

_____, or painful coitus, can affect men or women. The causes can be _____ (for example, vaginal infections, STIs, PID, smegma under the foreskin, endometriosis) or _____ (for example, guilt, anxiety, effects of sexual trauma). In women, the most common cause is _____ _____. Another sexual dysfunction, _____, occurs reflexively during attempts at vaginal penetration. It is caused by a _____ _____ _____, and these women often have histories of sexual traumas which resulted in _____ _____.

People with sexual dysfunctions are generally advised to have a physical exam to determine whether their problems are _____ based. Organic causes of sexual dysfunctions include _____, _____, _____ _____ _____, debilitating diseases, _____ or _____ disorders, etc. Medications and other _____ may impair sexual functioning. Many cases of sexual dysfunction involve the interaction of _____ and _____ factors.

Children reared in cultures or home environments that are _____ _____ may experience anxiety and guilt about sex. In the United States, the double standard has a greater impact on _____. Experiences such as rape, incest, or child molestation may cause _____ _____, which can stifle arousal or cause anxiety.

_____ _____ _____, such as little foreplay, lack of variety, or lack of clitoral stimulation, can contribute to sexual dysfunctions. High levels of _____ _____ are associated with lessened sexual interest and response. Troubled relationships are often characterized by _____ _____ about sex and other matters.

People who are overly concerned about how they will perform are experiencing _____ _____; a sexual failure can then lead to increased anxiety and begin a vicious cycle.

_____ and _____ pioneered the use of a male and female therapy team with a focus on direct behavior changes. Couples perform daily homework, including _____ _____ exercises, in which partners take turns giving and receiving stimulation. Kaplan's approach, termed _____ _____, combines _____ and _____ methods. Although Masters and Johnson reported high overall success rates (80%), their critics have suggested that their _____ were biased and their _____ data was disappointingly small. Other researchers have generally reported lower success rates.

By combining biological and other types of sex therapy, almost _____ erection problems can be treated successfully. Two methods of treating premature ejaculation are the _____ techniques and the _____ method. _____ _____ is one of the major treatments for anorgasmic women. Some predictors of the success of sex therapy with couples are _____ _____ and _____ _____.

A _____ _____ is a prosthetic device that is surgically implanted as a treatment for erectile dysfunction. _____ surgery may be used for specific blockages of blood vessels that supply the penis. For men with abnormally low levels of testosterone, _____ _____ may help restore sexual drive and erectile ability. _____ of phentolamine into the penis can produce long-lasting erections. A recently introduced treatment is the _____ _____ _____, which forces an increased flow of blood into the penis.

Short Answer Questions

(LO = Learning Objective)
1. List several factors which may contribute to lack of sexual desire. (LO 1 - p. 452)

2. How common is male erectile dysfunction? (LO 2 - p. 453)

3. What is the most common male sexual dysfunction? Explain the difficulty with defining this dysfunction. (LO 3 - p. 456)

4. Identify some prescription and illegal drugs which negatively influence sexual functioning. (LO 5 - p. 460)

5. Describe childhood experiences which may negatively influence sexual functioning. (LO 6 - pp. 460-461)

6. What characteristics are associated with individuals or couples who experience sexual dysfunctions? (LO 6 - pp. 459-465)

7. What is performance anxiety? How does it affect sexual performance? (LO 6 - pp. 464-465)

8. Name several treatments offered by sex therapists for treatment of sexual desire disorders. (LO 9 - p. 467)

9. Describe treatments offered by sex therapists for treatment of sexual arousal disorders. (LO 9 - pp. 468-469)

10. Name several treatments offered by sex therapists for treatment of orgasm disorders. (LO 9 - pp. 473-477)

11. Describe the treatments offered by sex therapists for sexual pain disorders. (LO 9 - p. 477-478)

12. How would you go about finding a qualified sex therapist? (LO 12 - p.480)

Matching Exercises

I. Vocabulary Exercise 1

Directions: Match each vocabulary term listed in the left-hand column with the correct definition in the right-hand column.

a. sexual dysfunctions (p. 451)   ____ A sexual dysfunction characterized by persistent or recurrent pain during sexual intercourse.

b. sexual desire disorders (p. 451)   ____ Sexual dysfunctions in which people persistently or recurrently have difficulty reaching orgasm or reach orgasm more rapidly than they would like, despite attaining a level of sexual stimulation of sufficient intensity to normally result in orgasm.

c. sexual arousal disorders (p. 451)   ____ A sexual dysfunction characterized by involuntary contraction of the muscles surrounding the vaginal barrel, preventing penile penetration or rendering penetration painful.

d. orgasmic disorders (p. 451)   ____ Sexual dysfunctions in which people have persistent or recurrent lack of sexual desire or aversion to sexual contact.

e. sexual pain disorders (p. 451)   ____ An endocrine disorder that reduces the output of testosterone.

f. dyspareunia (p. 451)   ____ Sexual dysfunctions in which people persistently or recurrently fail to become adequately sexually aroused to engage in or sustain sexual intercourse.

g. vaginismus (p. 451)   ____ Engorgement of blood vessels with blood, which swells the genitals and breasts during sexual arousal.

h. hypogonadism (p. 452)   ____ Persistent or recurrent difficulties in becoming sexually aroused or reaching orgasm.

i. vasocongestion (p. 453)   ____ Sexual dysfunctions in which people persistently or recurrently experience pain during coitus.

II. Vocabulary Exercise 2

Directions: Match each vocabulary term listed in the left-hand column with the correct definition in the right-hand column.

a. male erectile disorder (p. 453) ____ A role, usually taken on because of performance anxiety, in which people observe rather than fully participate in their sexual encounters.

b. performance anxiety (p. 453) ____ Never having reached orgasm.

c. neurotransmitter (p. 477) ____ Exercises in which sex partners take turns giving and receiving pleasurable stimulation in nongenital areas of the body.

d. anorgasmic (p. 456) ____ A sexual dysfunction in which ejaculation occurs with minimal sexual stimulation and before the man desires it.

e. premature ejaculation (p. 456) ____ Persistent difficulty achieving or maintaining an erection sufficient to allow the man to engage in or complete sexual intercourse.

f. tumescence (p. 460) ____ A method for treating premature ejaculation whereby the tip of the penis is squeezed temporarily to prevent ejaculation.

g. spectator role (p. 456) ____ Swelling; erection.

h. sex therapy (p. 465) ____ Anxiety concerning one's ability to perform behaviors, especially behaviors that may be evaluated by other people.

i. sensate focus exercises (p. 466) ____ A collective term for short-term behavioral models for treatment of sexual dysfunction.

j. squeeze technique (p. 476) ____ A chemical that transmits messages from one brain cell to another.

Multiple-Choice Questions

(LO = Learning Objective)

1. All of the following factors have been found to be related to desire disorders, *except*
   a. depression.
   b. marital dissatisfaction.
   c. certain medications.
   d. many premarital sexual relationships.
           pp. 452-453   LO 1

2. A generalized sexual dysfunction is
   a. when the dysfunction only occurs while masturbating.
   b. a dysfunction which occurs during any sexual activity.
   c. one which occurs only during coitus.
   d. the same as a situational dysfunction.
           p. 451   LO 2

3. Which is the most common male sexual dysfunction?
   a. inhibited male orgasm
   b. premature ejaculation
   c. erectile dysfunction
   d. dyspareunia
           p. 456   LO 3

4. What is dyspareunia?
   a. menstrual cramping
   b. painful anal intercourse
   c. painful coitus
   d. the inability to orgasm in females
           pp. 456-457   LO 4

5. The most common cause of vaginismus is
   a. a history of sexual or vaginal trauma.
   b. endometriosis.
   c. PMS.
   d. insufficient lubrication.
           p. 457   LO 4

6. Most contemporary sexologists believe that many or most cases of sexual dysfunction reflect
   a. organic causes.
   b. psychological causes.
   c. guilt caused by sexually deviant thoughts.
   d. psychosocial factors, or an interaction between organic and psychological factors
   　　　　p. 459　　　LO 5

7. Behavioral models of short-term treatment for sexual dysfunctions
   a. focus upon unconscious conflicts and traumas.
   b. focus upon relationship issues.
   c. modify the dysfunctional behavior directly.
   d. seek to identify the partner who is at fault for the dysfunction.
   　　　　p. 466　　　LO 7

8. When a couple takes turns giving and receiving nongenital stimulation as a part of their sex therapy homework, they are practicing
   a. mutual masturbation.
   b. tumescence.
   c. sexual shaping.
   d. sensate focus.
   　　　　p. 466　　　LO 8

9. Why is masturbation considered an important aspect of treatment for anorgasmia?
   a. The fear of STDs is eliminated.
   b. It allows the female to discover her own sexual responses without reliance on another.
   c. Orgasm can only occur with direct manual stimulation of the clitoris.
   d. Positive attitudes towards the partner are enhanced.
   　　　　p. 474　　　LO 9

10. If a couple seeks treatment for premature ejaculation, they are likely to utilize
    a. a penile implant.
    b. fellatio.
    c. the squeeze technique.
    d. the spectator mode.
    　　　　pp. 476-477　　LO 9

11. All of the following are accurate regarding penile implants, *except*
    a. Couples prefer the inflatable type of implant.
    b. Implants damage the spongy penile tissue.
    c. The implants may erode or become perforated.
    d. Most couples are dissatisfied with the results.
        p. 469   LO 10

12. Which is *not* an example of biological treatments for erectile dysfunction?
    a. vascular surgery
    b. stop-start technique
    c. vacuum constriction device
    d. a combination of papaverine and alprostadil
        pp. 469-471   LO 10

Chapter 16

Sexually Transmitted Infections

Chapter Summary

Sexually transmitted infections (STIs) are epidemic in the United States and the world. The most common bacterial STIs are gonorrhea, syphilis, and chlamydia. Symptoms of gonorrhea in men include a penile discharge and burning during urination; most women are asymptomatic. Syphilis develops through several stages. Although it may lie dormant for many years after the secondary stage, it may be lethal during the tertiary stage. Symptoms of chlamydial infections resemble those of gonorrhea but tend to be milder. Gonorrhea, syphilis, and chlamydia are treated with and respond to antibiotics.

Vaginitis is usually characterized by a foul-smelling discharge, genital irritation, and burning during urination. Most vaginitis is caused by bacterial vaginosis, candidiasis, or trichomoniasis. Candidiasis is caused by a yeast-like fungus and usually results from changes in the vaginal environment that allow the fungus to overgrow. Trichomoniasis is caused by a protozoan.

The human immunodeficiency virus (HIV) attacks and disables the body's immune system, making a person vulnerable to opportunistic diseases.

Shortly following infection, people may experience mild flu-like symptoms. They may then remain symptom-free for years. The beginnings of full-blown cases of AIDS are often marked by fatigue, "night sweats," persistent fever, swollen lymph nodes, diarrhea, and unexplained weight loss. The criteria for diagnosing AIDS includes the appearance of various opportunistic diseases and a severely lowered CD4 cell count.

HIV can be transmitted by infected blood, semen and vaginal secretions (as through vaginal or anal intercourse), oral-genital contact, transfusion with contaminated blood, sharing a needle with an infected person, childbirth, and breast-feeding. Several factors, including a history of STIs, heighten the risk of transmission. HIV infection can be diagnosed by a test that detects HIV antibodies in blood or saliva.

There is neither a cure nor an effective vaccine for AIDS. Drugs may slow the progress of AIDS, but they cause side effects and appear to have limited benefits. A new generation of drugs called protease inhibitors are more effective treatments for HIV and AIDS.

Viral STIs include herpes, viral hepatitis, genital warts, and molluscum contagiosum. Genital herpes produces painful shallow sores on the genitals. It can damage or kill babies who are infected by the mother during childbirth. There is no cure or vaccine for herpes, but acyclovir can relieve pain and speed healing during flare-ups. The several types of viral hepatitis are usually transmitted sexually or by contact with contaminated blood or fecal matter. A vaccine for hepatitis B (and D) is available. Genital warts, caused by the *human papilloma virus* (HPV), have been linked to cervical and penile cancer. Freezing the wart is the preferred treatment. The virus remains in the body afterwards, however, and there may be recurrences.

Pediculosis ("crabs") is caused by pubic lice, which attach themselves to pubic hair and cause itching. Scabies is caused by a tiny mite that causes itching. Both are usually treated with lindane.

Strategies for preventing STIs include abstinence, monogamy, remaining sober, inspecting oneself and one's partner, using latex condoms, avoiding high-risk sex, washing the genitals before and after sex, having regular medical checkups, and getting to know one's partner before engaging in sexual activity.

Learning Objectives

1. Summarize the statistics that illustrate that STIs are epidemic in the United States.
2. Discuss the incidence, transmission, symptoms, diagnosis, and treatment of gonorrhea.
3. Discuss the history, incidence, transmission, symptoms, stages, and treatment of syphilis.
4. Discuss the incidence, transmission, symptoms, diagnosis, and treatment of chlamydia.
5. Discuss the symptoms and treatment of several less common bacterial STIs.
6. Identify and discuss the symptoms, transmission, and treatment of the most common vaginal infections.
7. Summarize the history of the AIDS epidemic in the United States.
8. Discuss the incidence patterns and routes of transmission of HIV and AIDS in the United States and worldwide.
9. Describe how the immune system works to combat disease and how HIV attacks the immune system.
10. Identify the symptoms of HIV infection, beginning with the early symptom-free period through the typical opportunistic diseases that characterize full-blown AIDS.
11. Identify the known routes of HIV transmission, as well as factors that affect the risk of sexual transmission of HIV.
12. Identify the ways HIV is *not* transmitted.
13. Discuss the transmission, symptoms, diagnosis, and treatment of the two types of herpes.
14. Describe the transmission, symptoms, and treatment of the four types of hepatitis.
15. Discuss the symptoms, transmission, and treatment of genital warts (HPV).
16. Describe the symptoms, methods of transmission, and treatment of pediculosis (pubic lice).
17. Describe the symptoms, methods of transmission, and treatment of scabies.

18. Cite the many strategies that can be used to decrease one's risk of contracting an STI.

Fill-in-the-Blanks

_____ _____ _____ (STIs) are usually transmitted through sexual contact or through sharing _____ _____. Approximately ____ million new cases of STIs are reported in the U.S. each year.

Gonorrhea is highly _____, and nearly a million cases are reported each year. The symptoms in men include a yellowish-green _____ _____, burning on _____, and (in some) tenderness in the _____ _____ of the groin. _____ percent women have no symptoms in the early stages of infection. If left untreated, gonorrhea can spread through the _____ systems and affect the internal _____ _____, possibly causing infertility. Women can get PID (_____ _____ _____). _____ are the standard treatment for gonorrhea.

During the 1990s, there has been a large _____ in the number of cases of syphilis that are reported each year. The first, or primary, stage of syphilis is characterized by a painless _____, which disappears within a few weeks. The secondary stage (a few weeks to a few months later) consists of a _____ _____, usually accompanied by flu-like symptoms. These symptoms also fade. During the _____ stage (one to 40 years) the person has no symptoms, but the bacterium continues to multiply. During the _____ stage, the infection attacks the CNS or the cardiovascular system, and it may be fatal. The most frequently used blood test for syphilis is the _____. _____ is the treatment of choice.

Researchers estimate that as many as four million people contract _____ each year. Like gonorrhea and syphilis, it is caused by a _____. Babies born to infected mothers may develop _____ _____ or a form of _____. Infections caused by this bacterium are usually termed _____ in men. In men, the symptoms are less severe than those of gonorrhea and include a whitish _____ _____ and _____ on urination. Women may experience burning on urination and a mild vaginal discharge. As many as twenty-five percent of men and 70 percent of women are _____ . Like gonorrhea, chlamydia can cause _____ . About 50% of cases of _____ involve coexisting chlamydial infections. _____ is ineffective against chlamydia. Because of the large number of people who have no symptoms, treatment of _____ _____ is considered critical.

The text described four other less common bacterial STIs: _____, _____ , _____ _____ , and _____ _____ (LGV). These are all treated with specific _____ .

_____ is the term for any kind of vaginal infection or inflammation. Most vaginal infections involve _____ _____, _____, or _____ . Candidiasis is most commonly known as a _____ _____ , and is characterized by a maddening _____ and a thick, curdy _____ _____ . This infection may arise from changes in the _____ _____, and is *not* always sexually transmitted. About _____ percent of women will experience an episode during their reproductive years. It is advisable to treat both _____ , because it can be easily passed back and forth.

_____ is caused by a one-celled parasite, and is almost always sexually transmitted. In the U.S. about ____ million cases among women are reported annually. About _____ of infected women are asymptomatic. Both partners should be treated simultaneously.

The syndrome known as AIDS was first described in _____ (year). AIDS is the acronym for _____ _____ _____ _____, caused by the virus HIV (_____ _____ _____). It is estimated that ____ million people in the United States are infected with HIV. The rate of new cases of AIDS in _____ _____ has been declining, while _____ contact is the fastest growing exposure category.

AIDS is caused by a virus that attacks the body's _____ _____. _____ are the white blood cells which systematically envelop and kill _____ , like bacteria, viruses, and funguses. Infection by HIV may be determined by examining the blood for the presence of _____ to the virus. HIV attacks the immune system by invading and destroying the _____ cells, or _____ ___-_____ .

HIV-infected people may remain asymptomatic for ____ years or more. The diagnosis of AIDS requires the emergence of _____ _____, such as PCP or Kaposi's sarcoma, or _____ of the brain.

HIV can be transmitted by contaminated bodily fluids, namely _____, _____ , and _____ _____. It can also be transmitted from mother to fetus during pregnancy and mother to child during _____ or through _____ - _____. HIV is *not* transmitted through _____ _____.

The most widely used test for HIV infection is the _____, which tests for _____. The _____ _____ test can be performed to confirm the findings.

As of now, there is still no effective _____ for AIDS or for preventing HIV infection. Several drugs like _____ may slow the progress of AIDS, but a new generation of drugs called _____ _____ are more effective treatments for HIV infection and AIDS.

_____ STIs are the most dangerous because we have no cure for them. The _____ _____ _____ _____ ____ causes cold sores or fever blisters on the lips or mouth. However, it can be transferred to the genitals. _____ _____ , or herpes simplex virus type 2, causes painful shallow sores and blisters on the genitals. It can be transferred to the mouth through oral-genital contact. The antiviral drug _____ can help relieve pain and speed healing. When taken regularly, it may reduce the _____ and _____ of outbreaks. The _____ effects of coping with herpes may be more difficult than the physical effects. Most feel _____ , _____ , _____ , and _____ .

There are several types of _____ _____ . Hepatitis A appears to be transmitted primarily through contaminated _____ or _____. Hepatitis B is transmitted primarily through sexual contact. There is no cure for viral hepatitis, but a hepatitis B (and D) _____ is available.

The _____ _____ _____ (HPV) causes _____ _____, and is the world's most common sexually transmitted infection. _____ the wart with liquid nitrogen is the preferred treatment.

The text discusses two STIs caused by ectoparasites: _____ (pubic lice) and _____ . Pubic lice ("crabs") may be transmitted by sexual contact, _____ , _____ , and even toilet seats. The most prominent symptom is _____ . _____ is a parasitic infestation caused by a tiny mite. It is transmitted in the same ways that pubic lice are.

Short Answer Questions

(LO = Learning Objective)

1. What statistics lead the authors of your text to characterize the spread of STIs as an epidemic? (LO 1 - p. 485)

2. Name several factors cited by the text authors as leading to the increasing incidence of STIs in the United States. (LO 1 - p. 485)

3. What is PID and how does one get it? (LO 2 - p. 492)

4. In what ways is chlamydia different from gonorrhea and syphilis? (LO 4 - pp. 495-497)

5. When women speak of having a "yeast" infection, what do they have? How many women get "yeast" infections? (LO 6 - pp. 499-500)

6. Discuss the factors of ethnicity and gender in the distribution of AIDS cases in the United States. (LO 8 - p. 502)

7. Briefly summarize the effect of HIV on the immune system. (LO 9 - pp. 502-503)

8. Describe the diagnostic criteria used in the diagnosis of AIDS. (LO 10 - p. 506)

9. Describe the symptoms indicative of the progression from HIV infection to full-blown AIDS. (LO 10 - pp. 503-504)

10. How is HIV transmitted? How is it *not* transmitted? (LO 11 - pp. 504-505)

11. What factors affect the risk of transmission when a person engages in sexual behaviors with an HIV+ partner? (LO 11 - p. 505)

12. Why should a pregnant woman who has herpes be sure to inform her obstetrician? (LO 13 - p. 512)

13. In what ways is herpes different from gonorrhea, syphilis, and chlamydia? (LO 13 - pp. 510-514)

14. HPV is one of the least talked about STIs. What would you tell a fellow student who asked you about it? (LO 15 - pp. 515-516)

15. Why should women be especially concerned about contracting HPV? (LO 15 - p. 515)

16. What is the treatment for pubic lice ("crabs")? (LO 16 - pp. 516-517)

Matching Exercises

I. Vocabulary Exercise 1

Directions: Match each vocabulary term listed in the left-hand column with the correct definition in the right-hand column.

a. sexually transmitted infections (p. 485)

b. bacteria (p. 488)

c. gonorrhea (p. 488)

d. pharyngeal gonorrhea (p. 493)

e. ophthalmia neonatorum (p. 493)

f. cervicitis (p. 493)

g. asymptomatic (p. 493)

h. pelvic inflammatory disease (p. 493)

i. syphilis (p. 493)

j. chancre (p. 494)

k. congenital syphilis (p. 494)

l. neurosyphilis (p. 495)

____ Inflammation of the cervix.

____ Inflammation of the pelvic region—possibly including the cervix, uterus, fallopian tubes, abdominal cavity, and ovaries—that can be caused by organisms such as *Neisseria gonorrhoeae*. Its symptoms are abdominal pain, tenderness, nausea, fever, and irregular menstrual cycles. The condition may lead to infertility. Abbreviated *PID*.

____ Syphilitic infection of the central nervous system, which can cause brain damage and death.

____ Infections that are communicated through sexual contact. Abbreviated STIs.

____ An STI that is caused by a bacterium and which may progress through several stages of development—often from a chancre to a skin rash to damage to the cardiovascular or central nervous system.

____ A gonorrheal infection of the pharynx (the cavity leading from the mouth and nasal passages to the larynx and esophagus) that is characterized by a sore throat.

____ A sore or ulcer.

____ A class of one-celled microorganisms that have no chlorophyll and can give rise to many illnesses.

____ Without symptoms.

____ A syphilis infection that is present at birth.

____ An STI caused by a bacterium and characterized by a discharge and burning urination. Left untreated, it can give rise to pelvic inflammatory disease (PID) and infertility.

____ A gonorrheal infection of the eyes of newborn children who contract the disease by passing through an infected birth canal.

II. Vocabulary Exercise 2

Directions: Match each vocabulary term listed in the left-hand column with the correct definition in the right-hand column.

a. general paresis (p. 495) ____ An STI caused by the *Hemophilus ducreyi* bacterium. Also called *soft chancre*.

b. VDRL (p. 495) ____ A tropical STI caused by the *Chlamydia trachomatis* bacterium.

c. antibodies (p. 495) ____ A disease characterized by enlargement of parts of the body, especially the legs and genitals, and by hardening and ulceration of the surrounding skin.

d. chancroid (p. 497) ____ A progressive form of mental illness caused by neurosyphilis and characterized by gross confusion.

e. shigellosis (p. 497) ____ Specialized proteins produced by the white blood cells of the immune system in response to disease organisms and other toxic substances. They recognize and attack the invading organisms or substances.

f. granuloma inguinale (p. 498) ____ A tropical STI caused by the *Calymmatobacterium granulomatous* bacterium.

g. elephantiasis (p. 498) ____ A form of vaginitis usually caused by the *Gardnerella vaginalis* bacterium.

h. lymphogranuloma venereum (p. 498) ____ An STI caused by the *Shigella* bacterium.

i. vaginitis (p. 498) ____ A form of vaginitis caused by a yeastlike fungus, *Candida albicans*.

j. bacterial vaginosis (p. 499) ____ Any type of vaginal infection or inflammation.

k. candidiasis (p. 499) ____ The test named after the Venereal Disease Research Laboratory of the U.S. Public Health Service that tests for the presence of antibodies to *Treponema pallidum* in the blood.

III. Vocabulary Exercise 3

Directions: Match each vocabulary term listed in the left-hand column with the correct definition in the right-hand column.

a. acquired immunodeficiency syndrome (AIDS) (p. 501) ____ Redness and warmth that develop at the site of an injury, reflecting dilation of blood vessels that permits the expanded flow of leukocytes to the region.

b. human immunodeficiency virus (HIV) (p. 501) ____ A protein, toxin, or other substance to which the body reacts by producing antibodies.

c. immune system (p. 502) ____ Diseases that take hold only when the immune system is weakened and unable to fend them off. Kaposi's sarcoma and *pneumocystis carinii* pneumonia (PCP) are examples found in AIDS patients.

d. pathogen (p. 502) ____ Specialized proteins that attach themselves to foreign substances in the body, inactivating them and marking them for destruction.

e. leukocytes (p. 502) ____ White blood cells that are essential to the body's defenses against infection.

f. antigen (p. 502) ____ A term for the body's complex of mechanisms for protecting itself from disease-causing agents such as pathogens.

g. antibodies (p. 495) ____ A sexually transmitted virus that destroys white blood cells in the immune system, leaving the body vulnerable to life-threatening diseases.

h. inflammation (p. 503) ____ An agent, especially a microorganism, that can cause a disease.

i. opportunistic diseases (p. 504) ____ A condition caused by the human immunodeficiency virus (HIV) and characterized by destruction of the immune system so that the body is stripped of its ability to fend off life-threatening diseases.

IV. Vocabulary Exercise 4

Directions: Match each vocabulary term listed in the left-hand column with the correct definition in the right-hand column.

a. *Herpes simplex* virus type I (p. 511) ____ Parasites that live on the outside of the host's body—as opposed to *endo*parasites, which live within the body.

b. genital herpes (p. 511) ____ An inflammation of the liver.

c. *Herpes simplex* virus type 2 (p. 511) ____ An STI that is caused by the *human papilloma* virus and takes the form of warts that appear around the genitals and anus.

d. ocular herpes (p. 512) ____ A parasitic infestation caused by a tiny mite (*Sarcoptes scabiei*) that causes itching.

e. prodromal symptoms (p. 512) ____ A herpes infection of the eye, usually caused by touching an infected area of the body and then touching the eye.

f. hepatitis (p. 514) ____ A parasitic infestation by public lice (*Pthirus pubis*) that causes itching.

g. genital warts (p. 515) ____ Warning symptoms that signal the onset or flare-up of a disease.

h. ectoparasites (p. 517) ____ An STI caused by the *Herpes simplex* virus type 2 and characterized by painful shallow sores and blisters on the genitals.

i. pediculosis (p. 517) ____ The virus that causes oral herpes, which is characterized by cold sores or fever blisters on the lips or mouth. Abbreviated *HSV-1*.

j. scabies (p. 517) ____ The virus that causes genital herpes. Abbreviated *HSV-2*.

Multiple-Choice Questions

(LO = Learning Objective)

1. When left untreated, STIs
   a. are harmless.
   b. may damage the internal reproductive system.
   c. cannot be transmitted to another person.
   d. may be painful, but not lethal.
            p. 485   LO 1

2. Which statement is *not* accurate regarding STIs?
   a. Men are disproportionately affected.
   b. A person may have an STI but no noticeable symptoms.
   c. More than 13 million people in the U.S. contract an STI each year.
   d. Two of three cases of STIs afflict people under the age of 25.
            p. 485   LO 1

3. In the early stages of gonorrheal infection, most women
   a. develop cervicitis.
   b. have urethritis.
   c. discharge a pus-like substance from the vagina.
   d. are asymptomatic.
            p. 492   LO 2

4. In primary syphilitic infection, the chancre
   a. is usually a painful red sore.
   b. appears at the site of the infection.
   c. is accompanied by burning on urination or menstrual pain.
   d. quickly leads to PID.
            p. 494   LO 3

5. Newborns infected with chlamydia during the birth process are likely to
   a. develop skin ulcers and sores.
   b. develop eye infections and pneumonia.
   c. become blind and deaf.
   d. be mentally retarded.
            p. 496   LO 4

6. A potential outcome of untreated chlamydia is
   a. mental disorder.
   b. infertility.
   c. physical disability.
   d. death.
            p. 497   LO 4

7. Which term does *not* belong?
   a. candidiasis
   b. trichomoniasis
   c. flagyl
   d. bacterial vaginosis
           pp. 499-500   LO 6

8. In recent years, the rate of new cases of AIDS among gay men
   a. has continued to increase, despite the availability of safer sex programs.
   b. has held steady.
   c. has declined steadily because of the adoption of safer sex practices.
   d. has declined, but only among younger gay men.
           p. 501   LO 7

9. The fastest growing exposure category for cases of AIDS in the U.S. is
   a. male-male sexual contact.
   b. injecting drug use.
   c. male-female sexual contact.
   d. female-female sexual contact.
           p. 501   LO 8

10. Infection by HIV may be determined by examining the blood for the presence of _____ the virus.
    a. antibodies to
    b. white blood cells associated with
    c. antigens to
    d. inflammation caused by
            p. 502   LO 10

11. HIV disables the immune system by
    a. causing leukocytes to overreproduce themselves.
    b. directly attacking B-cells.
    c. preventing the production of antigens.
    d. destroying helper T-cells.
            p. 503   LO 9

12. All of the following have been documented as effective transmission routes of HIV, *except*
    a. blood
    b. vaginal secretions
    c. semen
    d. saliva
            pp. 504-505   LO 11

13. African American and Hispanic American women
    a. are relatively unaffected by the AIDS epidemic.
    b. account for 75% of AIDS cases among females in the United States.
    c. constitute only 22% of the female population.
    d. a and b
    e. b and c
         p. 502   LO 8

14. Which is the most widely used test to detect HIV antibodies?
    a. enzyme-linked protein screening evaluation (ELIPSE)
    b. enzyme-linked immunosorbent assay (ELISA)
    c. Western blot test
    d. Eastern blot test
         p. 506   LO 10

15. If taken regularly, acyclovir
    a. cures genital herpes.
    b. reverses organ damage due to the herpes virus.
    c. reduces the symptoms and frequency of flare-ups of genital herpes.
    d. functions as an antibiotic in the treatment of viral infections such as herpes.
         p. 513   LO 13

16. Genital warts are caused by the
    a. human immunodeficiency virus.
    b. human papilloma virus.
    c. human syphilitic virus.
    d. human wart bacteria.
         p. 515   LO 15

Other Activities

STIs: Their Symptoms and Treatments

Directions: Complete the following chart by supplying the correct information for each STI.

STIs	Symptoms	Treatments

Bacterial Diseases
  Gonorrhea
 	
  Syphilis
 	
  Chlamydia & NGU		

Vaginitis
  Bacterial Vaginosis
 	
  Candidiasis
 	
  Trichomoniasis		

Viral Diseases
  HIV/AIDS
 	
  Oral Herpes
 	
  Genital Herpes
 	
  Viral Hepatitis
 	
  Genital Warts		

Ectoparasitic Infestations
  Pediculosis
 	
  Scabies		

Chapter 17

Atypical Sexual Variations

Chapter Summary

Paraphilias involve sexual arousal in response to unusual stimuli, nonhuman objects, pain or humiliation. Except for sexual masochism, paraphilias are believed to occur almost exclusively among men.

In fetishism an inanimate object elicits sexual arousal, and in partialism people are excessively aroused by a particular body part. Transvestites become excited by wearing articles of clothing of the opposite gender. An exhibitionist experiences the compulsion to expose himself to unsuspecting strangers for the purpose of sexual arousal or gratification. The obscene phone caller becomes sexually aroused by shocking his victim, and he typically masturbates during the phone call or shortly afterwards. Voyeurs become sexually aroused by watching others naked, disrobing, or engaged in sexual relations. He may masturbate while "peeping" or later while engaging in voyeuristic fantasies. Sexual masochists become sexually aroused through having pain or humiliation inflicted on them by their sex partners. Sexual sadists become aroused by the infliction of pain on others. Sadomasochism involves mutually gratifying sexual interactions between consenting partners. Frotteurists experience arousal by rubbing against or touching nonconsenting persons, often in crowded places.

Five theoretical perspectives on paraphilias are discussed. The biological factors have yet to be fully researched. Classical psychoanalytic theory suggests that paraphilias are psychological defenses, usually against castration anxiety. Learning theorists argue that unusual stimuli acquire sexually arousing properties through association with sexual arousal or orgasm or through incorporation in masturbatory fantasies. According to one sociological model, the erotic appeal of S&M rituals may result from the opportunity to reverse the customary power relationships that exist in society. Money and Lamacz suggest that childhood experiences etch a "lovemap" in the brain that determines the types of stimuli and activities that become sexually arousing.

In treating paraphilias, psychoanalysis aims to bring unconscious Oedipal conflicts into awareness so that they can be worked through in adulthood. Behavior therapy employs techniques such as systematic desensitization, aversion therapy, covert sensitization, social skills training, and orgasmic reconditioning. Antiandrogen drugs or other drugs may help combat intense paraphilic urges by reducing sexual drives.

Learning Objectives

1. Define the term *paraphilia*, and describe the urges and behaviors characteristic of paraphiles.

2. Describe the behaviors associated with fetishism and partialism.
3. Describe the behaviors and characteristics typical of transvestites.
4. Describe the behaviors associated with exhibitionism, the characteristics of exhibitionists, and the effects on their victims.
5. Describe the behaviors typical of obscene telephone callers.
6. Describe the behaviors and characteristics typical of voyeurs.
7. Describe the behaviors and characteristics typical of masochists and sadists, and discuss the S&M subculture.
8. Describe the behaviors associated with frotteurism, zoophilia, necrophilia, and other less common paraphilias.
9. Discuss the role of biological factors in paraphilic behavior.
10. Present the psychoanalytic explanations for various paraphilias.
11. Discuss learning theory explanations of paraphilic behavior.
12. Discuss sociological explanations of paraphilic behaviors.
13. Discuss Money's theory of "lovemaps" and its application to the development of paraphilias.
14. Describe the psychoanalytic, behavioral, and biochemical approaches to treatment of paraphilias.

Fill-in-the-Blanks

The authors of the text prefer the term _____ _____ *in sexual behavior* to the term *sexual deviations*. The American Psychiatric Association labels these behaviors _____ .

_____ involve sexual arousal to unusual stimuli, nonhuman objects, or pain or humiliation. Paraphilic urges have a _____ quality; that is, people describe themselves as being overcome by seemingly irresistible urges. Except for sexual masochism, paraphilias are believed to occur almost exclusively in _____ (men/women).

In _____ , an inanimate object comes to elicit sexual arousal. In a related paraphilia, _____ , people are excessively aroused by a particular body part. Most fetishes and partialisms are _____ . In _____ , people become excited by wearing articles of clothing of the other gender.

_____ involves powerful urges to expose one's genitals to unsuspecting strangers for the purpose of sexual arousal or gratification. Although many people with this paraphilia are single males, the typical exhibitionist is _____ , _____ _____ , and _____ _____ . Exhibitionism usually begins before age ____ .

_____ _____, or obscene telephone calling, involves achieving sexual arousal by shocking the victims. Most exhibitionists and obscene telephone callers _____ (are/are not) dangerous. The typical obscene phone caller is a _____ _____ _____ male who has difficulty forming intimate relationships with women. Very few obscene phone callers are _____.

_____, found almost exclusively among males, involves urges to observe unsuspecting strangers who are undressing or engaging in sexual behaviors. The voyeur may _____ while "peeping" or afterward while "replaying" the incident in his mind. Compared to other types of sex offenders, voyeurs tend to be _____ (more/less) sexually experienced and they are _____ (more/less) likely to be married. Recent technology, such as _____, add new dimensions to voyeurism.

_____ _____ are people who associate pain or humiliation with sexual arousal. This paraphilia is the only one found with some frequency among women. Still, males may outnumber females by _____ to one. The association of sexual arousal with mildly painful stimuli is _____ (very rare/quite common). In _____, people may place plastic bags over their heads or nooses around their necks to become sexually aroused by being temporarily deprived of oxygen.

_____ _____ is characterized by urges and fantasies involving infliction of pain on others for sexual arousal and gratification. Sadomasochism involves _____ _____ sexual interactions between _____ partners. Participants often engage in elaborate rituals involving _____ and _____. If pain is employed, it is often mild or moderate. One survey showed that about ____ of four participants are male. Most were _____ (married/single).

_____ involves urges to rub against or touch a nonconsenting person. It has been reported exclusively among _____ (men/women). These acts usually take place in _____ _____. _____ is the persistent urge to fondle nonconsenting strangers.

_____ involves persistent urges to have, and fantasies about, sexual contact with animals. In most cases, it is associated with _____-_____ _____ _____ and difficulty relating to members of the other gender. In _____, a very rare paraphilia, a person desires sex with corpses. Many of the people with this paraphilia are clearly _____ _____ . In _____ , sexual arousal is derived from the use of enemas. In _____ , sexual arousal is connected to feces. And, in _____ , sexual arousal is associated with urine.

_____ is the term used for people who feel driven or compelled to engage in sexual acts and who have little regard for the consequences of their choice of partners. In women, this is sometimes labeled _____ . In men, it is labeled _____ or _____ _____ .

Little is known about the role of biology in paraphilic behavior. Efforts to link brain abnormalities or _____ levels have been generally unsuccessful. One study found elevated levels of a specific measure of testosterone among _____ .

Psychoanalytic theory views paraphilias as psychological defenses, usually against unresolved _____ _____. There is _____ (sufficient/a lack of) evidence to support this theory. Learning theorists believe that paraphilias are _____ _____ that are acquired through experience.

One proposal for a _____ explanation of sadomasochism focuses on the social and gender roles that exist in the larger society. Money and his colleagues propose a theory that incorporates multiple perspectives. _____ _____ etch a pattern in the brain, called a _____ , that determines the stimuli and activities that will be sexually arousing to the individual.

Paraphiles do not usually seek treatment _____ . Traditional _____ tends to be a lengthy process of exploration of the childhood origins of problem behaviors. _____ _____ is briefer and focuses directly on changing the problem behaviors. _____ _____ attempts to break the link between the sexual stimulus and the inappropriate response of sexual arousal by pairing relaxation (not arousal) with the stimulus. In _____ _____ , the undesirable sexual behavior is paired with an aversive stimulus, such as an electric shock. _____ _____ _____ focuses on helping the paraphile improve his ability to relate to the other gender.

210

_____ _____ focuses on pairing culturally appropriate imagery with orgasmic pleasure.

_____ drugs reduce the level of testosterone circulating in the bloodstream. _____-_____ is the drug most often used in the treatment of sex offenders. It reduces the intensity of sexual drives, fantasies, and urges, so that the man may feel less compelled to act upon them.

Short Answer Questions

(LO = Learning Objective)

1. Distinguish between the motives for cross-dressing among transvestites, transsexuals, female impersonators and some gays. (LO 3 - pp. 529-530)

2. How should a woman respond to an exhibitionist? (LO 4 - p. 533)

3. How should a woman respond to an obscene phone caller? (LO 5 - p. 534)

4. List the characteristics of the typical voyeur. (LO 6 - pp. 534-535)

5. What do surveys show about the prevalence of sadomasochistic behaviors among the general population? (LO 7 - p. 537)

6. Summarize the view of paraphilias as sexual addictions. (LO 14 - p. 540)

7. Describe the differences in our societal views of hypersexual men and hypersexual women. (LO 8 - pp. 542-543)

8. Briefly describe the learning perspective on paraphilias.
(LO 11 - pp. 543-545)

9. Briefly summarize Money's view of how paraphilias develop.
(LO 13 - pp. 545-546)

10. Evaluate the use of antiandrogens as a treatment for paraphilias.
    (LO 14 - p. 549)

Matching Exercises

I. Vocabulary Exercise 1

Directions: Match each vocabulary term listed in the left-hand column with the correct definition in the right-hand column.

a. paraphilia (p. 527) ____ Ritual restraint, as by shackles, as practiced by many sexual masochists.

b. fetishism (p. 528) ____ A paraphilia in which a person repeatedly cross-dresses to achieve sexual arousal or gratification, or is troubled by persistent, recurring urges to cross-dress.

c. partialism (p. 529) ____ A paraphilia characterized by strong, repetitive urges and related sexual fantasies of observing unsuspecting strangers who are naked, disrobing, or engaged in sexual relations.

d. transvestism (p. 529) ____ A paraphilia related to fetishism, in which sexual arousal is exaggeratedly associated with a particular body part, such as feet, breasts, or buttocks.

e. exhibitionism (p. 531) ____ A paraphilia characterized by the making of obscene telephone calls.

f. telephone scatologia (p. 533) ____ People who become sexually aroused by inflicting pain or humiliation on others.

g. voyeurism (p. 534) ____ A paraphilia in which an inanimate object, such as an article of clothing or items made of rubber, leather, or silk, elicit sexual arousal.

h. sexual masochism (p. 535) ____ A paraphilia characterized by the desire or need for pain or humiliation to enhance sexual arousal so that gratification may be obtained.

i. sexual sadists (p. 536) ____ A diagnostic category used by the American Psychiatric Association to describe atypical patterns of sexual arousal or behavior that become problematic in the eyes of the individual or society. The urges are recurrent and are either acted on or are distressing to the individual.

j. bondage (p. 536) ____ A paraphilia characterized by persistent, powerful urges and sexual fantasies involving exposing one's genitals to unsuspecting strangers to achieve sexual arousal or gratification.

II. Vocabulary Exercise 2

Directions: Match each vocabulary term listed in the left-hand column with the correct definition in the right-hand column.

a. sexual sadism (p. 537)   ____ A mutually gratifying sexual interaction between consenting sex partners in which sexual arousal is associated with the infliction and receipt of pain or humiliation. Commonly known as S&M.

b. sadomasochism (p. 537)   ____ A paraphilia in which sexual arousal is associated with urine.

c. frotteurism (p. 538)   ____ A practice related to frotteurism and characterized by the persistent urge to fondle non-consenting strangers.

d. toucherism (p. 539)   ____ A paraphilia in which sexual arousal is attained in connection with feces.

e. zoophilia (p. 539)   ____ A paraphilia characterized by the desire or need to inflict pain or humiliation on others to enhance sexual arousal so that gratification is attained.

f. necrophilia (p. 540)   ____ A paraphilia in which sexual arousal is derived from use of enemas.

g. klismaphilia (p. 540)   ____ A paraphilia characterized by recurrent, powerful sexual urges and related fantasies involving rubbing against or touching a nonconsenting person.

h. coprophilia (p. 540)   ____ An excessive or apparently insatiable sex drive that disrupts the person's ability to concentrate on other needs or leads to self-defeating behavior, such as indiscriminate sexual contacts.

i. urophilia (p. 540)   ____ A paraphilia characterized by desire for sexual activity with corpses.

j. hypersexuality (p. 541)   ____ An excessive, insatiable sexual appetite or drive in women.

k. nymphomania (p. 540)   ____ A paraphilia involving persistent or repeated sexual urges and related fantasies involving sexual contact with animals.

l. hypoxyphilia (p. 536)   ____ A practice in which a person seeks to enhance sexual arousal, usually during masturbation, by becoming deprived of oxygen.

III. Vocabulary Exercise 3

Directions: Match each vocabulary term listed in the left-hand column with the correct definition in the right-hand column.

a. satyriasis (p. 540) ____ Persons with pedophilia, a paraphilia involving sexual interest in children.

b. behavior therapy (p. 547) ____ A method for strengthening the connection between sexual arousal and appropriate sexual stimuli (such as fantasies about an adult of the other gender) by repeatedly pairing the desired stimuli with orgasm.

c. systematic desensitization (p. 547) ____ Behavior therapy methods for building social skills which rely on a therapist's coaching and practice.

d. aversion therapy (p. 547) ____ A form of aversion therapy in which thoughts of engaging in undesirable behavior are paired repeatedly with imagined aversive stimuli.

e. covert sensitization (p. 547) ____ The systematic application of the principles of learning to help people modify problem behavior.

f. pedophiles (p. 547) ____ A chemical substance that reduces the sex drive by lowering the level of testosterone in the bloodstream.

g. social skills training (p. 548) ____ An excessive, insatiable sexual appetite or drive in men.

h. orgasmic reconditioning (p. 548) ____ A method for terminating undesirable sexual behavior in which the behavior is repeatedly paired with an aversive stimulus, such as electric shock, so that a conditioned aversion develops.

i. antiandrogen drug (p. 549) ____ A method for terminating the connection between a stimulus (such as a fetishistic object) and an inappropriate response (such as sexual arousal to the paraphilic stimulus). Muscle relaxation is practiced in connection with each stimulus in a series of increasingly arousing stimuli, so that the person learns to remain relaxed (and not sexually aroused) in their presence.

Multiple-Choice Questions

(LO = Learning Objective)

1. Larry, a paraphile, has exposed his genitals to young children on several occasions. How is he likely to describe the emotions which precipitated these acts?
   a. "I didn't know what I was doing. I just felt such love for the children."
   b. "My urge just kept getting stronger. I couldn't help it."
   c. "Everybody does these kinds of things. It's no big deal."
   d. "I don't need to do it to become aroused, I just really enjoy doing this."
       pp. 531-532   LO 1

2. All of the following are true regarding fetishism, *except*
   a. they are practiced in private.
   b. they involve masturbation.
   c. they occur almost exclusively among males.
   d. they are harmful to others.
       pp. 528-529   LO 2

3. Most male transvestites are
   a. women in disguise.
   b. exceptionally feminine in nature.
   c. desirous of being females.
   d. married and heterosexual.
       p. 529   LO 3

4. All of the following characteristics are typical of exhibitionists, *except*
   a. young male.
   b. middle-aged or older male.
   c. sexually repressed.
   d. poor relationships with females.
       p. 532   LO 4

5. The typical obscene phone caller
   a. is an overly masculinized male who enjoys controlling women.
   b. is a depressed male with a history of sexual abuse.
   c. is a socially inadequate heterosexual male.
   d. is a gay male who hasn't acknowledged his homosexuality to himself and can only relate to women at a distance.
       p. 533   LO 5

6. Which is *not* typical of voyeurs?
   a. They usually started "peeping" before age 18.
   b. They have no intention of seeking sexual relations with the observed person.
   c. They often put themselves in situations in which they might be caught.
   d. They limit their voyeurism to observing women they know.
   pp. 534-535   LO 6

7. Which of the following statements is *not* accurate regarding masochism?
   a. It is the only paraphilia found among women with some frequency.
   b. Sexual excitement is achieved by being humiliated, bound or flogged.
   c. It is more prevalent among women than men.
   d. It is more prevalent among men than women.
   p. 536   LO 7

8. Frotteurists experience arousal when
   a. their victims become fearful or shocked.
   b. they rub or touch women unknown to them.
   c. they can entice children to submit to rubbing or touching.
   d. rubbing is followed by intercourse.
   p. 538   LO 8

9. Which statement is accurate regarding biological factors and paraphiles?
   a. Abnormal brain structures in the hypothalamus have been found.
   b. Elevated testosterone levels among all classes of paraphilic behavior have been found.
   c. No concrete evidence of brain damage or abnormalities have been found.
   d. Estrogen levels are elevated in the majority of paraphiles.
   p. 542   LO 9

10. Classical psychoanalytic theory views the paraphilias as
    a. expressions of unconscious rage against an indifferent father.
    b. a way to vent anger and hostility against the mother.
    c. originating in castration fears during the Oedipal period.
    d. a normal expression of fixated libidinal energy.
    pp. 542-543   LO 10

11. Which theory combines biological, psychological and sociocultural factors to explain the development of paraphilias?
    a. learning theory
    b. theory of "lovemaps"
    c. psychobiological theory
    d. theory of addictions
        pp. 545-546 LO 13

12. To increase sexual arousal to appropriate stimuli, which method would a therapist use?
    a. covert sensitization
    b. aversion therapy
    c. psychoanalysis
    d. orgasmic reconditioning
        p. 548   LO 14

Other Activities

I. Theoretical Perspectives on the Paraphilias

Directions: Summarize the explanations for paraphilias from each of the following theoretical perspectives.

Biological Perspectives:

Psychoanalytic Perspectives:

Learning Perspectives:

Sociological Perspectives:

**Integrated Perspective
   The "Lovemap":**

What have you concluded about the origins of paraphilias? _____
_____
_____
_____

Chapter 18

Sexual Coercion

Chapter Summary

Rape usually refers to obtaining sexual intercourse with a nonconsenting person by the use of force or the threat of force. The majority of rapes are not reported to the police. The types of rape include stranger rape, acquaintance rape, date rape, gang rape, male rape, marital rape, and rape by women. In the United States, sociocultural factors create a climate that encourages rape.

Sociocultural factors and psychological characteristics are important to consider. Traditional gender-role attitudes, condoning of rape and violence against women, and hostility toward women characterize self-identified sexually aggressive men. One group of researchers has identified three basic kinds of rape: anger rape, power rape, and sadistic rape.

Rape survivors often suffer physical injury, other physical symptoms, fear, anger, sadness, anxiety, and depression. They often develop signs of post-traumatic stress disorder. Treatment typically involves helping them through the crisis period and fostering long-term adjustment. Women are encouraged to take a number of precautions to avoid rape.

Verbal sexual coercion is persistent verbal pressure to manipulate a person into sexual activity. The use of verbal pressure and seduction "lines" is common, and it is difficult to recognize them as coercion.

Any form of sexual contact between an adult and a child is abusive. In most cases, the molesters are close to the victims: relatives, steprelatives, family friends, and neighbors. Genital fondling is the most common type of abuse. Pedophiles are almost exclusively male, and they usually molest many children. However, not all child molesters are pedophiles. Incest involves sexual relations between people who are closely related, and brother-sister incest is the most common type. Several theories about the origin of the incest taboo are presented. Incest victims often suffer social and emotional problems that persist into adulthood. Psychotherapy may help adult survivors improve their self-esteem and their ability to develop intimate relationships. The effectiveness of prison-based rehabilitation programs and antiandrogen drugs in treating child sexual abuse offenders remains to be demonstrated.

A large majority of sexual harassers are men. Since 1986, when the Supreme Court recognized sexual harassment as a form of sex discrimination, many workplaces have developed antiharassment programs and mechanisms to deal with complaints. Twenty-five to 30 percent of students report at least one incident of sexual harassment in college, with many more women than men reporting this. The suggestions for resisting harassment include conveying a professional attitude, avoiding being alone with the harasser, keeping a record of all incidents, filing a complaint, and seeking legal remedies.

Learning Objectives

1. Discuss the historical and current definitions of rape and the incidence of rape.
2. Discuss the types of rape, the incidence of each, and the characteristics of the perpetrators.
3. Discuss the myths, social attitudes, and sociocultural factors that encourage rape in the United States.
4. Examine the characteristics of rapists, and discuss their motives for rape.
5. Discuss the variations in rape victims' reactions to assault, including post-traumatic stress disorder and rape trauma syndrome.
6. List specific precautions women can take to reduce the risk of rape and strategies women can use if confronted by a rapist.
7. Define child sexual abuse, and examine the incidence of the problem.
8. Define pedophilia, and describe the characteristics of incarcerated pedophiles.
9. Discuss the incidence of incest, the most common types, and the characteristics of incest perpetrators and their families.
10. Describe the short-term and long-term effects on victims of child sexual abuse.
11. Describe child sexual abuse prevention programs, and describe treatment programs for victims and their families.
12. Describe treatment programs for rapists and child molesters, and evaluate their effectiveness.
13. List the EEOC guidelines for defining workplace sexual harassment, and discuss the research on its incidence.
14. Discuss the incidence of sexual harassment in schools and on college campuses, and list suggestions for resisting sexual harassment.

Fill-in-the-Blanks

_____ _____ is usually defined as sexual intercourse with a nonconsenting person by the use of force or the threat of force. _____ _____ refers to sexual intercourse with a person below the age of consent, even if the victim cooperates. The vast majority of rapes go _____ in the U.S. The best available evidence suggests between _____ and _____ percent of U.S. women are raped during their lifetimes.

_____ rape refers to a rape committed by an assailant not previously known to the victim. _____ rape refers to a rape committed by an assailant known to the victim. Of these two types, _____ rape is much less likely to be reported to the police. _____ rape is a form of acquaintance rape. About ____ to ____ percent of women report being forced into sexual intercourse by dates. Because date rape occurs within a context in which sex may occur voluntarily, the issue of _____ is usually the central question.

_____ rapes are those perpetrated by a group of assailants. Most _____ rapes occur in prison settings, but some occur elsewhere. Male victims are more likely to suffer _____ (greater/less) physical injury and are more likely to be attacked by (a) _____ (single/multiple) assailant(s). Most men who rape other men are _____ (homosexual/heterosexual).

A committee of the U.S. Congress estimated that one wife in _____ is likely to be the victim of _____ rape. This sexual coercion often occurs within a marriage where there is _____ , _____ _____ , and _____ intimidation. Rape by _____ is rare, but when it does occur, it often involves aiding or abetting _____ who are attacking another _____ .

College men who more closely identify with the _____ _____ gender role express a greater likelihood of committing rape and are more accepting of violence against women.

Studies of incarcerated rapists show that they are _____ (more/no more) likely to be mentally ill than comparison groups. The great majority of rapists _____ (are/are not) in control of their behavior, and they _____ (know/do not realize) that it is illegal. It is estimated that fewer than ____ percent of rapists are caught and eventually imprisoned. Evidence shows that student _____ commit a disproportionate number of sexual assaults.

Groth and Birnbaum believe there are three basic types of rape: _____ rape, _____ rape, and _____ rape. The _____ rapist uses more force than is needed and he uses rape as _____ against women. The _____ rapist is motivated by a desire to control and dominate the victim. _____ rapists often mutilate their victims.

Rape victims often show signs of _____ _____ _____ (PTSD), a stress reaction that is brought on by a traumatic event.

Two researchers identified the common response patterns of rape victims and labeled these the _____ _____ _____. The two phases are the _____ phase, characterized by _____ of the victim's lifestyle, and the _____-_____ phase, characterized by _____.

Researchers estimate that ____ to ____ percent of boys and over ____ percent of girls become victims of sexual abuse. In about ____ to ____ percent of cases, the molesters are relatives, family friends, and neighbors. Physical force is _____ (often/seldom) needed to gain compliance. Victimized children _____ (often/rarely) report the abuse. The overwhelming majority of child sexual abusers are _____.

_____ involves persistent or recurrent sexual attraction to children. _____ are almost exclusively _____ (male/female). Most _____ (do/do not) fit our image of the "dirty old man" hanging around the school yard. _____ involves sexual relations between people who are closely related. _____ incest is the most common type.

Many fathers who commit incest are _____ _____, _____, and _____. Incestuous abuse is _____ (often/rarely) repeated from generation to generation. Child sexual abuse often results in _____ (moderate/great) psychological harm to the child. Although reactions by boys and girls are similar in many ways, boys are more likely to become more _____ _____, and girls are more likely to become _____. The effects of childhood sexual abuse are often _____ (short-term/long-lasting).

The results of rehabilitative treatment programs for incarcerated sex offenders _____ (have been/remain to be) demonstrated. Drugs such as _____-_____ may be used to reduce testosterone levels.

_____ _____ is defined as deliberate or repeated unsolicited comments, gestures, or physical contact of a sexual nature that is unwelcome by the recipient. The great majority of the cases are perpetrated by _____ against _____. Sexual harassment may have more to do with abuse of _____ than with sexual desire. Only about _____ percent of women who have been sexually harassed in a workplace file a formal complaint. They fear they will not be believed, they will be branded as "troublemakers", or they will lose their _____. One survey found that _____ percent of Fortune 500 companies had received complaints of sexual harassment.

Overall, about _____ to _____ percent of college students report at least one incident of sexual harassment. Most forms of sexual harassment on college campuses involve _____ _____ relationships.

Short Answer Questions

(LO = Learning Objective)

1. Cite estimates of the incidence of date rape. List some beliefs commonly held by date rapists. (LO 2 - pp. 558-559)

2. How common is marital rape? What are some of the rapist's motives? (LO 2 - p. 561)

3. Identify the cultural factors that make our society a breeding ground for rapists. (LO 3 - pp. 562-563)

4. Summarize the information in the text comparing rape-prone and rape-free societies. (LO 3 - p. 565)

5. List some common reactions of women to being raped. (LO 5 - pp. 566-567)

6. What suggestions would you give women to help them avoid being raped? (LO 6 - pp. 569-570)

7. What is verbal sexual coercion and what is the best way to respond? (LO 14 - pp. 571-573)

8. What characteristics are common to families in which incest occurs? (LO 9 - pp. 578-579)

9. Discuss some new methods for determining the truth in cases of child abuse.
(LO 10 - p. 580)

10. What steps can you take if you are sexually harassed at a college or a workplace? (LO 14 - pp. 585-587)

Matching Exercises

I. Vocabulary Exercise 1

Directions: Match each vocabulary term listed in the left-hand column with the correct definition in the right-hand column.

a. forcible rape (p. 555)

b. statutory rape (p. 555)

c. stranger rape (p. 558)

d. acquaintance rape (p. 558)

e. anger rape (p. 564)

f. power rape (p. 564)

g. sadistic rape (p. 565)

h. posttraumatic stress disorder (p. 567)

i. rape trauma syndrome (p. 567)

j. incest (p. 577)

k. sexual harassment (p. 583)

____ Marriage or sexual relations between people who are so closely related (by "blood") that sexual relations are prohibited and punishable by law.

____ A highly ritualized, savage rape in which the person who is attacked is subjected to painful and humiliating experiences and threats.

____ A two-phase reaction to rape that is characterized by disruption of the survivor's life-style (the acute phase) and reorganization of the survivor's life (the long-term phase).

____ Rape by an acquaintance of the person who is assaulted.

____ Sexual intercourse with a person who is below the age of consent. Sexual intercourse under such conditions is considered statutory rape even though the person attacked may cooperate.

____ Deliberate or repeated unsolicited verbal comments, gestures, or physical contact of a sexual nature that is considered to be unwelcome by the recipient.

____ A type of stress reaction brought on by a traumatic event and characterized by flashbacks of the experience in the form of disturbing dreams or intrusive recollections, a sense of emotional numbing or restricted range of feelings, and heightened body arousal.

____ A vicious, unplanned rape that is triggered by feelings of intense anger and resentment toward women.

____ Sexual intercourse with a nonconsenting person obtained by the use of force or the threat of force.

____ Rape that is motivated by the desire to control and dominate the person assaulted.

____ Rape that is committed by an assailant previously unknown to the person who is assaulted.

Multiple-Choice Questions

(LO = Learning Objective)

1. For most of recorded history, rape was considered
   a. a violent crime that curtailed the rights of women.
   b. a crime against the property rights of fathers or husbands.
   c. the act of mentally deranged men.
   d. an act of adultery by the victim.
           p. 555   LO 1

2. Acquaintance rapists
   a. tend to believe in sexual equality.
   b. are less sexually aggressive.
   c. tend to believe myths which serve to legitimize their behavior.
   d. are more likely than stranger rapists to be reported to the police.
           p. 558   LO 2

3. All of the following statements about marital rape are accurate, *except*
   a. marital rape generally leads the couple to become involved in marital counseling.
   b. marital rape is motivated by the need to dominate, intimidate, and subjugate.
   c. many survivors of marital rape fear physical injury and/or death.
   d. marital rapes are probably more common than date rapes.
           p. 561   LO 2

4. The lessons learned by males in competitive sports may
   a. increase their willingness to accept limits in sexual encounters.
   b. teach them that rules of proper conduct are to be obeyed.
   c. predispose them to sexual violence.
   d. bear no relationship to how they behave in sexual interactions.
           p. 563   LO 3

5. All of the following are features of posttraumatic stress disorder, *except*
   a. intrusive flashbacks of the rape
   b. heightened arousal
   c. numbing or blunting of feelings
   d. unpredictable rage
           p. 567   LO 5

6. After a rape, it is suggested that the survivor do all of the following, *except*
   a. seek medical help.
   b. consider reporting the rape to the police.
   c. ask questions regarding medical rights.
   d. wash herself and obtain clean clothes as soon as possible.
           p. 568   LO 5

7. Resisting rape decreases the chances of the rape being completed, and it
   a. increases pregnancies among survivors.
   b. decreases the chances of being hurt.
   c. increases the chances of being physically injured.
   d. none of the above
           p. 570   LO 6

8. Which of the following is accurate regarding verbal sexual coercion?
   a. It is common in dating relationships and is thus not recognized as sexual coercion.
   b. It employs devious means to exploit the person's emotional needs.
   c. It includes persistent verbal pressure or use of seduction "lines" to manipulate the person into sexual activity.
   d. all of the above
           p. 571   LO 6

9. Parents are least likely to report the sexual abuse of their child if the perpetrator is
   a. a strange to the child.
   b. a family acquaintance.
   c. an older teenager.
   d. a relative of the child.
           p. 575   LO 7

10. Which of the following statements is accurate regarding childhood sexual abuse?
    a. The child is usually abused by a stranger.
    b. The abuser usually uses physical force to obtain compliance by the child.
    c. Submission to adult authority aids the abuser to gain compliance.
    d. Most children enjoy the sexual behaviors.
            pp. 574-575   LO 7

11. Which statement regarding pedophilia is *untrue*?
    a. It involves a persistent or recurrent sexual attraction to children.
    b. All child molesters are pedophiles.
    c. The prevalence in the general population in unknown.
    d. Pedophiles are almost exclusively male.
           pp. 576-577   LO 8

12. According to the U.S. Supreme Court, sexual harassment is held to involve behavior of a sexual nature that
    a. causes psychological harm to the victim that require psychological treatment.
    b. must be flagrant and demeaning to the victim.
    c. creates a hostile work environment or interferes with an employee's work performance.
    d. must involve outright sexual advances.
           p. 585   LO 13

Chapter 19

Commercial Sex

Chapter Summary

In the United States, prostitution is illegal everywhere except in some rural counties in Nevada. The decrease in experience with prostitutes among young men seems to be linked to the decay of the sexual double standard. The major types of female prostitutes today are streetwalkers, brothel prostitutes, prostitutes who work in massage parlors and escort services, and call girls. Poverty and sexual and/or physical abuse figure prominently in the backgrounds of many prostitutes. Teenage runaways with marginal skills and limited means of support may find few alternatives to prostitution. Most patrons of female prostitutes are "occasional johns" who also have regular sex partners. Many customers are more interested in sexual novelty or companionship than sexual release per se. Male prostitutes typically begin selling sex in their teens. They may gay or heterosexual, but most service gay men.

Prostitutes are at greater risk of HIV transmission because they have sexual relations with many partners, often without protection. Many prostitutes, their clients, and their other sex partners also inject drugs and share contaminated needles.

Pornography is "writing, pictures, etc. intended to arouse sexual desire." Erotica refers to sexual material that is artistically produced. The United States Supreme Court's definition of obscenity includes whether the work "appeals to prurient interest," whether it "lacks serious literary, artistic, political, or scientific value," and the application of "community standards." Although both genders can become physiologically aroused by erotic materials, men are more interested in sexually explicit pictures and films. Millions of people around the world are surfing the internet to find websites that promote sex and erotica. Research in laboratory settings suggests that it is the violence in violent pornography that may promote violence against women.

When using sex in advertising, advertisers hope that people will link the product with the sexual imagery in the ad. Men tend to react more positively than women to sex in advertising. In television advertising, women are still generally stereotyped as wives, mothers, brides, waitresses, actresses, and so on.

Learning Objectives

1. Summarize the cross-cultural history of prostitution and the changing incidence of prostitution in the United States.

2. Describe the types of female prostitution, including where prostitutes conduct business and the types of customers they service.
3. Describe the economic and family influences characteristic of most prostitutes.
4. Discuss the demographic profiles and motives of customers of female prostitutes.
5. Describe the family backgrounds and the customers of male prostitutes.
6. Examine the dangers to prostitutes and to society posed by the AIDS virus.
7. Discuss the continuing social debate over the definition of pornography.
8. Discuss the legal battles that led to current definitions of obscenity.
9. Discuss the current use of pornography in the United States, the people who use it, and the gender differences in attitudes and responses.
10. Summarize the results of research that has investigated the link between pornography and sexual coercion.
11. Describe the purpose of using sexual themes in advertising and the impact of such ads.
12. Discuss the common gender-role stereotypes found in advertisements.

Fill-in-the-Blanks

In the United States, _____ is illegal everywhere except in some counties in Nevada. In this activity, a person exchanges _____ _____ for money or items of value. Although _____ is also illegal in many states, police rarely arrest customers. Most prostitutes are _____ (male/female) and virtually all customers are _____ (male/female). The major motive for prostitution throughout history and currently is _____.

Kinsey's data indicated a decrease in sexual experience with prostitutes that seems to be linked to the decay of the _____ _____ _____. Of the different types of prostitutes, most are _____, who hold the lowest status and earn the lowest income. They are also most likely to be abused by _____ and _____. Many were _____ _____ who initially became prostitutes in order to survive on their own.

_____ prostitutes have a higher status than streetwalkers. Except in Nevada, these prostitutes are most likely to work in _____ _____ or for _____ _____. _____ _____ provide "outcall" services and are listed in the yellow pages of telephone directories. They are typically, but not always, fronts for prostitution. Prostitutes who work for these businesses are often from _____ - class backgrounds and are _____ educated.

_____ _____ occupy the highest status in female prostitution. They are usually the most attractive and most well educated. They are expected to provide not only sex but _____ _____ and _____. They usually work _____ (on their own/with a pimp).

Two factors which figure prominently in the backgrounds of many prostitutes are _____, and _____ and/or _____ _____. Studies of female teenage prostitutes in the U.S. show that _____ to _____ have been sexually abused as children.

According to some information, most men who use female prostitutes are _____ (single/married) and of _____ - class backgrounds.

Male prostitutes who service female clients — _____ — are rare. They may or may not offer sexual services. The overwhelming majority of male prostitutes, usually called _____, service other men. The average age of male prostitutes is _____ (14-15, 17-18, 20-22). The majority come from _____ - class or _____ - class backgrounds. The majority were survivors of _____ _____. About half or more are _____ (heterosexual/gay) in orientation. Their major motive is _____.

Hustlers typically _____ (are/are not) attached to a pimp. _____ _____ hold the highest status. _____ _____ work on their own or through an agency or escort service. _____ _____ and _____ _____ occupy the lowest status and are the most likely to be arrested. The _____ the hustler, the higher the price.

_____ is writing, pictures, etc. intended to arouse sexual desire. Legislative bodies usually write laws about _____, but they have great difficulty defining it. _____ refers to sexual materials that are artistically produced or motivated. The 1873 _____ Act banned information about _____ _____ and made it a felony to _____ obscene material.

The report of the 1960s Commission on Obscenity and Pornography found _____ (persuasive/no) evidence that pornography led to crimes of violence or sexual offenses. A recent review of the research literature found _____ (significant/little or no) differences in the level of exposure to pornography between incarcerated sex offenders and felons who had committed nonsexual crimes.

The 1986 Meese Commission (the United States Attorney General's Commission on Pornography) claimed they _____ (found/were unable to find) a causal link between sexual violence and exposure to violent pornography. Laboratory studies have measured sympathy toward rape victims after viewing X-rated nonviolent films, R-rated violent films ("Slasher" films), or R-rated nonviolent films; men who watched the _____ _____ films showed the least sympathy. One researcher, Linz, concluded that it is _____ (sex/violence), with or without _____ (sex/violence), that has the most damaging effects on those who see, hear, or read it. Although studies on the effects of nonviolent pornography do not yet allow firm conclusions, _____ (significant new/no) research has linked sexual explicitness per se with undesirable effects.

Sex in advertising operates according to the principle of _____; the message is that if you use their product, you can get the sexual rewards the person in the commercial seems to have received. Studies of TV commercials show that _____ (males/females) are more likely to be portrayed visually and _____ are more likely to be featured as the off-camera "voice of authority". Commercials tend to portray _____ (men/ women) in a wider variety of occupational roles. _____ (Men/ Women) are more likely to be seen in traditional roles, usually in _____ settings. Heavier TV viewing is linked to the adoption of more _____ (traditional/nontraditional) gender-role attitudes among children.

Short Answer Questions

(LO = Learning Objective)
1. Describe the factors which seem to explain entry into female prostitution. (LO 3 - pp. 600-601)

2. What are the customers' most common motives for using prostitutes? (LO 4 - p. 602)

3. Describe the typical backgrounds of male prostitutes. (LO 5 - pp. 603-604)

4. In the U.S. and other countries, what is the link between prostitution, HIV, and AIDS? (LO 6 - p. 605)

5. In the United States, how widely used are sexually explicit materials? (LO 9 - p. 606)

6. What criteria have the U.S. courts used in their attempts to define obscenity? (LO 8 - pp. 607-608)

7. Describe the gender differences in responses to pornography. (LO 9 - p. 611)

8. From the research results given in the text, what conclusions can you reach regarding the effects of the various types of pornography?
   (LO 10 - pp. 612-614)

9. What does research show about the effects of nonviolent pornography?
   (LO 10 - pp. 613-614)

10. How does the use of sexual themes fit into the goals of advertisers?
    (LO 11 - pp. 615-616)

Matching Exercises

I. Vocabulary Exercise 1

Directions: Match each vocabulary term listed in the left-hand column with the correct definition in the right-hand column.

a. prostitution (p. 594)   ____ Written, visual, or audiotaped material that is sexually explicit and produced for purposes of eliciting or enhancing sexual arousal.

b. streetwalkers (p. 596)   ____ Prostitutes who arrange for their sexual contacts by telephone. *Call* refers both to telephone calls and to being "on call."

c. pimps (p. 596)   ____ Books, pictures, and so on that have to do with sexual love. Many contemporary writers use this term to refer to sexual material that is artistically produced or motivated by artistic intent.

d. call girls (p. 599)   ____ Customers of hustlers.

e. whore-madonna complex (p. 602)   ____ The sale of sexual activity for money or goods of value, such as drugs.

f. hustlers (p. 603)   ____ Tending to excite lust; lewd.

g. scores (p. 603)   ____ A rigid stereotyping of women as either sinners or saints.

h. pornography (p. 606)   ____ That which offends people's feelings or goes beyond prevailing standards of decency or modesty.

i. prurient (p. 606)   ____ Prostitutes who solicit customers on the streets.

j. obscenity (p. 607)   ____ Men who engage in prostitution with male customers.

k. erotica (p. 607)   ____ Men who serve as agents for prostitutes and live off their earnings.

Multiple-Choice Questions

(LO = Learning Objective)

1. The major motive for young women becoming prostitutes has been
   a. sexual gratification.
   b. the satisfaction of an abnormally high sex drive.
   c. economics.
   d. emotional instability.
       p. 600 LO 1

2. Streetwalkers typically experience all of the following, *except*
   a. choice regarding customers.
   b. vulnerability to abuse by pimps and customers.
   c. childhood history of incest or sexual abuse.
   d. a background of poverty and deprivation.
       pp. 596-597 LO 2

3. Prostitutes who are survivors of child sexual abuse
   a. often learn to enjoy sex and therefore enter prostitution.
   b. learn that their sexuality can help them gain attention or love from adults.
   c. learn to detach themselves emotionally from sex.
   d. a and b
   e. b and c
       p. 601 LO 3

4. In contemporary America, the most frequent use of prostitutes occurs among men
   a. who are away from home.
   b. who regularly use escort services.
   c. who seek social companions to impress business associates.
   d. who have problems with sexual performance.
       pp. 601-602 LO 4

5. Which is the rarest type of prostitute?
   a. call girl
   b. house prostitute
   c. streetwalker
   d. gigolo
       p. 603 LO 5

6. One difference between hustlers and female prostitutes is that the hustlers
   a. are better paid.
   b. typically do not have pimps.
   c. are less vulnerable to abuse and injury.
   d. are part of a well-connected community.
          p. 604   LO 5

7. Sex with prostitutes increases the risk of HIV transmission for all of the following reasons, *except*
   a. many prostitutes have unprotected sex with many partners.
   b. many prostitutes are injecting drug users.
   c. the clients can spread the infection to their wives and other sex partners.
   d. prostitutes not HIV-infected can serve as carriers of the virus to clients.
          p. 605   LO 6

8. Gender differences in response to pornography indicate
   a. that males and females both prefer visual pornography over other forms.
   b. males actually prefer reading erotic passages to heighten sexual arousal.
   c. females are more likely to become sexually aroused from visual pornography than are males.
   d. males prefer visual pornography more than do females.
          p. 611   LO 9

9. The 1960s Commission on Obscenity and Pornography concluded that
   a. pornographic materials perpetuate violence against women.
   b. there was no causal link between pornography and sexual violence against women.
   c. males were more likely to engage in obscene acts after watching pornography.
   d. pornography should be regulated by the government.
          p. 611   LO 10

10. Opposition to the findings of the Meese Commission argued that the commission failed to
    a. distinguish child pornography from artistic expression.
    b. distinguish between the effects of violent pornography and sexually explicit materials.
    c. admonish Playboy and Hustler for their contributions to the increased sexual violence against women.
    d. include Playgirl in their examination of pornography.
          p. 612   LO 10

11. Short-term or prolonged exposure to sexual violence, whether sexually explicit or not,
    a. increases sympathy toward survivors of rape.
    b. lowers arousal levels overall.
    c. has no effect upon attitudes about forced sexual encounters.
    d. lessens sensitivity towards survivors of rape.
        pp. 612-613   LO 10

12. In general, female models in advertisements
    a. are depicted in egalitarian terms.
    b. still reflect stereotypic gender roles.
    c. are portrayed in a wide variety of occupational roles.
    d. are degraded, humiliated and presented as sex objects.
        p. 616   LO 12

Chapter 20

Making Responsible Sexual Decisions—

An Epilogue

Chapter Summary

The epilogue explores the process of decision making when choices about sexual behavior involve value conflicts. Information alone cannot form the basis for these decisions, but information is very important for an individual to predict the outcomes of specific decisions. People experience psychological conflict when the alternatives they are weighing involve both negative and positive aspects or have serious negative aspects.

Information is not the only guide for people to use when weighing alternatives. Value systems provide another framework that an individual can refer to when evaluating the acceptability of sexual options available. The authors describe seven value systems: legalism, situation ethics, ethical relativism, hedonism, asceticism, utilitarianism, and rationalism.

Another strategy for weighing the pluses and minuses of alternatives is presented -- using a balance sheet. The balance sheet suggests that, when making decisions, the individual list the projected gains and losses for each alternative according to five criteria. Although the balance sheet does not yield a "correct" decision, it does help people organize and process their perceptions of various alternatives.

Learning Objectives

1. Examine the role information can play in sexual decision making when a person's choices involve value conflicts.

2. Describe the basis for decision making that characterizes each of the seven value systems discussed in this chapter.

Fill-in-the-Blanks

The text has provided the _____ you will need for making responsible sexual decisions, but _____ alone cannot determine your choices. *You* must determine which behaviors you find morally acceptable. In addition to information, _____ systems provide another framework for decision-making.

The text describes seven value systems: _____, _____ _____, _____ _____, _____, _____, _____, and _____.

The _____ approach determines what behavior is ethical on the basis of a code of moral laws derived from an external source, such as a religious creed. Another view, known as _____ _____, advocates that ethical decisions should be guided by genuine love for others rather than by moral rules. This value system argues that decisions should be based on the _____ of the particular situation.

_____ _____ reject the idea that there is a single correct moral view, and they believe that there is no objective way of justifying one set of moral values over another. To them, the essence of human morality is to derive _____ _____ principles and apply them.

_____ are guided by the pursuit of pleasure. However, there is _____ and _____ hedonism; basing decisions on what feels good now may fail to account for the consequences of one's actions.

_____ choose self-denial of material and sexual pleasures in order to devote themselves to spiritual pursuits.

The core ethic of _____ is that moral conduct is determined by what brings about "the greatest good for the greatest number." _____ view behavior as ethical when it does the greatest good and causes the least harm.

_____ involves the use of reason as the means of determining a course of action. The _____ attempts to assess the facts in a sexual situation and then logically weigh the consequences of each course of action before making a decision.

Short Answer Questions

(LO = Learning Objective)
1. Define psychological conflict. (LO 1 - p. 620)

2. Describe the decision making methods you use when faced with choices about sexual behaviors. (LO 1 - p. 630)

3. List some of the sources of our value systems or sexual standards. (LO 2 - p. 621)

4. Which of the value systems described in the text does your value system most closely resemble? Explain your answer. (LO 2 - pp. 621-624)

Multiple-Choice Questions

(LO = Learning Objective)
1. Psychological conflict is characterized by
    a. indecision.
    b. vacillation between alternative options.
    c. stress.
    d. all of the above.
          p. 620   LO 1

2. Factual information gathering
    a. enables us to predict the possible outcome of our decisions.
    b. forces us to make logical choices.
    c. absolves us of moral decision making.
    d. should outweigh all other factors in decisions regarding sexual behavior.
          p. 621   LO 1

3. The legalistic approach to ethical behavior is formulated on the basis of
   a. scientific fact.
   b. Supreme Court laws.
   c. an external code of moral laws.
   d. individualistic legal interpretation.
         p. 621   LO 2

4. Which does *not* belong?
   a. flexible rules
   b. situation ethics
   c. guided by love for others
   d. legalism
         pp. 621-623   LO 2

5. Opponents of ethical relativism believe
   a. all humans are basically evil and need social control.
   b. social chaos and decay would result from individuals determining their own moral code of conduct.
   c. that a diversity of values is a fundamental human quality.
   d. more hedonistic moral values create social order.
         pp. 622-623   LO 2

6. Which viewpoint is guided by the pursuit of pleasure rather than what is morally right?
   a. asceticism
   b. utilitarianism
   c. situation ethics
   d. hedonism
         p. 623   LO 2

7. Ethical behavior which does the greatest good for the greatest number and causes the least harm is the core ethic of
   a. hedonism.
   b. asceticism.
   c. utilitarianism.
   d. ethical relativism.
         p. 623   LO 2

8. The rationalist
   a. makes decisions based upon blind obedience.
   b. believes good decisions stem from doing what feels good.
   c. takes a vow of celibacy for ascetic reasons.
   d. assesses facts and logically weighs consequences when making decisions.
      p. 624   LO 2

9. Ethical systems provide us with
   a. absolute guidelines regarding sexual behavior.
   b. a general framework of moral reasoning for decision making.
   c. pathways for judging the moral acceptability of our behaviors.
   d. a and c
   e. b and c
      p. 624   LO 2

10. Using a Balance Sheet to help weigh the positive and negative factors involved in decision making is most similar to which value system?
    a. hedonism
    b. rationalism
    c. ethical relativism
    d. asceticism
      p. 624   LO 2

Appendix

Answers to Chapter Exercises

Chapter 1:

Fill-in-the-Blanks: Human sexuality, values, prehistoric, 9000, incest, Pederasty, fellatio, cunnilingus, fornication, *Kama Sutra*, middle ages, Luther, Calvin, prostitution, Havelock Ellis, 30s, 40s, mid-1960s, mid-1970s, genetic, hormonal, neural, cross-species, Sociobiologists, cross-cultural, polygamy, monogamy, Freud, psychoanalysis, psychosexual development, oral, anal, phallic, latency, genital, Behaviorists, Social-learning, Sociocultural theorists, gender roles.

Short Answer Questions:
1. Unwanted pregnancies, STIs, sexual harassment, rape, sexual dysfunctions, and the impact of aging and disability on sexual functioning, etc.
2. See list on pages 7-10.
3. Cave drawings, stone carvings, figurines, statues, archeological remains, jewelry, etc.
4. Saint Paul associated sex with sin. Celibacy was the ideal, and sex within marriage was supposed to occur without passion and only with the goal of reproduction. Sex outside marriage was clearly sinful, but nonprocreative sexual behaviors were most sinful.
5. There is little evidence of universal sexual attitudes and behaviors across time. Throughout history, religion has been a major influence on sexual values and behaviors.
6. Mechanisms of reproduction, biological processes of sexual maturation, the physiological mechanisms of sexual arousal and response, etc.
7. All species evolve over time from other species. The individuals who are better adapted to the environment are more likely to survive, reproduce, and pass on their genetic traits.
8. A great variety of sexual behaviors exists among nonhumans. Experience and learning play more important roles as we travel up the evolutionary ladder. Animal sexual behavior is not a good yardstick by which to judge the "naturalness" of human sexual behavior.
9. Reproductive success is increased for men if they impregnate large numbers of women and it is increased for women when they are selective about mates, because they can produce only a few offspring in their lifetimes.
10. Sexual practices vary widely across cultures, but all societies regulate sexual behavior in some fashion. All societies have *some* form of incest taboo.
11. Behaviorists emphasize the importance of rewards and punishments, which increase or decrease the likelihood of behaviors being learned and repeated.
12. Refinement of hormone replacement therapy for postmenopausal women, increase in number of men who become proactive about their sexual health, decline in gender polarization around the world, development of improved contraceptives, more effective ways to prevent teen pregnancies, improvement in treatment of sexual dysfunctions, etc..

Matching Exercises:
I. Individuals and Their Contributions:
c, h, f, j, g, b, a, i, e, d

II. Vocabulary Exercise 1:
k, h, j, l, g, n, e, m, a, f, b, o, c, i, d

III. Vocabulary Exercise 2:
j, f, g, d, k, h, i, c, a, b, e

Multiple-Choice Questions:
1. c; 2. d; 3. c; 4. c; 5. c; 6. a; 7. b; 8. a; 9. c; 10. b; 11. c; 12. c.

Chapter 2:

Fill-in-the-Blanks: scientific method, case-study, survey, observational, correlational, experimental, sample, generalize, random, probability sample, case study, survey, less expensive, volunteer bias, faulty estimation, social-desirability response bias, exaggeration, denial, observational, anthropologists, participant observation, observer effect, Correlational, cause and effect, predictions, experimental, independent, dependent, experimental, control, Ethics review committees, pain, stress, confidentiality, informed consent, deception, benefits.

Short Answer Questions:
1. Formulating a research question. Framing the research question in the form of a hypothesis. Testing the hypothesis. Drawing conclusions.
2. Describe, explain, predict, and control.
3. If researchers are to be confident that they are studying the same events, they must define their concepts in ways that link their meaning to the methods used to measure them. For example, sexual arousal may be defined as a subjective feeling of arousal, a self-report of genital sensations, or a physiological measure of vasocongestion.
4. In a random sample, every member of a population has an equal chance of participating. In a stratified random sample, known subgroups of a population are represented in proportion to their numbers in the population.
5. Magazine readers or subscribers do not constitute a representative sample of the U.S. population. Additionally, because of volunteer bias, the survey respondents may not even be a representative sample of the magazine readers or subscribers. Therefore, the results of such surveys are not generalizable to either the magazine readers or to the U.S. population.
6. Survey (interviews). The team wished to know the sexual behavior patterns of the people in the United States. They wanted to know how many people engaged in which behaviors with what frequency.
7. Survey respondents may attach different meanings to different terms, or they may not know the meaning of some terms.
8. Volunteer bias, observer effect, altered responses, bias of observer, etc.
9. All conditions are held the same for both groups, with only one exception - the treatment, or independent variable. Therefore, researchers can conclude that any differences in the groups are *caused* by the treatment.
10. If studies with humans would be impractical or unethical, other animals may be used.
11. They mistakenly conclude that a correlation means that a change in one variable *causes* the change in the other variable.

Matching Exercises:
I. Research Reports and Their Descriptions:
f, i, g, b, h, d, a, c, j, e

II. Vocabulary Exercise 1:
c, f, g, l, i, n, m, k, b, e, d, j, a, h

III. Vocabulary Exercise 2:
c, f, h, a, i, k, d, j, b, g, e

Multiple-Choice Questions:
1. c; 2. c; 3. c; 4. a; 5. b; 6. a; 7. b; 8. d; 9. a; 10. a; 11. c.

Chapter 3:

Fill-in-the-Blanks: vulva, mons veneris, labia majora, labia minora, clitoris, vestibule, urethral, Cystitis, hymen, perineum, episiotomy, vagina, cervix, Pap smear, uterus, Fallopian tubes, ovaries, Breast, eight, Menstruation, proliferative, 28, ovulatory, secretory, menstrual, Menopause, Dysmenorrhea, Amenorrhea.

Short Answer Questions:
1. Clitoridectomy is the surgical removal of the clitoris. Infibulation entails the surgical removal of the clitoris, the labia minora, and the inner layers of the labia majora, followed by stitching together the labia majora. The reasons include social custom, "curing" female masturbators, and ensuring a girl's chastity.
2. Drink two quarts of water a day, drink orange or cranberry juice, decrease use of alcohol and caffeine, wash hands prior to touching genitals, prevent objects that have touched the anus from touching the vulva, urinate immediately after intercourse.
3. Vaginal lubrication results from the engorgement of vaginal tissues during sexual excitement. The engorgement causes moisture from the small blood vessels in the vaginal wall to be forced out and to pass through the vaginal lining.
4. Exercises performed to strengthen the P-C muscle. To improve urinary control and heighten genital sensations during coitus.
5. Wash the vulva and anus regularly, wear cotton panties, avoid wearing pants that are tight in the crotch, have sexual partners wash well, use K-Y jelly if lubrication is needed, avoid intercourse that is painful, avoid diets high in sugar and refined carbohydrates, perhaps douche with a plain water or vinegar or baking soda solution, take care of your general health.
6. One woman in three by the age of 60. They are usually performed when women develop cancer of the uterus, ovaries, or cervix, or when women develop diseases that cause pain or excessive bleeding from the uterus.
7. Women should have pelvic exams once a year by age 18 or earlier if they are sexually active, and twice a year if they are over 35 or use BC pills. The physician does an external exam for abnormalities, takes a sample of vaginal discharge to test for STIs, and does a Pap smear.
8. Women should do breast self-exams at least once a month, preferably about a week after their periods end. Women between 35 and 39 should have a baseline mammogram; women age 40 to 50 should have a mammogram every year or two and women over 50 should have one a year. Physicians exam breasts during a yearly exam.
9. Abstain: religious prohibition, the "mess," etc. Engage: relieve menstrual cramps, satisfy sexual desire, etc.
10. Night sweats, hot flashes, hot flushes, cold sweats, headaches, tingling in hands or feet, sleep problems, etc.
11. Any four of the ten myths and accompanying facts listed on pages 92 and 93.
12. Nearly three in four women have some symptoms of PMS during the four to six days that precede their menses. The symptoms include anxiety, depression, irritability, weight gain, and abdominal discomfort.
13. Any five of the ten suggestions listed on pages 96 and 98 of the text.

Matching Exercises:
I. Vocabulary Exercise 1:
d, f, g, i, m, l, a, e, j, b, h, k, c

II. Vocabulary Exercise 2:
d, h, f, l, a, o, j, n, b, m, i, k, c, g, e

Multiple-Choice Questions:
1. c; 2. c; 3. b; 4. b; 5. b; 6. a; 7. c; 8. b; 9. e; 10. d; 11. a; 12. c.

Chapter 4:

Fill-in-the-Blanks: penis, scrotum, Semen, urine, erection, Circumcision, Physicians, scrotum, androgens, sperm, seminiferous tubules, sex chromosome, vasectomy, vas deferens, seminal vesicles, prostate, Cowper's, seminal vesicles, prostate glands, Cowper's glands, Urethritis, Testicular, survival rate, self-examinations, prostate, prostate, Prostatitis, nocturnal erections, are not, reflexes, autonomic, parasympathetic, sympathetic, emission stage, expulsion stage, retrograde ejaculation.

Short Answer Questions:
1. Advocates believe it eliminates a site where bacteria might grow; opponents believe regular cleaning reduces the risks sufficiently. Uncircumcised male infants have more urinary tract infections; uncircumcised males may be at greater risk of becoming infected by the AIDS virus. It is unlikely that there are significant differences in coital sensitivity.
2. Penis size has little to do with sexual performance. Women rarely mention it as an important element in their sexual satisfaction. The diameter of the penis *may* have a greater bearing on satisfaction than does length.
3. The scrotum's ability to raise the testicles when a man is cold and lower them when a man is hot allows optimal sperm production. Optimal sperm production occurs at 93_ F or 5.6_ lower than body temperature.
4. The lobes of the testicles are filled with seminiferous tubules which manufacture sperm cells. In an early stage sperm cells, then called spermatocytes, have 46 chromosomes. Each divides into two spermatids, each having 23 chromosomes. The manufacture of a mature sperm cell takes 72 days.
5. Bladder and urethral inflammations. Drink more water, drink cranberry juice, lower your intake of alcohol and caffeine.
6. Urethritis—urinary frequency and urgency, burning during urination, penile discharge.
Cancer of the testes—in early stages, no symptoms other than the mass.
Enlargement of the prostate—urinary frequency and urgency, difficulty starting urination.
Cancer of the prostate—urinary frequency and difficulty urinating, or no symptoms in the early stages.
Prostatitis—ache or pain between scrotum and anal opening, painful ejaculation.
7. The scrotum should be examined for pea-sized lumps. Each testicle should be rolled gently between the thumb and fingers. Warning signs include: enlargement or change in consistency of a testicle, a dull ache in the lower abdomen or groin, a feeling of heaviness in a testicle.
8. Almost all men over 50. Urinary frequency, urinary urgency, difficulty starting the flow of urine.
9. The two corpus cavernosa and the corpus spongiosum become engorged with blood, causing the penis to enlarge. The firmness is caused by the tough, fibrous covering surrounding the two corpus cavernosa.
10. Nocturnal erections occur throughout the night every 90 minutes or so, generally during the REM stage of sleep.
11. This tactile stimulation causes sensory neurons to transmit signals to an erection center in the sacral portion of the spinal cord. Messages are then sent from the spine to the penis. These messages cause arteries carrying blood to the penis to dilate. More blood moves into the tissues and the penis becomes erect.

12. It occurs when there is no tactile stimulation of the penis. The brain sends messages (sexual memories, fantasies, visual stimuli) to an erection center in the lumbar region of the spinal cord.
13. The nerves that cause penile arteries to dilate during erection belong to the parasympathetic branch. The nerves governing ejaculation belong to the sympathetic branch. Anxiety, fear, etc. can interfere with erection or cause premature ejaculation.

Matching Exercises:
I. Vocabulary Exercise 1:
c, k, f, m, h, g, a, j, d, b, l, e, i

II. Vocabulary Exercise 2:
i, d, m, g, l, b, j, e, k, c, a, f, h

Multiple-Choice Questions:
1. c; 2. a; 3. b; 4. b; 5. d; 6. b; 7. b; 8. c; 9. d; 10. c; 11. c.

Chapter 5:

Fill-in-the-Blanks: vision, smell, Pheromones, menstrual synchrony, Erogenous zones, hearing, aphrodisiac, Psychoactive, depressant, dampens, none, cerebral cortex, limbic system, pleasure centers, Hormones, Testosterone, estrogen, progesterone, secondary sex characteristics, sexual desire, erection, ejaculate, do not, estrus, androgens, Masters, Johnson, sexual response cycle, excitement, plateau, orgasm, resolution, vasocongestion, myotonia, Helen Singer Kaplan, desire, excitement, orgasm, sexual dysfunctions, multiple, clitoral, vaginal, Grafenberg spot.

Short Answer Questions:
1. Research by several investigators suggests that exposure to other women's sweat can modify the menstrual cycle. Underarm secretions may contain an as yet unidentified pheromone.
2. Primary erogenous zones are parts of the body that are especially sensitive to tactile sexual stimulation because they are richly endowed with nerve endings. Secondary erogenous zones are parts of the body that become erotically sensitized through experience. Genitals, inner thighs, perineum, buttocks and anus, breasts, ears, mouth, lips, tongue, neck, navel, armpits.
3. Anaphrodisiacs inhibit sexual response. Tranquilizers, CNS depressants, antihypertensive drugs, some antidepressants, nicotine, antiandrogen drugs, etc.
4. Alcohol is a central nervous system depressant that biochemically dampens sexual arousal. However, because of expectations, people who drink moderate levels of alcohol may feel more sexually aroused. Ingestion of large amounts can severely impair sexual performance in men and women. Alcohol can induce feelings of euphoria and impair the ability to weigh information (reduce inhibitions).
5. Sex hormones that have an *organizing* effect influence the *type* of behavior that is expressed. Ones that have an *activating* effect influence the frequency or the intensity of the drive that motivates the behavior.
6. Minimal levels of androgens are critical to male sexuality, but there is no one-to-one correspondence between hormone levels and sex drive or sexual performance in adult men. Sexual responsiveness in women is also influenced by androgens. For men and women, learning, fantasies, attitudes, memories, and other psychosocial factors have a large influence on sexual interest.
7. Vasocongestion: swelling of the genital tissues with blood. Myotonia: muscle tension that causes voluntary and involuntary muscle contractions.

8. Men enter a refractory period during which they are physiologically incapable of experiencing another orgasm or ejaculation. Women do not undergo a refractory period and can become quickly rearoused to the point of repeated orgasms.
9. Men are more similar to other men than are women to other women in their patterns of sexual response. See descriptions of patterns, p. 141.
10. Kaplan designates desire as a separate phase of sexual response; Masters and Johnson do not. Masters and Johnson view the order of the sexual response stages as successive and invariant; Kaplan sees the stages as relatively independent components and the sequence as somewhat variable.
11. Some men seem to be capable of two or more nonejaculatory orgasms preceding a final ejaculatory orgasm. Most of the evidence, however, is anecdotal.
12. Clitoral orgasms, those achieved through direct clitoral stimulation, were seen as immature. Vaginal orgasm, those achieved through deep penile thrusting, were seen as a sign of mature sexuality.

Matching Exercises:
I. Vocabulary Exercise 1:
c, g, d, l, a, k, i, j, f, d, h, b, e

II. Vocabulary Exercise 2:
e, g, a, j, d, i, k, b, l, h, c, f

Multiple-Choice Questions:
1. d; 2. d; 3. a; 4. c; 5. b; 6. a; 7. b; 8. b; 9. c; 10. c; 11. d; 12. a.

Chapter 6:

Fill-in-the-Blanks: 23, 23, X, X or Y, father, female, Y, seventh, Klinefelter's, Turner, gender identity, Pseudohermaphrodites, gender assignment, hermaphrodites, Transsexuals, early childhood, gender reassignment surgery, male-to-females, female-to-males, Gender roles, small, environmental, men, Sociobiologists, prenatal sex hormones, cultural expectations, identification, Social-learning, observational, socialization, schemas, gender schema, aggressive, passive, initiate, overaroused, underaroused, psychologically androgynous, masculine, feminine.

Short Answer Questions:
1. For the first six weeks following conception, male (XY) and female (XX) embryos develop similarly. During the seventh week, in XY embryos, the Y chromosome stimulates the production of H-Y antigen, which triggers the development of the testes. The testes begin to produce androgens which spur differentiation of the Wolffian ducts.
2. Hermaphrodites may have one gonad of each gender or gonads that combine testicular and ovarian tissue. Pseudohermaphrodites have gonads which match their chromosomal gender, but their external genitals and sometimes their internal reproductive anatomy are ambiguous or resemble those of the other gender.
3. Most conclude that gender identity is influenced by complex interactions between biological and psychosocial factors.
4. A clear majority have improved psychological adjustment following surgery. However, many had poor adjustment prior to surgery and remain lonely and isolated afterwards. About half incur postoperative medical complications.
5. The gender differences are small and narrowing. The variation within genders is larger than between genders. The small differences may reflect environmental influences and cultural expectations.

6. Sociobiologists attribute complex social behaviors, such as aggression and gender roles, to heredity. They imply that "men as breadwinners" and "women as homemakers" reflect the natural order of things and are our destiny.
7. Anthropologists believe that cultural differences in gender roles can be explained in terms of the adaptations that cultures make to their social and natural environments.
8. Socialization is the process of guiding people into socially acceptable behavior patterns by means of information, rewards, and punishments. Mothers, fathers, parental roles, schools, the popular media, etc.
9. Sexism is widespread. Some science and math teachers ignore girls in favor of boys. Some tests remain biased against girls. The gender gap in math scores is narrowing.
10. Men usually ask women for dates, and men usually initiate sexual interactions. Women are usually expected to wait for men to initiate dates and sexual interactions, and they are expected not to indicate sexual desire. In many cases, men also determine sexual positions and techniques.
11. Masculine and androgynous males and females tend to have higher self-esteem and be generally better adjusted psychologically. Feminine traits in both males and females tend to predict success in intimate relationships.

Matching Exercises:
I. Vocabulary Exercise 1:
k, h, i, a, m, f, e, b, l, c, j, g, d

II. Vocabulary Exercise 2:
k, f, h, m, g, j, b, l, d, a, e, c, i

Multiple-Choice Questions:
1. c; 2. c; 3. b; 4. d; 5. d; 6. b; 7. b; 8. d; 9. b; 10. c; 11.b; 12. c.

Chapter 7:

Fill-in-the-Blanks: Physical attractiveness, plumpness, physical characteristics, relative youth, earning capacity, kind-understanding, intelligent, honesty, matching hypothesis, attitudes, Reciprocity, romantic love, *storge, agape, philia, eros,* Infatuation, intense physiological arousal, cognitive appraisal, romantic, game-playing, friendship, logical, possessive/excited, selfless, triangular, intimacy, passion, decision/commitment,.

Short Answer Questions:
1. Most college men think they are close to ideal and appealing to women. Most college women believe they too heavy. Women generally prefer men a little leaner than men think, and men generally prefer women a little heavier than women think.
2. Men prefer mates younger than themselves, and women prefer mates older than themselves. In all 37 cultures, men placed greater value on a partner's "good looks" than did women. In almost all of the cultures women placed greater emphasis on "good earning capacity." In all 37 cultures, both men and women placed greatest emphasis on "kind-understanding" and "intelligent."
3. Sociobiologists view these as part of our genetic heritage. The physical features that are universally appealing to both genders might predict better reproductive potential.
4. We tend to develop relationships with people who are similar in physical attractiveness, attitudes, and personality traits. We may do this to avoid rejection.
5. Similarity in attitudes and tastes contributes greatly to initial attraction, friendships, and love relationships. People also prefer to work with others who have similar attitudes.

6. Reciprocity is a powerful determinant of attraction. When others admire and compliment us, we tend to return these feelings. We tend to be more warm and helpful toward those we believe like us.
7. They believe romantic love is a prerequisite for marriage. Young people rate it as the most important reason for marriage.
8. Sexual arousal; elation; general physiological arousal; difficulty sleeping, working, and carrying out routine chores.
9. College men are more likely to develop game-playing and romantic love styles. College women are more likely to develop friendly, logical, and possessive love styles.
10. At the outset, passions may be strong but intimacy weak. Over the years, passion tends to lessen while intimacy and commitment grow stronger.
11. Major differences exist between the partners on all three components: intimacy, passion, and decision/commitment.

Matching Exercises:
I. Vocabulary Exercise 1:
g, h, b, i, d, a, e, c, f

Multiple-Choice Questions:
1. c; 2. b; 3. d; 4. b; 5. c; 6. d; 7. b; 8. c; 9. d; 10.d.

Chapter 8:

Fill-in-the-Blanks: romantic, attraction, building, continuation, deterioration, ending, small talk, self-disclosure, mutuality, continuation, Sexual jealousy, deterioration, Ending, Loneliness, intimacy, trust, caring, acceptance, communication, Nonverbal communication, touch, eye contact, irrational, paraphrasing, specific, tolerate, agree.

Short Answer Questions:
1. Small talk is a realistic way to begin a relationship, and the topics usually involve the weather, movies, hobbies, vacations, etc. If small talk goes well, a relationship may begin.
2. Similarity in level of physical attractiveness and attitudes, mutual liking, positive evaluations of the other person, careful self-disclosure, and establishing mutuality.
3. They are rated as less mature, secure, well-adjusted and genuine. They may be viewed as emotionally distraught or socially awkward.
4. Jealousy puts stress on a relationship and makes it less rewarding. Partners may feel inadequate and constantly mistrustful. In extreme cases jealousy can cause depression or give rise to spouse abuse, suicide, or murder.
5. The factors include failure to invest time and energy in the relationship, and permitting the deterioration to proceed (passive response).
6. Lack of social skills, lack of interest in other people, lack of empathy, fear of rejection, failure to self-disclose, cynicism about human nature, demanding too much too soon, pessimism about life, and external locus of control.
7. See page 217.
8. A person can become emotionally intimate with friends, family members, or partners. Sexual intimacy with partners does not necessarily lead to emotional intimacy, which involves the exchange of inmost thoughts and feelings.
9. Voice tone, gestures, body posture, facial expressions, touching, eye contact, etc. People may place more weight on *how* something is said rather than *what* is said.
10. You should learn to listen actively, to draw the other person out, to provide information to your partner, to make requests, to deliver criticism without inducing defensiveness, and to receive criticism.

11. Take turns petting, directing your partner's hand, and signaling.
12. Relationships can continue if the partners decide to tolerate their differences and agree to disagree on some issues.

Matching Exercises:
1. Vocabulary Exercise 1:
g, f, b, a, d, e, c.

Multiple-Choice Questions:
1. c; 2. c; 3. b; 4. b; 5. d; 6. e; 7. b; 8. d; 9. c; 10. a; 11. a; 12. c.

Chapter 9:

Fill-in-the-Blanks: Masturbation, physically, mentally, men, women, manual manipulation, vaginal insertion, mons, labia minora, clitoris, sexual fantasy, having intercourse with a loved one, Foreplay, longer, kissing, breast, fellatio cunnilingus, African, White, simultaneous oral-genital, Coitus, missionary, ejaculation, failed to, African American males, White American males, females, Anal, 20-26%, anilingus.

Short Answer Questions:
1. The Judeo-Christian tradition has been to strongly condemn masturbation as sinful. Both Jews and Christians have condemned this and other sexual practices that can not lead to pregnancy.
2. Masturbation is not physically or psychologically harmful. Negative attitudes toward masturbation cause anxiety and guilt in some people. Most people have masturbated at some point in their lives. Masturbation is prevalent among married as well as single people. Masturbation may have therapeutic benefits for women who have difficulty achieving orgasm.
3. Most people do not intend to act out their fantasies, nor do they necessarily want the events to occur. Women who fantasize about coercive sexual encounters do not wish to be raped. It is common for heterosexuals to have homosexual fantasies (and vice versa) but have no interest in acting on these fantasies.
4. They parallel traditional gender stereotypes. Men reported more fantasies about making love to a stranger, making love to more than one person at a time, and forcing someone to engage in sexual activity. Women reported more fantasies about being forced to engaged in sex and about engaging in sexual acts they would never do in reality.
5. Broude and Greene found that prolonged foreplay was the norm in one half of the cultures they studies; it was almost absent in one third of these cultures. Generally, women want longer periods of foreplay than men do.
6. More than 90% of young married couples engage in fellatio and cunnilingus at least occasionally. African-American couples are less likely than White Americans to engage in oral-genital stimulation.
7. Several studies show that African American men and women are significantly less likely to engage in oral-genital sex than their White American counterparts.
8. Stereotype: African Americans are more promiscuous than White Americans. See pages 256-257. The Belcastro and Wyatt surveys fail to support the stereotypes, although neither surveyed a national sample.
9. It may be used to enhance arousal and response. A large majority of men and women report fantasies during coitus. It does not indicate sexual dissatisfaction in a relationship.

10. They should use a water soluble lubricant like K-Y jelly. Slow penetration helps avoid pain or tearing of sensitive rectal tissue. People who are not sure that their partners are free of sexually transmitted diseases should avoid anal sex or use a condom and a spermicide known to kill the AIDS virus.
11. The 1994 NHSLS survey found that one in four men and one in five women have engaged in anal sex sometime during their lives. A higher incidence is found among more highly educated people. Religion seems to be a restraining influence.

Matching Exercises:
I. Vocabulary Exercise 1:
d, e, i, f, b, h, g, a, c

Multiple-Choice Questions:
1. c; 2. b; 3. a; 4. b; 5. d; 6. d; 7. c; 8. d; 9. b; 10. d; 11. c; 12. b.

Chapter 10:

Fill-in-the-Blanks: Heterosexual orientation, Homosexual orientation, Bisexuality, 7, continuum, do not, Storms, independent dimensions, condemned, masturbation, oral-genital sex, anal sex, require, lesbian, heterosexual, no, Homophobia, stereotypic gender roles, Heterosexual males, heterosexual females, anal intercourse, oral-genital contact, sex with animals, decriminalized, effeminate, butch, sex hormones, desire, preference, genetic, structural differences, Oedipus complex, Castration anxiety, penis envy, gender-nonconformity, has failed to show, Coming out, gays, lesbians, lesbians.

Short Answer Questions:
1. Gay males and lesbians have gender identities that are consistent with their anatomic gender, and they are attracted to members of their own gender. Transsexuals see themselves as trapped in the body of the other gender.
2. Many heterosexuals and gays identify their orientation long before they engage in sexual behaviors with partners. Some people who identify themselves as having a heterosexual orientation engage in male-male or female-female sexual behaviors. This includes adolescents, some prisoners, and some males who engage in prostitution. Some people with a gay orientation marry and do not engage in male-male or female-female sexual behaviors.
3. Whether the question dealt with sexual identify, sexual behavior, or sexual attraction, and over what period of time. Whether the survey was face-to-face or an anonymous written survey. The gender of the interviewer. Possible volunteer bias. The social desirability of the behavior asked about, etc.
4. It may be more difficult to acquire data about female sexuality. Female sexual behavior in general may be more repressed. Female-female sexual interest and activities may be less common.
5. Monkeys have been observed engaging in manual manipulation of the genitals, oral-genital stimulation, and rear mounting with occasional penetration. One can not conclude that the motivation for these animal behaviors is similar to that for humans.
6. Generally, a majority of people are negative, but a decreasing percentage say they would bar gays from teaching in a college or university. A 1992 national Gallup poll indicated that a majority now favor equal employment opportunities and health insurance and inheritance rights for gay spouses.
7. Myth: Gay men and lesbians will recruit children into a homosexual lifestyle. (There is no evidence of teachers luring children into homosexuality or that children reared by gay men or lesbians are more likely to become homosexuals.) Myth: Gays are swishy and lesbians are butch. (About 15% of gays fit these stereotypes.) Myth: Among gay couples, one

assumes a masculine and one a feminine role. (Most lesbians and gay men reject traditional roles.)
8. The 1993 National Cancer Institute research indicates that the end tip of the X chromosome may hold a gene that predisposes men to a gay male sexual orientation. Other studies support a genetic influence on sexual orientation, but further research is needed.
9. Faulty resolution of the Oedipus complex causes men to become effeminate and gay. Faulty resolution of the Electra complex results in penis envy, masculine traits, and lesbianism.
10. Gay males and lesbians report a greater incidence of gender nonconformity as children than do heterosexual reference groups, with lesbians showing less difference than gay males. Very effeminate boys often become gay or bisexual adults. It is not clear which psychosocial or biological factors are involved.
11. Researchers have *not* found that gay men and lesbians suffer from more psychological distress than heterosexuals.
12. Generally, gay men have had more sexual partners than lesbians. Fewer gay men than lesbians are in steady relationships. In committed relationships, gay men are more likely than lesbians to have sexual contacts outside the relationship. Since the advent of AIDS, the behavior of gays has been changing and research should continue.

Matching Exercises:
I. Vocabulary Exercise 1:
k, i, a, l, g, j, m, e, h, f, c, d, b

II. Vocabulary Exercise 2:
k, f, g, l, a, j, d, c, i, e, b, h.

Multiple-Choice Questions:
1. c; 2. d; 3. b; 4. d; 5. a; 6. d; 7. c; 8. d; 9. d; 10. c; 11. b; 12. b.

Chapter 11:

Fill-in-the-Blanks: Conception, Ova, sperm, 120, 150, spontaneous abortion, Fallopian tube, 60, 90, 4, 20, basal body temperature, vaginal mucus, urine, luteinizing hormone, Shettles's, sperm separation, infertility, low sperm count, artificial insemination, in vitro fertilization, missed period, breast tenderness, morning sickness, frequent urination, HCG, miscarriages, 16, throughout pregnancy, 266, ten, germinal, embryonic, cephalocaudal, proximodistal, amniotic, amniotic, placenta, umbilical, placenta, fetal, one ounce, two pounds, fourth, age of viability, minority, teratogens, fetal alcohol syndrome, smoke, Amniocentesis, chorionic villus sampling, Braxton-Hicks, efface, dilate, Twelve, 24, Transition, cervix, birth, episiotomy, placenta, Lamaze, Caesarean section, birth center, home birth, anoxia, 37, five, post-partum depression, Breast-feeding, six.

Short Answer Questions
1. Sperm swim up the Fallopian tubes. Sperm that reach the ovum secrete an enzyme that briefly thins the gelatinous layer on the outside of the ovum. This allows one sperm to penetrate the ovum.
2. Using a variety of techniques they can identify the time of ovulation and engage in coitus in the male-superior position near that time. The man should penetrate deeply, remain still during ejaculation, and then withdraw slowly. Following ejaculation, the woman should lie on her back with her knees drawn up. She should lie still for 30-60 minutes following ejaculation.
3. Shettles's approach, which relies on the fact that Y sperm swim faster but are less durable than X sperm. Sperm separation combined with artificial insemination with X or Y sperm.

4. A. In vitro fertilization -- Mature ova are surgically removed from an ovary, fertilized in a laboratory dish by the father's sperm, and injected into the mother's uterus.
    B. GIFT -- gamete intrafallopian transfer -- Sperm and ova are inserted together into a Fallopian tube.
    C. ZIFT -- zygote intrafallopian transfer -- Sperm and ova are combined in a laboratory dish; the zygote is placed in the mother's Fallopian tube.
    D. Donor IVF -- The ovum is taken from another woman, fertilized, and then injected into the uterus or Fallopian tube of the intended mother.
    E. Embryonic Transfer -- A woman is artificially inseminated with the sperm of the intended father. After 5 days the embryo is removed from her uterus and implanted in the mother-to-be.
    F. Surrogate mothers -- A woman is artificially inseminated by the sperm of the husband and carries the baby to term. She signs a contract to turn the baby over to the couple.
5. The amniotic sac provides a protective environment in the uterus; the amniotic fluid cushions the embryo/fetus from shocks due to the mother's movements and helps maintain a steady temperature.
6. Approximately 25 pounds. The placenta, amniotic fluid, and fetus together weigh about 20 pounds.
7. If an Rh negative mother (one who does not carry the Rh blood protein) is pregnant with an Rh+ fetus, she may produce antibodies which may harm the fetus if an exchange of blood occurs during childbirth. This does not usually affect a first pregnancy. In this case, the woman will be injected with Rhogam within 72 hours of giving birth, to prevent this problem in subsequent pregnancies.
8. An underdeveloped upper jaw, flattened nose, widely spaced eyes, smaller than average brains and developmental lags. They may be mentally retarded, lack coordination, and have deformed limbs and heart problems.
9. Amniocentesis and chorionic villus sampling (CVS)
10. The pregnant woman and her coach are educated about childbirth, relaxation, breathing exercises, etc. The coach will help her time contractions, offer emotional support, and coach her in breathing and relaxation. She may or may not *choose* to request anesthetics. It enhances the woman's self-esteem and helps her gain a sense of control over the delivery.
11. Advantages: Breast-feeding transmits the mother's antibodies to the baby. It reduces the incidence of allergies in babies. The milk is always ready and the right temperature.
    Disadvantages: The woman cannot share the feedings with another person; she must do all the night feedings. It is very difficult, if not impossible, to do if she must return to work shortly after childbirth.

Matching Exercises:
I. Vocabulary Exercise 1:
i, g, a, k, f, c, j, d, l, b, h, e

II. Vocabulary Exercise 2:
l, f, j, i, m, h, c, k, g, d, a, e, b

III. Vocabulary Exercise 3:
l, j, m, h, o, k, a, n, d, g, b, i, c, f, e

IV. Vocabulary Exercise 4:
n, i, g, o, j, a, m, h, d, l, e, b, f, c, k

Multiple-Choice Questions:
1. d; 2. c; 3. b; 4. a; 5. d; 6. b; 7. b; 8. b; 9. c; 10. b; 11. d; 12. b

Chapter 12:

Fill-in-the-Blanks: birth control pills, combination pills, minipills, suppressing ovulation, thickening the cervical mucus, rendering the uterine lining less receptive to a fertilized egg, Morning-after, Norplant, ovulation, cervical mucus, 24 hours, five years, one, intrauterine device, uterus, implantation, diaphragm, spermicidal cream, jelly, two, six, Spermicides, six, eight, failure rate, cervical cap, spermicide, eight, condoms, spermicide, STIs, Douching, Withdrawal, fertility awareness, ovulation, avoid, calendar, eighteen, basal body temperature method, cervical mucus, Ovulation-prediction, Sterilization, vasectomy, vasovasotomy, Fallopian tubes, 100, women, female condom, Depo-Provera, 20s, first trimester, Roe, Wade, Vacuum aspiration, first, dilation, curettage, dilation, evacuation, second, general, Intra-amniotic infusion, hysterotomy, RU-486, methotrexate, misoprostol.

Short Answer Questions:
1. Many methods were available in the nineteenth century. In 1873, Comstock was responsible for the passage of a law that prohibited the dissemination of birth-control information through the mail. Dismantling this law began in 1918 and was completed in 1965.
2. Convenience, Moral acceptability, Cost, Sharing responsibility, Safety, Reversibility, Protection against STIs, and Effectiveness.
3. If one believes that life begins with conception, one would probably be morally opposed to the use of minipills and the IUD, which may prevent implantation but not fertilization.
4. Pills with high doses of estrogen and progestin which stop fertilization or prevent implantation. They are not intended for regular use.
5. Although "skins" allow greater sexual sensations, they do not protect as well as latex condoms against STIs. The "pores" permit the AIDS virus and other STD viruses to pass through.
6. For those who have religious objections to other methods of birth control. For those who may have health concerns about other artificial methods of birth control. For couples who communicate well and wish to share the responsibility for birth control.
7. Through the mid-nineteenth century, women were allowed to terminate pregnancies prior to the time of "quickening". During the period from about 1860 through 1900, all states passed laws banning abortion any time during pregnancy, except to save the life of the mother. During the late 1960s and early 1970s, some states liberalized their abortion laws. In 1973, the Supreme Court ruled that abortion was protected under the right to privacy. The Court also set varying restrictions on abortions during each trimester.
8. The decision legalized abortion nationwide for any reason during the first trimester. States may regulate abortion to protect the woman's health during the second trimester (for example, require that it take place in a hospital). States may prohibit abortion (because of viability) during the third trimester except to protect a woman's health or life.
9. About 90% occur during the first trimester. It is safer than continuing a pregnancy to term. Overall, including all abortions, there is fewer than one death per 100,000 procedures.
10. Generally, the sooner the abortion occurs, the less stressful it is. However, almost all women have some feelings of guilt, remorse, sadness, and anger. After an abortion, most women feel a sense of relief.

Matching Exercises:
I. Vocabulary Exercise 1:
i, e, l, a, h, c, j, f, m, b, k, d, g

II. Vocabulary Exercise 2:
g, b, i, d, a, l, k, c, e, h, j, f

Multiple-Choice Questions:
1. b; 2. c; 3. c; 4. d; 5. c; 6. a; 7. c; 8. c; 9. d; 10. b; 11. d; 12. c.

Chapter 13:

Fill-in-the-Blanks: erections, Pelvic thrusting, Masturbation, orgasm, genital play, same-gender sexual, heterosexual, six, ten, same, peers, puberty, reproduction, has failed to demonstrate, puberty, take on adult responsibility, secondary sex characteristics, pubic hair, menarche, ejaculation, 12 1/2, 13, Estrogen, two years, 13, 14, nocturnal emissions, 17, gynecomastia, half, one-fourth, coitus during high school, less, more, more, Petting, oral sex, oral sex, 15, 16, 5, peers, one million, one, 40, 500 thousand, misconceptions, inconsistently.

Short Answer Questions:
1. Some boys are born with erections, and most have erections within the first few weeks of life. Ultrasound has shown erections in male fetuses.
2. Possibly as early as four or five months of age, but rarely before the second year of life.
3. Permissive societies permit masturbation, sexual expression among peers, open discussion of sex, possibly observation of sexual behavior of adults. Restrictive societies generally punish childhood sexual experimentation, masturbation, premarital sex and watching adults.
4. Kissing, curiosity about the others' bodies, "playing doctor," showing each other their genitals, etc.
5. Research does *not* support a causal relationship. Some comprehensive sex education programs show a small delay in first intercourse.
6. At least part of the decrease is due to improved nutrition and health care. Another view is that girls must achieve a critical body weight or accumulate a certain percentage of body fat to trigger menarche, and girls today reach that weight or fat percentage sooner.
7. It stimulates growth of breast tissues, growth of the uterus and the thickening of the vaginal lining, growth of fatty and supporting tissue in the hips and buttocks, growth of the labia, and (with androgens) stimulates development of pubic and underarm hair.
8. It prompts growth of the testes, scrotum, and penis; growth of facial, body, and pubic hair; and the deepening of the voice. The prostate and seminal vesicles increase in size and semen production begins.
9. Hormones, "love", a way for girls to "reward" boys for being loyal, as a sign of maturity, peer pressure, pressure from dating partners.
10. Lower school performance, early steady dating, divorced or separated parents, being less able to talk to their parents, permissive parents.
11. About 5%. The vast majority of the experiences (90%) are with peers.
12. African-American teens tend to begin coitus about two years earlier, on the average, than White teens. The prevalence of premarital sex among Asian-American college students is low compared with the general U.S. college population. Hispanic American students tend to be more conservative and traditional, report less sexual experience, and are less likely than non-Hispanics to use contraception. Rates of adolescent pregnancy occur in the following order: African Americans, Hispanic Americans, Whites. Whites are much more likely to resolve adolescent pregnancy by abortion, African Americans by single parenting, and Hispanic Americans by having the baby and marrying or living with the father.
13. Women are more likely than men to be disappointed. Only 28% of women said that their first time was physically or psychologically satisfying; 81% of males said it was physically satisfying and 67% said it was psychologically satisfying. A majority of boys reported feeling "glad" and a majority of girls expressed ambivalence.

14. Half quit school and go on public assistance. One in five will become pregnant again within a year. The children are at greater risk of prematurity; birth complications; infant mortality; and physical, emotional and intellectual problems in preschool years.

Matching Exercises:
I. Vocabulary Exercise 1:
c, g, e, a, f, b, h, d

Multiple-Choice Questions:
1. c; 2. c; 3. c; 4. a; 5. a; 6. d; 7. a; 8. b; 9. c; 10. c; 11. d; 12. d

Chapter 14:

Fill-in-the-Blanks: Singlehood, four, well-adjusted, content, serial monogamy, celibacy, POSSLQ, doubled, less, less, twice, marriage, 65, 60, 26.5, 24.4, patriarchy, chattel, right, duty, love, monogamy, polygamy, polygyny, polyandry, homogamy, race/ethnic background, educational level, religion, social class, one, sexual revolution, frequency, variety, age, years of marriage, foreplay, intercourse, orgasmic consistency, pleasurable, more, conventional adultery, consensual adultery, 90, 75, disapprove, Swinging, partner, 2000, half, 1/4, women, men, higher, retain, men, women, no, the availability of a sexually interested and supportive partner, Cerebral palsy, spinal-cord injuries, pregnant, Sensory disabilities, mental retardation.

Short Answer Questions:
1. More people postponing marriage to pursue an education or a career. Many people living together instead of marrying. People getting married at later ages. Increased prevalence of divorce. Lessened stigma attached to remaining single.
2. Couples are not *randomly assigned* to the two groups. Cohabitors tend to be more committed to personal independence, and to be less traditional and less religious. Cohabitors' attitudes, not cohabitation itself, may account for these results.
3. A strong tradition of patriarchy can be seen in the cultures of the Ancient Hebrews, classical Greece, and Rome. In these cultures women were viewed as chattel. The Christian tradition is also strongly patriarchal. Even in the 19th century sex was viewed as a husband's right and a wife's duty. Today, although some marriages still adhere to traditional roles, many are changing.
4. We tend to marry those who are similar in social class, geographical area, physical characteristics, intelligence, race/ethnic background, religion, attitudes, values, age, etc.
5. The sexual revolution, greater availability of books on sex, sexually explicit films for home VCRs, mobility and exposure to ideas and attitudes of many other people, effective contraceptives, etc.
6. Relaxed restrictions on divorce (no-fault divorce), increased economic independence of women, higher expectations of marriage today, marriage at later ages, etc.
7. Emotional: feelings of failure, loneliness, depression, higher rates of physical and mental illness, higher rates of suicide; eventually few regret their decision to divorce. Financial: women may find it difficult to find employment that supports them and their children. The man may find it difficult to pay child support.
8. Females: reduced myotonia, vaginal lubrication, elasticity of the vaginal walls, and muscle spasms at orgasm; smaller increases in breast size during arousal.
   Males: Longer time for erection and orgasm, longer refractory period, less firm erections, greater need for direct stimulation, less semen emitted, less intense orgasmic contractions.
9. In one study, half of the 60- to 91-year-olds reported regular sexual relations, and half of these, at least once a week. A 1988 study of 80-to-102-year-olds reported that 30% of women

and 62% of men still engaged in intercourse. 70% of healthy 70-year-olds are sexually active, having sex at least once a week.
10. Most people with disabilities experience the same sexual needs and feelings as do able bodied people. Parents may try to deny the sexuality of their disabled children. People may see the disabled as sexless, dependent, childlike. The disabled may receive less or no sex education.

Matching Exercises:
I. Vocabulary Exercise 1:
c, e, a, g, b, d, f

II. Vocabulary Exercise 2:
h, m, d, l, g, c, e, i, j, b, a, k, f

Multiple-Choice Questions:
1. c; 2. a; 3. c; 4. a; 5. c; 6. a; 7. c; 8. a; 9. c; 10. b; 11. a; 12.d

Chapter 15:

Fill-in-the-Blanks: sexual desire, sexual arousal, orgasmic, sexual pain, Hypoactive sexual desire, depression, emotional stress, relationship, sexual aversion, impotence, frigidity, erectile dysfunction, orgasmic disorders, women, men, anorgasmic, preorgasmic, premature ejaculation, Dyspareunia, physical, psychological, inadequate lubrication, vaginismus, fear of penetration, vaginal injuries, biologically, diabetes, MS, spinal cord injuries, hypertension, psychiatric, drugs, organic, psychological, sexually repressive, women, psychosexual trauma, Ineffective sexual techniques, emotional stress, poor communication, performance anxiety, Masters, Johnson, sensate focus, psychosexual therapy, behavioral, psychoanalytic, samples, follow-up, all, squeeze, stop-start, Directed masturbation, high motivation, good relationships, penile implant, Vascular, hormone treatments, Injections, vacuum constriction device.

Short Answer Questions:
1. Hormone deficiencies, depression, marital dissatisfaction, medical conditions, emotional stress, anxiety, a history of sexual assault, negative parental attitudes toward sex, some medications, etc.
2. An estimated 10 to 15 million men in the U.S. suffer from erectile dysfunction. Perhaps another 10 million suffer from partial dysfunction. It affects approximately one-third of men over 60. Occasional problems are even more common.
3. Premature ejaculation. The question is how to define premature. Is it a period of time, number of thrusts, satisfaction of the couple, etc.
4. Antidepressant and antipsychotic meds may impair erectile functioning and inhibit orgasm. Tranquilizers may delay or prevent orgasm. CNS depressants can reduce sexual appetite and impair functioning. Marijuana has been associated with reduced sex drive and performance. Regular cocaine use can cause erectile dysfunction, inhibited orgasm, and reduced sexual desire.
5. Sexually repressive cultural or home environments, exposure to negative attitudes about sex, lack of accurate information, the sexual double standard, rape, incest, sexual molestation.
6. Ineffective sexual techniques, fear of "letting go," depression, high levels of emotional stress, lack of communication regarding preferences for stimulation, relationship problems, difference in level of sexual activity desired, lack of sexual knowledge and skills, performance anxiety.

7. Performance anxiety occurs when a person is overly concerned with how she or he will perform. The person focuses on self-doubts and fears instead of on erotic sensations. It can inhibit erection, increase the potential for premature ejaculation, reduce vaginal lubrication, and contribute to female orgasmic dysfunction.
8. Self-stimulation exercises, sensate focus exercises, sexual skills training, treatment for depression or hormonal deficiencies, communication training, couples therapy (if a relationship problem exists).
9. Information regarding orgasm as a reflex when arousal occurs under relaxed circumstances. Nondemand sexual contacts (to reduce performance anxiety).
10. Nondemand sensate focus exercises for men and women. Directed masturbation for women. For premature ejaculation, either the stop-start or the squeeze technique can be used.
11. Medical treatment of any underlying physical problems. For vaginismus, vaginal dilators of increasing size are inserted. The woman controls the pace. The idea is to reduce her fears of penetration. Because vaginismus often occurs among women who have experienced rape or incest, psychological therapy for these effects may accompany the use of dilators.
12. The American Association of Sex Educators, Counselors, and Therapists (AASECT) will provide you with the names of certified sex therapists in your area. Ask any therapist you contact about his/her professional degrees, license or certification, fees, treatment plans, and training in sex therapy.

Matching Exercises:
I. Vocabulary Exercise 1:
f, d, g, b, h, c, i, a, e

II. Vocabulary Exercise 2:
g, d, i, e, a, j, f, b, h, c

Multiple-Choice Questions:
1. d; 2. b; 3. b; 4. c; 5. a; 6. d; 7. c; 8. d; 9. b; 10. c; 11. d; 12. b

Chapter 16:

Fill-in-the-Blanks: Sexually transmitted infections, contaminated needles, 13, contagious, penile discharge, urination, lymph glands, 80, urogenital, reproductive organs, pelvic inflammatory disease, Antibiotics, decrease, chancre, skin rash, latent, tertiary, VDRL, Penicillin, chlamydia, bacterium, eye infections, pneumonia, NGU, penile discharge, burning, asymptomatic, PID, gonorrhea, Penicillin, sex partners, chancroid, shigellosis, granuloma inguinale, lymphogranuloma venereum, antibiotics, Vaginitis, bacterial vaginosis, candidiasis, trichomoniasis, yeast infection, itch, vaginal discharge, vaginal environment, 75, partners, Trichomoniasis, 2-3, half, 1981, Acquired Immunodeficiency Syndrome, Human Immunodeficiency Virus, 1, gay men, male-female, immune system, leukocytes, pathogens, antibodies, CD4, helper t-cell, 10, opportunistic diseases, toxoplasmosis, blood, semen, vaginal secretions, childbirth, breast-feeding, casual, everyday, contact, ELISA, antibodies, Western Blot, vaccine, AZT, protease inhibitors, herpes simplex virus type 1, Genital herpes, Acyclovir, frequency, duration, psychological, anger, depression, isolation, shame, viral hepatitis, food, water, vaccine, human papilloma virus, genital warts, Freezing, pediculosis, scabies, towels, bedding, itching, Scabies.

Short Answer Questions:
1. Studies show perhaps 1 to 1.5 million Americans are infected with HIV and about 56 million are infected with some other STI. As high as 1 in 500 college students is HIV+, and possibly 10% of college students are infected with HPV. More than 13 million people in the U.S.

contract an STI each year. Two of every three cases affect people under age 25. 100,000 to 150,000 women become infertile each year due to STIs.
2. More young people are having sex at earlier ages. Many of them practice unprotected sex. The birth control pill, one of the most commonly used methods of contraception, provides no protection from STIs. Many people, particularly women, initially have no symptoms when they have an STI.
3. Pelvic inflammatory disease is usually the result of untreated bacterial STIs that spread through the cervix, uterus, Fallopian tubes, ovaries, etc. It can cause scarring of the Fallopian tubes, resulting in infertility.
4. Physicians are not required to report cases of chlamydia. The incidence is especially high among teenagers and college students. Twenty-five percent of infected men and 70 percent of infected women are asymptomatic. Babies born to infected women can develop eye infections or a form of pneumonia. Untreated chlamydia results in about 500,000 cases of PID annually.
5. "Yeast" infections are technically known as candidiasis and are caused by a yeast-like fungus. They may develop when there are changes in the vaginal environment and they are not acquired only through sexual contact. However, they can be transmitted back and forth between sex partners. About 75 percent of women will have a yeast infection sometime during their reproductive years. About half of these women will have recurrent episodes.
6. Forty-six percent of the men and three-fourths of the women with AIDS in the U.S. are African American or Hispanic American. Death rates are more than twice as great among African Americans and Hispanic Americans than among white Americans. AIDS is increasing more rapidly among women than men; most of these women are poor, urban minority women. Children with AIDS are also disproportionately poor and African American or Hispanic American.
7. HIV invades and destroys a type of lymphocyte called the CD4 cell. (CD4 cells signal killer T-cells to destroy infected cells.) When these cells are destroyed, the immune system is disabled and cannot fight off infections and diseases.
8. Diagnosis of AIDS is based on the appearance of various indicator diseases, such as PCP, Kaposi's sarcoma, toxoplasmosis, etc. (There are now 26 indicator diseases.) Since 1992, an additional criterion has been when an individual's CD4 cell count falls below 200 cells per cubic millimeter, about one fifth the normal amount.
9. Shortly following infection, people may experience mild flu-like symptoms which usually disappear within a few weeks. Usually they then enter an asymptomatic stage, which may last as long as ten years or more. The beginning symptoms are swollen lymph nodes, fatigue, fever, "night sweats," diarrhea, and weight loss. To be diagnosed as having AIDS, people must have one or more of several specific opportunistic diseases or a significantly lowered CD4 cell count.
10. It *is* transmitted through anal sex, penile-vaginal sex, oral-genital sex, sharing contaminated needles, needle sticks with contaminated needles, during pregnancy to the fetus, during birth to the infant, through breast-feeding to the infant, and very rarely now through blood transfusions. It is *not* transmitted through touching, handling objects HIV-infected people have handled, swimming pools, insect bites, or sharing eating utensils or toothbrushes.
11. The probability of transmission rises with the number of coital contacts. A history of STIs heightens the risk. Other factors include a higher risk from anal intercourse than from other sexual behaviors, the amount of virus in the semen, uncircumcised men being more vulnerable, alcohol consumption before, during or shortly after sex, etc.
12. Her doctor may recommend she have a C-section. Newborns exposed to chlamydia can acquire serious chlamydial eye infections or a specific form of pneumonia.
13. Herpes simplex virus type 2 is a viral, not a bacterial, STI. There is no cure for herpes, and flare-ups can occur over a lifetime. The psychological effects (anger, shame, fear of transmitting it to partners) distinguish it from the bacterial STIs.

14. HPV (human papilloma virus) causes genital warts. About 20-30% of sexually active Americans have the virus. HPV is present in 85% or more of cases of cervical cancer. The majority of the people who have HPV have warts too small to be visible to the eyes. Women are particularly susceptible to HPV.
15. Genital warts may not cause symptoms, or the warts may occur in locations that cannot be detected during visual examination. Women with HPV are much more likely to develop cervical cancer than are other women.
16. Prescription (Kwell) or nonprescription creams, lotions or shampoos, which must be applied according to directions. All the person's bedding, towels, and clothes must be washed in hot water. Because the eggs they lay may take up to 7 days to hatch, the person should reexamine him/herself in 7 days (and possibly repeat the treatment and washing).

Matching Exercises:
I. Vocabulary Exercise 1:
f, h, l, a, i, d, j, b, g, k, c, e

II. Vocabulary Exercise 2:
d, h, g, a, j, e, k, i, b, c, f

III. Vocabulary Exercise 3:
h, f, i, g, e, c, b, d, a

IV. Vocabulary Exercise 4:
h, f, g, j, d, i, e, b, a, c

Multiple-Choice Questions:
1. b; 2. a; 3. d; 4. b; 5. b; 6. b; 7. c; 8. c; 9. c; 10. a; 11. d; 12. d; 13. e; 14. b; 15. c; 16. b

Chapter 17:

Fill-in-the-Blanks: atypical variations, paraphilias, Paraphilias, compulsory, men, fetishism, partialism, harmless, transvestism, Exhibitionism, young, unhappily married, sexually repressed, 18, Telephone scatologia, are not, socially inadequate heterosexual, women, Voyeurism, masturbate, less, less, videophones, Sexual masochists, 20, quite common, hypoxyphilia, Sexual sadism, mutually gratifying, consenting, dominance submission, three, married, Frotteurism, men, crowded places, Toucherism, Zoophilia, deep-seated psychological problems, necrophilia, mentally disturbed, klismaphilia, coprophilia, urophilia, Hypersexuality, nymphomania, satyriasis, Don Juanism, hormone, exhibitionists, castration anxiety, a lack of, learned behaviors, sociological, Childhood experiences, "lovemap," voluntarily, psychoanalysis, Behavior therapy, Systematic desensitization, aversion therapy, Social skills training, Orgasmic reconditioning, Antiandrogen, Depo-Provera.

Short Answer Questions:
1. Transvestites cross-dress for sexual arousal. Transsexuals do so because of extreme discomfort with their gender or as one step in a gender-reassignment process. Female impersonators do so to earn a living. Some homosexuals do so because it is fashionable, but rarely do so for purposes of arousal.
2. It is best to show no response at all, or to just continue on one's way. If a woman responds she could say "You need professional help for this problem." She should report the incident to the police.

3. Remain calm. Do not reveal shock or fright. Say nothing and hang up, or say "I think you should seek professional help for this problem." If calls are repeated, a woman can request an unlisted number and/or notify the police.
4. Almost all are male, usually began this behavior before age 15, often put themselves in risky situations to "peep", and most are nonviolent. Voyeurs are usually less sexually experienced and less likely than other sex offenders to be married.
5. Kinsey reported that 22% of men and 12% of women experienced at least some sexual response to sadomasochistic stories.
6. Carnes suggests that some paraphiles suffer from a nonchemical addiction. He argues that sexual addicts use sex like drug addicts and alcoholics use drugs or alcohol: to alter their moods and temporarily relieve psychological states of discomfort, such as depression or anxiety. Although this view has met with controversy, self-help groups have been set up.
7. The term nymphomania is more widely known than is its counterpart, satyriasis. This reflects our cultural double standard that allows men much greater sexual liberties. A man who is "oversexed" is likely to be viewed positively and admiringly. A woman exhibiting the same behavior is likely to be viewed much more negatively.
8. Learning theorists believe paraphilias are learned behaviors that are acquired through experience. The explanations focus on association of objects or behaviors with arousal or orgasm. The mechanisms include classical and operant conditioning and, possibly, modeling.
9. Paraphilias can best be examined from a framework that incorporates multiple perspectives. Childhood experiences etch a pattern in the brain, called a "lovemap," which determines the types of stimuli and activities that will be arousing. "Lovemaps" can become distorted by early traumatic experiences. Genetic predispositions, hormonal factors, brain abnormalities, etc., may make one more vulnerable to vandalized "lovemaps."
10. Drugs do not cure paraphilias. They reduce sexual desire and lower the intensity of the fantasies and urges, so that the paraphile may feel less compelled to act on them. The effects of antiandrogens are reversible when treatment is terminated. Questions about side effects, ethics, and usefulness remain.

Matching Exercises:
I. Vocabulary Exercise 1:
j, d, g, c, f, i, b, h, a, e

II. Vocabulary Exercise 2:
b, i, d, h, a, g, c, j, f, k, e, l

III. Vocabulary Exercise 3:
f, h, g, e, b, i, a, d, c

Multiple-Choice Questions:
1. b; 2. d; 3. d; 4. b; 5. c; 6. d; 7. c; 8. b; 9. c; 10. c; 11. b; 12. d

Chapter 18:

Fill-in-the-Blanks: Forcible rape, Statutory rape, unreported, 14, 25, Stranger, Acquaintance, acquaintance, Date, 10, 20, consent, Gang, male, greater, multiple, heterosexual, seven, marital, battering, marital violence, physical, women, men, woman, traditional masculine, no more, are, know, four, athletes, anger, power, sadistic, anger, revenge, power, Sadistic, posttraumatic stress disorder, rape trauma syndrome, acute, disorganization, long-term, reorganization, 4, 16, 20, 75, 80, seldom, rarely, men, Pedophilia, pedophiles, male, do not, Incest, Brother-sister, religiously devout, fundamentalist, moralistic, often, great, physically aggressive, depressed, long-lasting, mixed, Depo-Provera, Sexual harassment, men, women, power, three, jobs, 90, 25, 30, unequal power.

Short Answer Questions:
1. About 10 to 20% of women report they have been victims of date rape. Date rapists often believe: acceptance of a date is consent to coitus; women in singles bars have already given tacit consent; resistance is just a ploy, not really a refusal to have sex; women who consent to go in a car or to their residence have given tacit consent.
2. A committee of the U.S. Congress estimated that one wife in seven is likely to be raped by her husband. To dominate, to degrade, to "teach" the wife a lesson, to "solve" marital disputes, or within the context of other marital violence.
3. Men are often reinforced from childhood for aggressive behavior. Women are socialized to be submissive, passive, cooperative, and obedient to male authority. Images from books and movies often reinforce stereotypical roles. Men often view sex as a conquest or a sport in which the goal is to "score."
4. Rape-prone societies are characterized by interpersonal violence, male domination, and the treatment of women as property. Rape-free societies are characterized by sexual equality and the economic independence of women to control their own resources.
5. Fear for their lives while being raped. In the days and weeks afterward, women may be distraught, have difficulty sleeping, cry frequently, experience eating problems, anxiety, depression, irritability, mood changes, etc.
6. See the lists of suggestions on page 569.
7. Persistent verbal pressure or the use of seduction "lines" to manipulate a person into sexual activity. See lists of suggestions on pages 572-573.
8. General family disruption (spousal abuse, dysfunctional marriages, alcoholic or abusive parents). Many fathers who commit incest are religiously devout, fundamentalist, and moralistic. Factors such as poverty, overcrowded living conditions, and social or geographical isolation may contribute.
9. See box on page 580.
10. Convey a professional attitude. Discourage harassing behavior. Avoid being alone with the harasser. Maintain a record. Talk with the harasser and/or write a letter to the harasser. Seek support. File a complaint. Seek legal remedies.

Matching Exercises:
I. Vocabulary Exercise 1:
j, g, i, d, b, k, h, e, a, f, c

Multiple-Choice Questions:
1. b; 2. c; 3. a; 4. c; 5. d; 6. d; 7. c; 8. d; 9. d; 10. c; 11. b; 12.c

Chapter 19:

Fill-in-the-Blanks: prostitution, sexual activity, soliciting, female, male, economic, sexual double standard, streetwalkers, customers, pimps, teenage runaways, Brothel, massage parlors, escort services, Escort services, middle, well, Call girls, gracious company, conversation, on their own, poverty, sexual, physical abuse, 1/2, 2/3, married, middle, gigolos, hustlers, 17 - 18, working, lower, sexual abuse, gay, economic, are not, Kept boys, Call boys, Bar hustlers, street hustlers, younger, Pornography, obscenity, Erotica, Comstock, birth control, mail, no, little or no, found, R-rated violent, violence, sex, no, association, females, males, men, Women, domestic, traditional.

Short Answer Questions:
1. Poverty, sexual and/or physical abuse, conflict-ridden homes, marginal skills and limited means of support, teenage runaways.
2. Sex without a negotiation, Sex without commitment, Sex for eroticism and variety, Prostitution as sociability, Sex away from home, Problematical sex.
3. Begin prostitution at an average age of 14, less than 11th grade educations, few if any marketable skills, working- or lower-class backgrounds, troubled families, majority have been victims of sexual abuse or rape, half or more are gay and may be throw-aways.
4. Prostitutes are at greater risk of HIV because they have many partners and often use no protection. Many prostitutes, their clients, and their other sex partners are injectable drug users who share contaminated needles. In Thailand and Africa, transmission of HIV by prostitutes is widespread.
5. Nearly everyone has been exposed to some type of sexually explicit material. Polls show 25 - 40% of people had seen an X-rated video in the last year, either at a theater or on their VCR. One survey of Midwesterners showed that over 90% had been exposed to a sexually explicit magazine. Over 90% had seen at least one sexually oriented R-rated film.
6. In *Roth*, the Supreme Court ruled that expression was protected under the First Amendment unless its dominant theme dealt with "sex in a manner appealing to prurient interest". In *Miller*, obscenity was to be determined by contemporary community standards; it must be viewed as a whole; and the work had to lack "serious literary, artistic, political, or scientific value". In *Pope*, the judgment was to be left up to a "reasonable" person, not "an ordinary member of any given community."
7. Men express a higher interest in pornography. Men are generally the consumers of pornographic visual materials, which are generally made for men by men. Women are often disgusted by portrayals of women as subservient to the sexual demands of men and portrayals of women as aroused by domination and coercion. Women prefer erotic romance novels.
8. The research on the effects of violent pornography (and violent nonpornographic films) indicates that it produces greater acceptance of rape myths, increased reported willingness to force a woman into sexual activity, and greater reported likelihood of engaging in rape. Research on nonviolent pornography is not conclusive, but it portrays women in degrading and dehumanizing roles. It *may* affect men's sensitivity toward female victims. Other researchers argue that it loosens traditional family values. No research has yet linked sexual explicitness per se with undesirable effects.
9. Males may become more callous in their attitudes toward women, although the evidence is mixed. One researcher found support for a loosening of traditional family values and decreased satisfaction with one's partner's physical appearance and sexual performance.
10. The goals of using sexual images are to capture attention and to make the message persuasive and memorable. However, if there is too much sexual content or the ad is considered offensive, the viewer may concentrate on the message and forget the product, or the viewer may boycott the product.

Matching Exercises:
I. Vocabulary Exercise 1:
h, d, k, g, a, i, e, j, b, f, c

Multiple-Choice Questions:
1. c; 2. a; 3. e; 4. a; 5. d; 6. b; 7. d; 8. d; 9. b; 10. b; 11. d; 12. b

Chapter 20:

Fill-in-the-Blanks: information, information, value, legalism, situation ethics, ethical relativism, hedonism, asceticism, utilitarianism, rationalism, legalism, situation ethics, context, Ethical relativists, one's own, Hedonists, short-sighted, long-term, Ascetics, utilitarianism, Utilitarians, Rationalism, rationalist

Short Answer Questions:
1. Psychological conflict occurs when we are pulled in different directions at the same time. It occurs when the choice is between alternatives that each have positive and negative aspects or that each have very negative aspects.
2. Requires individual answer.
3. Parents, peers, religious training, ethnic subculture, larger culture, etc.
4. Requires individual answer.

Multiple-Choice Questions:
1. d; 2. a; 3. c; 4. d; 5. b; 6. d; 7. c; 8. d; 9. e; 10. b

NOTES

NOTES

NOTES

NOTES

NOTES

NOTES

NOTES

NOTES